GEONOMICS INSTITUTE FOR INTERNATIONAL ECONOMIC
ADVANCEMENT SERIES
Michael P. Claudon, Series Editor

Debt Disaster? Banks, Governments, and Multilaterals Confront the Crisis
edited by John F. Weeks

DEBT DISASTER?
Banks, Governments, and Multilaterals Confront the Crisis

Edited by
JOHN F. WEEKS

NEW YORK UNIVERSITY PRESS
New York and London

Library of Congress Cataloging-in-Publication Data

Debt disaster? : banks, governments, and multilaterals confront the crisis /
    edited by John F. Weeks.
        p.   cm.
    Bibliography: p.
    Includes Index.
    ISBN 0-8147-9233-2
    1. Debts, External—Developing countries. 2. Debt relief—Developing
countries. 3. Developing countries—Economic policy.
I. Weeks, John.
HJ8899.D434   1989
336.3'435'09172409048—dc20   89-9207
                                                                        CIP

New York University Press books are printed on acid-free paper,
and their binding materials are chosen for strength and durability.

CONTENTS

List of Figures   ix

List of Tables   xi

Acknowledgments   xiii
—*John F. Weeks*

Foreword   xv
—*Michael P. Claudon*

Introduction   xix
—*John F. Weeks*

PART I   *DEBT CRISIS IN THE THIRD WORLD*   1

Chapter 1
The Outlook for Development
—*Barry Herman*   3

Chapter 2
External Shocks, Adjustment, and Income
Distribution
—*Rolph van der Hoeven*   21

Chapter 3
Losers Pay Reparations, Or How the Third
World Lost the Lending War
—*John F. Weeks*   41

PART II   THE DEBT CRISIS AND
           COMMERCIAL BANKS   65

Chapter 4
Background to the Debt Crisis: Structural
Adjustment in the Financial Markets
—*Karin Lissakers*   67

Chapter 5
Safe Passage Through Dire Straits: Managing
an Orderly Exit from the Debt Crisis
—*Paul M. Sacks and Chris Canavan*   75

PART III   STRUCTURAL ADJUSTMENT:
           SOLUTION OR PART OF THE PROBLEM?   89

Chapter 6
World Bank-Supported Adjustment Programs
—*Robert Liebenthal and Peter Nicholas*   91

Chapter 7
Assessing Structural Adjustment Programs:
A Summary of Country Experience
—*Robin A. King and Michael D. Robinson*   103

Chapter 8
Undervaluation, Adjustment, and Growth
—*Richard D. Fletcher*   125

Chapter 9
Old Wine in New Bottles: Policy-Based
Lending in the 1980s
—*José D. Epstein*   131

*PART IV   STRUCTURAL ADJUSTMENT:
            IMPACT IN THE THIRD WORLD*   141

Chapter 10
Social Costs of Adjustment in Latin America
—*William L. Canak and Danilo Levi*   143

Chapter 11
Political Change and Economic Policy in
Latin America and the Caribbean in 1988
—*Louellen Stedman and Peter Hakim*   165

Chapter 12
The Demise of the Labor Aristocracy in Africa:
Structural Adjustment in Tanzania
—*Vali Jamal*   175

PART V   SEEKING A SOLUTION   193

Chapter 13
Facing the Realities of the Debt Crisis
—*Rep. Bruce Morrison*   195

Chapter 14
From Adjustment with Recession to
Adjustment with Growth
—*Rudiger Dornbusch*   207

Chapter 15
From Adjustment and Restructuring to
Development
—*Osvaldo Sunkel*   223

Chapter 16
Is to Forgive the Debt Divine?
—*William Darity, Jr.*   233

Chapter 17
Foreign Lending at the Brink
—*Michael P. Claudon*   243

Bibliography	255
Index	271
About the Contributors	285
About the Editor	289

LIST OF FIGURES

1-1   Output Per Capita   8
1-2   Net Resource Transfers and Investment in
      Middle Income and African Country Groups   15

ix

LIST OF TABLES

1-1	The Growth of Per Capita Output	11
1-2	Net Transfer of Resources of Capital-Importing Developing Countries	13
2-1	Nonfuel-Exporting Developing Countries: External Shocks, 1978-1987	22
2-2	Cumulative Change in Real Industrial Wages and Open Unemployment Rates in Selected Countries, 1981-1985	26
2-3	Index of Nonagricultural Real Wages, Employment and Labor Force	31
2-4	Central Government Fiscal Balances	33
7-1	Economic Variable Comparisons, 1974-1984	111
7-2	Economic Variable Comparisons, 1974-1984	111
7-3	Economic Variable Comparisons	113
7-4	Three-Year Percent Changes in Economic Variables Following a Rescheduling Episode	113
7-5	Simulations of the Impact of a Rescheduling Episode	115
7-6	Probability of Debt Service Difficulty	117
7-A1	Vector Autoregression of Macroeconomic Variables	121-122
7-B1	Countries in Data Base and Reschedulings	123
12-1	Wages in Current and Real (1969) Terms, 1957-1983	179
12-2	Indices of Crop Prices and Minimum Wage in Current Terms, 1963-1988	184
12-3	Poverty Line for an Urban Family, December 1985	187
17-1	Exposure of U.S. Banks to Six Troubled Developing Countries, 1984	248
17-2	Financial Resource Balance	249

ACKNOWLEDGMENTS

If the success of a conference can be measured by the enthusiasm of its participants and the quality of its papers, then the seminar sponsored by the Geonomics Institute over the weekend April 27-29, 1988, was an unqualified success. Particular thanks go to Michael P. Claudon, President and Managing Director of Geonomics, who not only provided the inspiration for the meeting, but also found time to contribute to this volume.

As in all such endeavors, many people made for its success. Foremost among them was Colleen Duncan, Senior Editor and Conference Coordinator, whose contributions went far beyond the administrative, for she gave invaluable counsel in the process of selecting participants and editing and enriching the final manuscript. Elizabeth Leeds, Editorial Assistant, earned the debt of conference participants for her organizational assistance. The amiable and collegial ambiance of the conference sessions and informal gatherings owed much to their site, Middlebury College's Bread Loaf Mountain Campus, and College officials provided generous support.

Finally, I wish to thank those members of the faculty who took their valuable time to chair sessions of the conference, Elizabeth Dore, David Rosenberg, and Alicia Andreu. And I would be remiss were I not to thank the undergraduates from the College who attended sessions and contributed insightful comments. One hopes their enthusiasm and seriousness is indicative of the awareness and concern of their generation for the problems of the Third World.

John F. Weeks

FOREWORD

The surge of unprecedented private, commercial credit from Northern financial centers to the developing countries of the South, which originated about 1973, erupted in 1982 into a global debt crisis, a crisis that today is still very much with us.

Economists are fond of assuming "other things equal," but the most important "other things" are very different in 1988 than they were fifteen years ago. The post-World War II economic boom has finally run its course. Growth in the 1990s is unlikely to match, or possibly even come close to, that of the last two decades. The OPEC surpluses of the 1970s disappeared as real oil prices fell, and were subsequently replaced by Japanese and West German trade surpluses. Northern commercial banks, their credibility and profitability severely, and potentially mortally, wounded by their exposure to debt service moratoria, reschedulings, and outright Latin American debt repudiation, have turned their collective back on the South. The large, multinational banking community turned away from the LDCs and toward industrial country markets. Globalization of financial markets continued, but was and is increasingly limited to the developed economies in the North.

Most of the orthodox strategies that have been adopted produced little more than momentary breathing room before the crisis resurfaced. Heavily indebted developing economies are now faced with an impossible equation: The $30 billion to $50 billion annual financial resource transfer to the North, averaging more than 5 percent of their GDPs, is exhausting desperately needed investment among debtor nations. Without substantial additional productive investment, growth is impossible. Without a resumption of economic growth, continued debt servicing promises accelerating real wages losses, growing human misery, and increasing domestic instability within developing debtor nations.

Now is the time to design a facility aimed at dramatically decreasing debt service, thereby hastening recovery of private banks' and debtor countries' financial health as soon as possible. To be successful, such a plan must facilitate, even provide an impetus to, debtor growth by somehow transforming interest payments destined for the North into productive investment in the South. Options to be considered include payment of interest in local currencies, legislated decreases in the interest rate paid by debtors, and establishment of debt-investment rather than debt-equity swap options, as well as new multilateral financial intermediaries between debtor and creditor countries. It is hoped that this volume will stimulate such consideration to begin in earnest. Continued financial and economic health in the North, and resumption of true economic development in the South are securely tethered to resolving the global debt crisis.

Growing out of the Geonomics Institute for International Economic Advancement's 1988 North-South conference, The World Debt Crisis: Transnational Policy Alternatives on Trial, organized by Middlebury College Professor of International Politics and Economics John F. Weeks, and held at Middlebury College's Bread Loaf Mountain Campus, this volume focuses on the origins of the global debt crisis, ensuing developments, and the current situation. It offers a fresh perspective on the crisis, proposes new and unorthodox strategies, and provides an intriguing mix of normative and positive analysis.

That the papers in this volume do not all speak in one voice allows the compilation to contribute to our understanding of the range of possible outcomes. As such, the volume will assist policymakers formulating possible legislation, business leaders assessing the potential for investing in Latin America and Africa, and students of North-South relations trying to gain a fuller understanding of the debt crisis and what it portends.

The Geonomics Institute seeks to promote a clearer and more complete understanding of international economic issues within and among the business, academic, and government communities. The Geonomics Institute is dedicated to sponsoring and publishing policy-oriented research and seminars, and providing advice and consultation to policymakers on domestic and international economic policy. Annual conference series for North-South and East-

West projects provide sustained forums for diverse groups of academic and business researchers and government representatives to examine, debate, and illuminate specific sets of issues. Geonomics is privately funded, nonpartisan, and not for profit.

We welcome ideas and opinions for better achieving our goals.

Michael P. Claudon

INTRODUCTION

From the end of World War II until the late 1970s, the field of development economics focused on the structural problems of underdevelopment in the context of growth: the population explosion, the desirable balance between agriculture and industry, and, particularly in the 1970s, the equitable distribution of the gains from growth. A fundamental characteristic of the development literature was the presumption that the growth of per capita income in the Third World was the rule, almost a given, and the issue was growth—growth at what rate, its composition, and for whom. The debt crisis changed all that. It is no longer the case that growth of per capita income be presumed the natural course. The 1980s have brought stagnation and decline throughout the Third World, catastrophically so in Sub-Saharan Africa, less virulently but across-the-board in Latin America, and with enough frequency in Asia to generate substantially increased poverty.[1] Indeed, the growth performances of most Third World countries have been so depressing that it has become common to refer to the 1980s as the "Lost Development Decade," and has provoked some writers to abandon the term *developing* countries as a misnomer.

At the end of April 1988, the Geonomics Institute for International Economic Advancement brought together a group of distinguished experts in the development field at the Bread Loaf Mountain Campus of Middlebury College to discuss, debate, and propose solutions for the current malaise in the

1. The relatively good performance of Asian countries taken as a whole is the result of the growth performances of India and China, which together total over half the population of the Third World. It is true, however, that the debt burden is least in the Asian countries.

Third World.   While participants came from varied backgrounds and institutions—the private financial sector, multilateral organizations, and academia—and entered into what proved a heated debate, all were motivated by a concern that the Lost Development Decade might stretch to the end of the century (indeed, millenium) and beyond.   In 1985, Middlebury College sponsored a conference on Third World debt (with some of the same participants), and the 1988 gathering was inaugurated with the sober realization that three years later the debt crisis was not only alive and well, but by most indicators worse than before.[2]

That the dismal economic performances of indebted countries is the result of the debt burden itself is hardly controversial, though the emphasis of authors varies.   One can go further and say that there is a growing consensus of the existence of a clear and present trade-off between growth and debt service. Shafiqul Islam of the Council on Foreign Relations has put it starkly:

> . . . [T]he primary reason half a decade of hard work to resolve the debt problem has resulted in failure and fatigue, and not in success and relief, is that the international debt managers have spent more time and energy on ensuring interest is collected in full and on time [for the private banks], and less working out a viable long-term solution.[3]

This emerging consensus that matters could no longer "muddle through" did not come easily.   In August 1982, the government of Mexico formally initiated the crisis by announcing its inability to meet payments on its huge foreign debt. From that time until August 1985, the international financial community—creditor governments, the two Bretton Woods multilaterals (the International Monetary Fund and the World Bank), and private commercial banks—pursued a strategy with regard to the debtor countries that came to be called "muddling through," a policy basically involving stop-gap rescheduling of debts (stretching out payments over time) and policy packages foisted upon debtor governments, usually designed by the IMF. By 1985, it was clear to all that while a general default on debt (or default by one or several of the major debtors) had been avoided, it had been achieved by the stifling of economic growth.   Indeed, a large number of countries in Latin America and Africa suffered economic decline.

The formal recognition that "muddling through" could not continue in its orginal form came in a proposal by James A. Baker III, U.S. Secretary of the

2. This point is documented in Chapter 14 by Dornbusch.
3. Islam (1988: 7-8).

Treasury, in a speech before the annual meeting of the Bretton Woods "twins."[4] There was little new in the proposal, but it had two major consequences. First, in the view of many, it successfully prevented the emergence of a Latin American debtors' cartel, which would have altered the balance of power between the financial community and the governments of the Third World.[5] Second, it rendered formal the mediating roles of the IMF and the World Bank in the debt crisis. The vehicle for such mediation would be multilateral lending to Third World countries coupled with strong policy conditionality, with these policy-contingent packages referred to generically as "structural adjustment programs." The essence of these programs was and is the conservative economic philosophy that calls for deregulation of markets, "supply side" actions such as tax changes and elimination of labor regulations, "liberalization" of external trade and finance, and moves to encourage greater foreign investment.

It is this policy package the April 1988 conference addressed. In particular, debate and discussion centered on whether these policies could be the vehicle by which the end would be brought to the Lost Development Decade. The issue of the appropriateness of these policies presents itself on several levels. At the most fundamental, there is the question of whether it is appropriate for multilateral agencies, whose officials are beholden to no constituency in the Third World, to play such a dominant role in the affairs of nations, involving themselves in matters that are as political as they are economic. The resolution of this first question probably makes little difference in practice, but it leads naturally to a second: If the debtor countries accept the legitimacy of the multilateral's policy conditionality, can they expect to reap the alleged benefits? The most important of these benefits in the short term is increased private bank financing, promised but not forthcoming under the Baker Plan. Structural adjustment programs frequently have a high domestic political cost in the adjusting country, and their main attraction for the debtor government is the new finance they would bring. In other words, without new finance, there is no reason a government should not design its own program without pressure from the multilaterals. The World Bank has always been quite clear that it sees new commercial bank finance as central to the success of the structural adjustment strategy.

4. Christine Bogdanowicz-Bindert, Senior Vice President of Shearson Lehman Hutton, wrote in 1986, "The Baker declaration was significant as it had taken three years of muddling through crises for the Reagan Administration to recognize the debt crisis for what it is: a long-term economic and political barrier to development that is slowly strangling world economic growth" (Bogdanowicz-Bindert 1986).

5. "My own assessment of the Baker Plan is that its major impact was to defuse any discussion of a debtor cartel in Latin America" (Bogdanowicz-Bindert 1986).

> . . . [B]anks must show . . . that they intend to play a full part in supporting
> essential adjustment and investment programs. Without adequate financing,
> these programs will continue to give results discouraging to debtors and
> creditors alike.[6]

The issue of whether accepting conditionality brings "fresh money" to a debtor government is perhaps the single most important political issue, because it raises the spectre of unilateral debt default. If the benefits are not positive, then perhaps default is not such a costly strategy on the part of debtor governments. But even more fundamental, it may be that new finance is not part of the solution, but part of the problem.

> The fundamental problem with [the structural adjustment strategy] is that it
> requires the debtors to raise their already intolerably heavy debt burden to even
> higher levels and transfer massive amounts of scarce resources year after year to
> service loans that are not generating new income.[7]

The other proposed source of benefits from structural adjustment is the alleged efficiency gains from a more optimal allocation of resources. The authors in this volume are quite divided on this issue. But out of the disagreement emerges a sense of humility about the ability of economists to prescribe optimal remedies, which represents a significant step forward in moving from debate to consensus. Closely related to the putative efficiency gains is the issue of who carries the burden of adjustment in the debtor countries, which is an issue with wide-ranging implications, including the support for the multilaterals by taxpayers in the developed countries. Few people in the creditor countries would support policies that systematically had the effect of transferring income from the poor in the Third World to the commercial banks in the First World.[8]

The foregoing issues are treated in the essays that follow. The reader will find as he or she proceeds a sense of urgency and even passion underlying the contributions. The conference participants agreed on one issue: The deterioration of living standards in the Third World has gone on too long, and action to foster development out of the ashes of debt and decline is tragically overdue.

John F. Weeks

6. World Bank (1987-1988: xvi).
7. Islam (1988: 11).
8. This issue is treated in Chapter 13 by Representative Bruce Morrison.

▌ DEBT CRISIS IN THE THIRD WORLD

In August 1982, just as the International Monetary Fund was about to convene its annual meeting in Toronto, the government of Mexico stunned the international financial community by announcing its inability to service its debt. Most date the "debt crisis" from that time, and it is still very much with us. The subsequent approach of the international financial community, both private and official, to the debt crisis has been to foster (impose, some would say) a package of policy measures in developing countries ostensibly designed to facilitate repayment of debt. The three essays in this first section of the volume deal with the context in which those policies have been applied.

In Chapter 1, Barry Herman considers a key unknown in the structural adjustment/debt equation—the global prospects for growth for developing countries as a whole. This is clearly a crucial issue, for if the prospects for growth in the aggregate are not propitious, then the likelihood of success with "muddling through" the debt crisis is not great. Closely complementary to Herman's analysis is the survey of the impact of changes in the world economy on developing countries by Rolph van der Hoeven in Chapter 2. His essay indicates that "external shocks" to the economies of developing countries have been severe indeed; further, the author demonstrates that it has been the poorest countries, and perhaps the poorest within those countries, that have suffered most.

In Chapter 3, John F. Weeks launches a frontal attack against the conventional wisdom of the financial community, arguing that the debt crisis

1

can be likened to a war that the developing countries lost, and that the debt service is equivalent to reparations paid by the defeated nations. In this interpretation, structural adjustment programs do not represent policy reform or growth strategies, but the international equivalent of blood-letting.

Each of these essays raises issues that are pursued in more detail in subsequent chapters, and each provides the reader with a context (if a sometimes controversial one) in which to evaluate the analyses and proposals that follow.

1 THE OUTLOOK FOR DEVELOPMENT

Barry Herman

We wish to say something about the outlook for development in the rest of the century. In essence, that is the same as wanting to say something about the experience of development in the 1980s. Whether done through estimated models or informal projections, futurology is based on the relationships we see today. The objective of this paper is to try to look to the future by saying some things about the present and by observing some things about economic attributes shared by most developing countries, though interestingly enough not by all.

WHICH COUNTRIES?

In a field like economic development, some definitional issues must first be settled to establish a common groundwork. One is to identify the countries that are included in the analysis and at least ask about the defining charac- teristics of the group. Low average income is not the key criterion, unless Kuwait and the United Arab Emirates are to be excluded, as they are two of the four countries with the highest per capita incomes in the world (the other two being Switzerland and the United States). Similarly, Ireland and Spain are

The views expressed in this paper are those of the author and do not necessarily represent those of the United Nations.

usually not thought of as developing countries, although Hong Kong, Singapore, and Trinidad and Tobago, which are, have higher income per head.[1]

The structure of trade also does not define development status: Australia and New Zealand are thought of as developed countries, yet the share of manufactures in their exports are 15 and 21 percent respectively, whereas the share for Bangladesh is 66 percent.[2] Nor is a relatively recent colonial past the key indicator: the Argentine Republic was declared in 1810, Colombia has been independent since 1819, and Turkey was the seat of the Ottoman Empire and a cradle of western civilization. The structure of production, skills of the labor force, health indicators, energy consumption, number of telephones, and statistically complicated combinations of these and many other indicators have offered possibilities for defining development status.[3] But, in fact, there is no analytically clean solution to this definitional dilemma and, not surprisingly, different authors draw different boundaries around the countries to be included.

Making definition is a particular difficulty for the official international institutions where government representatives express definite preferences for how they wish to be classified. The institutions meet the problem in various ways. The International Monetary Fund makes perhaps the largest grouping of developing countries, classifying all but twenty-one industrialized countries as developing (the Soviet Union, should it join the IMF, would presumably become the twenty-second developed country). Thus, the socialist countries of Eastern Europe, as well as Greece, Israel, Portugal, and South Africa, are included among the developing as far as IMF data—and statistical aggregates—are concerned. A smaller group is used by the United Nations Secretariat, as in its *World Economic Survey* and several other reports of the Department of International Economic and Social Affairs. It excludes all the countries just listed except Israel and Yugoslavia. Self-definition is a major aspect of the grouping—for example, through membership in the Group of 77, or being a major recipient of official development assistance.

In one sense, any definition will do as long as it is explicit. But in assessing the economic performance and financial situation of "the developing countries," it matters a great deal to the final statistics which countries are included or not, or at least which *big* countries are included or not, as the example of China will make clear below.

---

1. As measured for cross-country comparisons as of 1985 in World Bank (1987a).

2. This is due largely to jute products and, increasingly, garments. Data are for 1985; see United Nations (1987a: table 4.1).

3. See, for example, McGranaham et al. (1985).

DEVELOPMENT OF WHAT?

Economic development has always meant growing per capita output and income. It has entailed growing employment opportunities and rising productivity of labor. In the United States, at least since the days of Alexander Hamilton, it also meant a diversified economy with a manufacturing base. Later, Frank Knight made economists think about nurturing the ability to bear uncertainty, as well as take risks, while Joseph Schumpeter sensitized the profession to entrepreneurship, Veblen to culture, Hobson to empire, and Lenin to the state. The list may seem somewhat arbitrary, depending on where the reader went to school, but, in any event, things changed.

By the early 1960s, the physics metaphor was ascendant in economics and development became economic engineering. National planning was the rage for low-income countries. Largely private, technologically backward, and incompletely integrated economies were supposed to be guided into efficient production structures by price incentives (taxes and subsidies) derived from a central analysis of relative scarcities, and by direct state investment in selected areas of production, indicated by programming models for project selection. Algebra was everything. Even Schumpeter's "winds of creative destruction" became McClelland's "n-achievement" or Leibenstein's "x-efficiency." In 1965, the United Nations set up a Committee for Development Planning, composed of internationally prominent economists and headed by Jan Tinbergen, and charged it with elaborating planning techniques to share with developing countries.

Twenty-three years later, the United Nations committee still exists and still comprises prominent economists from around the world, but it never discusses planning as such. Perhaps coming full circle, a working group of the committee has recently produced a report that takes as its starting point the following quote from Amartya Sen: "The process of economic development can be seen as a process of expanding the capabilities of people."[4] By the same token, the received engineering-style wisdom that donor governments, the IMF, and the World Bank insist upon in programs of balance of payments adjustment has now been critiqued by another formulation—albeit not yet fully articulated—called "adjustment with a human face" (Cornia et al. 1987).

The picture just sketched is admittedly something of an exaggeration, made to emphasize a point. Twenty to thirty years ago one could push aside protests largely from sociologists and historians and talk about the growth of economic output, and do so using the more inclusive term "development." Of course, it

4. Taken from Sen (1983: 755), quoted in United Nations (1988a: 1).

was understood that there was more to development than the growth of output. But, surely, it was believed, the correlations were strong among economic growth, rising standards of living of the poor, emergence of an entrepreneurial class, and political development (the latter generally defined, at least in academic circles in the United States, as evolution of political institutions to increasingly resemble those of the industrial democracies). Unfortunately, it did not quite work out that way, and "growth without development" became a watchword in the development profession in the 1970s.

Somebody discovered that, "Despite unprecedented rates of aggregate economic growth in much of the 1950s and 1960s and impressive gains in health and literacy, more people in developing countries were living in deep poverty at the end of the 1960s than a decade earlier" (Martin 1985: 49). The result was to introduce broader considerations into policy planning exercises for developing countries, most notably through the country missions of the World Employment Programme of the International Labour Office, followed by the call of the president of the World Bank, Robert McNamara, to address poverty alleviation in the design of World Bank lending programs. At least there were efforts to measure and analyze income distribution and poverty in poor countries.

The critique of development practice was important to donor country governments. Whatever the *realpolitik* in disbursing official development assistance (ODA), it is sold to public opinion in donor countries as aid to the poor. As the wide public response to the last African famine demonstrated, people are deeply moved by acute suffering, especially if it occurs far away. If people believed that a larger aid appropriation did not reduce poverty, legislators would be hard-pressed to support it, and the leverage of governments in disbursing ODA would suffer. In the Third World, the anti-poverty critique of economic growth had a mixed reception. Representatives of developing country governments in international forums were distrustful, as is now again the case in response to the donor community's new enthusiasm for environmentally sound development. These ideas promised interference by outside meddlers, however well-intentioned, in domestic policy, politics, and the making of wealth.

This is not to defend developing country elites, who are as surely part of the problem as they are likely to be part of the solution.[5] But the developing country delegations were on to something, namely, that social policy was not development policy. Lord Peter Bauer was not King Lear, but there seems to

5. An interesting analysis to this effect is by one of the fathers of development economics and North-South negotiations, Raul Prebisch, in a series of long articles in English and Spanish in *CEPAL Review* (United Nations Economic Commission for Latin America and the Caribbean, Santiago), from 1976 to 1981, collected into Prebisch (1981).

be a kernel of truth in his writing about "relief of poverty or some other purpose unrelated to development" (Bauer 1981: 101).[6] Of course, this is put too strongly, but it seems that the social process that can be called economic development is consistent with a variety of policies toward poverty. The point can be asserted positively: "It is possible . . . for governments successfully to pursue distributive equity objectives as well as growth objectives" (United Nations 1988a: 5). Equivalently, distributive equity does not seem a part of the definition or measure of development. It may be an important determinant— many things are—but it is not part of the thing itself; neither is the emergence of friendly looking political institutions, nor consistently "good" macro-economic management or efficient resource allocation.

What does seem central to economic development is that there is a long run of rising per capita output and income, that a large share of income is continuously plowed back into the expansion, upgrading, and renewal of production capacity, that an increasing variety of commodities is produced and an increasing proportion designed locally, that people invest in themselves, and that a significant portion of the high- and low-income strata of the population is optimistic about the future.

FORTY YEARS OF DEVELOPMENT POLICY: HOW MUCH GROWTH?

A further perspective on the development prospect is gained from a review of some broad orders of magnitude at the global level. World economic analysis by the United Nations Secretariat, for example, divides the nations of the globe into three broad classifications: developed market economies (DMEs), centrally planned economies (CPEs), and the developing countries. About 75 percent of the people of the world live in the developing countries (defined to include China), 8 percent in the CPEs, and 17 percent in the DMEs. Average productivity differences among the groups—even after many decades of development efforts—are simply enormous, as is illustrated in Figure 1-1.[7] This is not to deny that there has been progress. Before 1990, output per capita in the developing countries as a whole is expected to reach twice that of 1960.

---

6. Taken from Bauer (1981), quoted by Michael Lipton (1984a: 44-50) in his Comment on Bauer that is highly recommended.

7. The level of output of the CPEs (the Soviet Union and Eastern Europe, excluding Yugoslavia) is somewhat understated compared to that of the other groups of countries because the data that the CPE governments report to the United Nations are net material product rather than gross domestic product, which includes more service activities.

Figure 1-1. Output Per Capita
(Thousand 1980 Dollars)

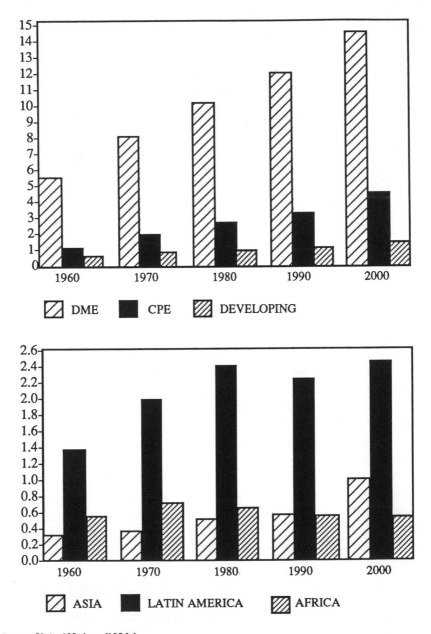

Source: United Nations (1986c).

However, excluding China, it will take almost until the year 2000 to double the 1960 per capita output level.

The growth rate of per capita output over the forty years from 1960 to 2000 is estimated on the basis of current projections to be almost the same in the developing as in the developed world, averaging 2.4 percent annually in the DMEs and 2.5 percent in the developing countries. However, excluding China, the developing countries' average rate of growth per capita drops significantly lower, to 2 percent per year. Certainly, the long-run rate of growth of output itself has been higher in the developing countries (4.7 percent annually on average) than in the DMEs (3.2 percent), but the difference is eaten away by the higher rate of growth of population in the former.[8] Such numbers are often used to buttress the argument for active population policies in developing countries, as indeed are warranted. But for purposes of the present discussion, attention should focus on the per capita growth trends per se, as over such a long period these may be taken as rough indicators of relative trends in productivity growth.

At such a gross level of aggregation and such an approximate level of analysis, the development enterprise does not seem to have been a success at all. The story is somewhat different at the regional level, where growth has been greatest over the long run in the developing countries of Asia.[9] Per capita output almost doubled from 1960 to 1980 and is forecast to almost double again by the year 2000 (see the second panel of Figure 1-1). Considering the low level of Asian per capita income in 1960—$254 at 1980 prices and exchange rates—this development was desperately needed.

At the other extreme, per capita output in Africa is lower now than it was in 1980, and it is not expected to regain even that level by the end of the century. Despite the vast oil wealth of the continent and considerable other resources, developing Africa (defined to exclude South Africa) will have become the poorest region in the world by 1990. The Latin America and Caribbean region has exhibited another form of tragedy. The economic structure of the region is generally more complex here than elsewhere, indicated by the fact that per capita output in 1980 was about three times that of the Asian and African average. It was said at the beginning of the international debt crisis in 1982 that Latin America might lose a decade of development. Measured by per capita output, that forecast seems to be coming true, and the 1990s do not yet hold out the promise of a greatly improved situation.

8. Population growth was 2.1 percent in all developing countries, but 2.3 percent excluding China, versus 0.8 in the DMEs.

9. Asia is defined here to range from Turkey in the west, through the Middle Eastern oil exporters, to the Pacific island countries in the east.

Figure 1-1 can be used to show that the gap between the developing countries as a whole (and each of the main regions) and the other groups of countries has been growing and is projected by the Secretariat to continue growing. However, the widening of the gap between developed and developing countries at the aggregate level was almost inevitable. Given the 1960 difference in income per capita levels, the developing countries would have had to grow by unrealistically rapid rates just to keep the absolute size of the gap from widening.[10] Indeed, even with the more rapid growth in the CPEs, the gap between them and the DMEs also grew, which can be seen as well in Figure 1-1.

The arithmetic is such that the only way the developing countries could narrow the gap with the industrialized countries is if the latter slowed their growth appreciably, which has already happened to a degree. A slowdown did take place in the 1980s, and only a partial recovery is forecast for the 1990s, but a slowdown also took place in the growth of the developing countries, and, again, only a partial recovery is projected for the 1990s (Table 1-1). The slowdown occurred in each of the three main regions, but in Africa and Latin America it took the form of an actual decline in output per capita. In Latin America, a certain developmental momentum was broken. For the 1970s as a whole, eight countries of the region (Brazil, Colombia, Costa Rica, the Dominican Republic, Ecuador, Guatemala, Mexico, and Paraguay) saw their GDP grow by more than 5 percent per year on average. In the 1980s, no country has seen that kind of growth year in and year out. In Africa, aside from certain major exporters of oil, Côte d'Ivoire, Kenya, Morocco, and Tunisia averaged over 5 percent GDP growth per year in the 1970s. Nevertheless, with population growing at about 3 percent per year and the output of other countries growing more slowly, growth of per capita output for the region was virtually nonexistent. For the 1980s as a whole, a drop of 1.4 percent per year on average is estimated.

Now, the usual analysis is that the developing countries need a rapid rate of growth in the DMEs so that the latter expand their imports of the exports of the developing countries and raise international commodity prices. Whether or not the industrialized world has been a generalized engine of growth for

10. A constant gap requires that the absolute change in per capita output in the developing countries be the same as that in the developed countries. If x is the output per capita of the developing countries and y is the same for the DMEs, then the criterion of a constant gap requires that $xx' = yy'$, where x' and y' are rates of growth. Thus, a constant gap requires $x' = (y/x)y'$. In 1960, $x = \$411$, $y = \$5445$ (both in 1980 dollars), and for the forty-year period, $y' = 2.4$ percent a year on average. To have maintained a fixed gap, the average annual rate of growth per capita would thus have had to be 32 percent per year over forty years.

Table 1-1. The Growth of Per Capita Output
(Average Annual Percentage Change)

	1960s	1970s	1980s	1990s
Developed Market Economies	3.8	2.3	1.6	2.0
Centrally Planned Economies	5.6	4.2	2.4	3.2
Developing Countries	3.2	2.9	1.3	2.6
Asia	2.8	4.0	3.2	3.8
China	0.0	5.3	6.9	5.5
Other Asia	3.6	3.5	1.8	3.1
Africa	3.4	0.2	-1.4	0.5
Latin America	3.3	2.3	-0.4	1.1

Source: United Nations Department of International Economic and Social Affairs (data 1960-1985, estimates 1986-1987, forecasts based on Project LINK to 1990, long-run projections to 2000).

development, there are reasons to wonder if the post-war period of rapid growth has not already ended.[11] The fact that Europe has been so politically tolerant of slow growth and high rates of unemployment, especially unemployment of youth, gives one pause. Nevertheless, authors have seen the "stationary state" on the horizon at least since the English classical economists and so far have been wrong.

One can envision a more attractive scenario for global growth than a stagnating center and a dependent periphery. The developing countries—in particular, the middle income countries—should become the world's new growth pole, pulling up global demand, generating new products and production processes, and so on. To a very limited degree, it has begun, for example, with Hong Kong designers showing at the *prêt à porter* exhibition in Paris, Indian engineering firms doing contract work abroad, Brazil exporting small aircraft (not to mention weapons), and Korean multinational firms establishing production facilities in North America. This kind of development, however, grows out of a long period of domestic economic dynamism, and one striking difference between the current decade and the 1970s is the far smaller number of countries that are experiencing sustained, rapid economic growth. For example, out of a sample of eighty-three developing economies, thirty-three had an average rate of growth of GDP of at least 5 percent per annum in the 1970s,

11. See, for example, Glyn et al. (1988).

while only ten have had this much growth on average thus far in the 1980s.[12] The countries that have undergone a significant growth slowdown are either major exporters of petroleum or countries whose foreign debt burden became impossible to bear. It is very hard to say anything with much confidence about petroleum prices or their outlook, but the role of the debt problem as a constraint on development is something else.

DEBT AND THE NET TRANSFER OF FINANCIAL RESOURCES

Not all the developing countries have a debt problem, but the difficulties of the highly indebted countries weigh so heavily that they have swung certain statistical aggregates of overall financial relationships. One, the net transfer of financial resources, which is the flow of financing net of the flow of financial service payments, has been the focus of international attention. For direct investments, this means the net increment to the stock of direct investment minus the net payment of dividends. For credit flows, it means the change in the net stock of foreign debt outstanding (aside from the valuation effects of exchange rate or price changes) minus the net payment of interest income. As the net stock of debt is the gross debt minus the foreign assets of developing country residents, the net credit flow includes outflows from the developing countries as well as foreign lending to those countries.[13] Finally, official transfers—mainly ODA and military assistance in grant form—are also included.

What is noteworthy about the aggregate net transfer is that it was significantly positive in the 1970s, but since the onset of the debt crisis it has become significantly negative. The results for the past ten years for a large sample of countries that have been net users of foreign capital over the past few decades are shown in Table 1-2. In the first four years of the period shown, from $37 billion to $42 billion was added to developing-country purchasing ability beyond what had been generated domestically. Since 1985, in contrast,

12. The 1980s list comprises Burma, Cameroon, Hong Kong, the Republic of Korea, Oman, Pakistan, Singapore, Thailand, Turkey, and Uganda. (Uganda qualifies only in the purely statistical sense, as it is recovering from a disastrous decade in which GDP *fell* on average by 1.7 percent per year.)

13. The convention followed by the United Nations Secretariat, the United Nations Economic Commission for Latin America and the Caribbean, and others, is to exclude additions to official reserve assets from the credit outflow of residents. The Secretariat explicitly treats reserve accumulation as a particular form of domestic inventory investment, namely accumulation of foreign currency assets. For further details, see United Nations (1986a: 163-164).

Table 1-2. Net Transfer of Resources of Capital-Importing Developing Countries

(Billions of Dollars, 98 Countries)

	1978	1979	1980	1981	1982	1983	1984	1985	1986	1987[a]
Direct Investment Transfer										
Net Investment Flow	4.6	7.2	6.4	10.2	7.9	6.6	6.2	7.5	5.7	7.5
Net Investment Income	-7.0	-8.6	-10.9	-10.3	-10.0	-9.7	-8.8	-8.1	-7.0	-8.5
Net Transfer	-2.4	-1.4	-4.5	-0.1	-2.1	-3.0	-2.6	-0.6	-1.3	-1.0
Private Credit Transfer										
Net Credit Flow	33.8	33.6	34.0	35.8	24.2	12.2	8.8	2.0	1.6	-1.0
Net Interest Paid	-11.8	-17.7	-18.5	-29.0	-42.4	-38.9	-41.4	-39.3	-33.6	-31.3
Net Transfer	22.0	15.9	15.6	6.9	-18.2	-26.7	-32.5	-37.2	-32.0	-32.3
Official Flows Transfer										
Grants	7.3	12.3	13.5	13.7	11.3	11.6	12.5	14.4	14.4	15.0
Net Credit Flow	14.1	15.4	22.0	28.4	29.5	27.8	25.0	14.2	15.0	13.8
Net Interest Paid	-4.4	-5.1	-6.2	-7.1	-8.8	-10.3	-11.8	-13.5	-16.2	-17.7
Net Transfer	16.9	22.6	29.2	35.0	32.0	29.2	25.7	15.2	13.1	11.1
Total Net Transfer	36.5	37.1	40.3	41.7	11.8	-0.6	-9.5	-22.7	-20.1	-22.2

a. Preliminary.

Source: United Nations Department of International Economic and Social Affairs, based on IMF data, national official, and other sources and estimates.

at least $20 billion of domestically generated purchasing power had to be transferred abroad instead of being used at home. That swing of roughly $60 billion is the heart of the debt problem and why it is so intractable.

The culprit is clearly visible in the table. It is not direct investment, although it has exhibited a negative financial transfer in every year. The amount of that transfer has been small overall and relatively smaller still in recent years. Official financial flows have come down quite sharply from their high in 1981, but they have remained positive (although the net transfer on account of official credit flows per se have been negative since 1986). Private credit, on the other hand, has been absorbing in excess of $30 billion a year in net transfers, whereas in the pre-crash years it had provided transfers of $15 billion or more a year.[14]

A few years ago, several authors emphasized that the swing in net credit transfers was not solely the fault of the private banks that had lost enthusiasm for extending new credits to debtor countries when the old loans could no longer be serviced. The problem, they said, was also and very much one of "capital flight." A number of observations are in order on that phenomenon. First, some of the banks that complained loudly about capital flight had themselves competed to attract such resources into accounts in their own banks, so if there is sin here, the banks are not innocent of it. Second, while the concept itself is elusive, estimates indicate that the outflow peaked in 1979-1982.[15] During those years, the overall net transfer of financial resources was at its most positive. In short, the negative net transfer problem is very much the result of the negative cash flow vis-à-vis the foreign private creditors.

The effect of the shift in net overall resource transfers can be seen most clearly if the grouping of countries is narrowed somewhat. Figure 1-2, for example, shows the net transfer and investment as a share of GDP for two groups of heavily indebted countries, one largely middle income and the other relatively poor. It may be seen that in the first group of countries—which are the fifteen countries usually associated with the proposal of the United States Secretary of the Treasury[16]—the net transfer of financial resources dropped from 2 percent of GDP at the beginning to -4 percent in the mid-decade years. The

14. The role of private credit flows in the fluctuation in overall net transfers can be put a bit more systematically. The variability of the overall net transfer measured as the standard deviation relative to the absolute value of the mean from 1978 to 1987 was 2.8. For direct investment it was 0.6, for official flows it was 0.3, but for private credit it was 1.9.

15. For an analysis and review of estimates, see Deppler and Williamson (1987: 39-58).

16. See the statement by Treasury Secretary James A. Baker III in IMF (1985a: 50-58). The countries, which were not an explicit part of the proposal, are Argentina, Bolivia, Brazil, Chile, Colombia, Côte d'Ivoire, Ecuador, Mexico, Morocco, Nigeria, Peru, Philippines, Uruguay, Venezuela, and Yugoslavia.

Figure 1-2. Net Resource Transfers and Investment in
Middle Income and African Country Groups
(Percent of GDP)

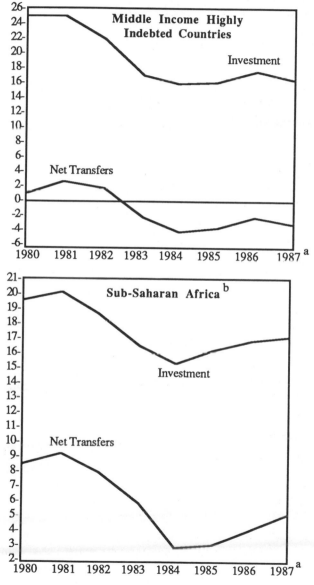

a. Preliminary.
b. Sub-Saharan Africa excludes Nigeria.
Source: United Nations (1988c: 54).

investment share of GDP moved almost in parallel. Development requires that it return to previous levels.

A similar pattern appears for the countries of Sub-Saharan Africa, which in the second panel of Figure 1-2 excludes Nigeria (which would otherwise swamp the data for the smaller countries of the region). The region has enjoyed a positive resource transfer throughout the period, but the swing in the size of that transfer has been almost as great as in the case of the middle-income countries, from around 8 percent of GDP in the early 1980s, to around 3 percent at mid-decade. Relative to the trough in 1984, the resource transfer and investment share have improved somewhat more for this group of countries than for the former, but the level remains below what was already an inadequate investment share in the early 1980s.

The swing in the net transfer of financial resources does not explain all the economic difficulties of the middle income countries or of the African countries. There have also been other international factors, with the weakness of international commodity prices in the 1980s having been a special burden. In Sub-Saharan Africa (again excluding Nigeria), it has been estimated that the net deterioration in the external financial position between 1979-1981 and 1985-1987 was almost equally split between terms of trade losses and losses through changes in the net transfer of resources.[17]

But, undoubtedly, there is still something more. Representatives of developed country governments and multilateral financial institutions have argued strongly in many forums that the developing countries have created their own difficulties through bad policy. Not that the developed countries have been so well managed themselves, but developing country representatives do acknowledge that they have made policy mistakes. Given present circumstances, that is an easy admission to make. What is not so simple is to provide an answer to the question of what to do next, an answer that takes into account political conditions in the developing countries and international economic prospects.

WHAT DO WE LEARN FROM
THE "SUCCESS" STORIES?

It has been noted above that while all the developing regions experienced a slowdown in growth in the 1980s, the Asian economies as a whole have been less seriously disrupted (again, see Table 1-1). Indeed, the United Nations

---

17. The total deterioration between the two periods expressed as an annual flow was estimated at $6.5 billion, of which $2.9 billion was terms of trade losses. See United Nations (1988b: 14).

Secretariat undertook a study of fourteen developing economies, all but two of which (Cameroon and Congo) were Asian, that were relatively fast growing in the first half of the 1980s. In comparing those economies to the other developing countries, certain patterns emerged.[18]

First, agricultural production grew faster in the faster-growing countries (for example, 4 percent for faster-growing energy importers versus 2 percent for other energy importers), continuing a difference in agricultural output trends of the 1970s. The 1980s difference in agricultural growth was attributed to the greater importance attached to agriculture in the development policy of the faster growers. This was given effect through an emphasis on the use of modern inputs and investment in infrastructure, especially irrigation, but it also included agricultural policies that provided effective incentives to farmers. It is significant as well in this context that food production was emphasized in countries that had been satisfying some of their food needs with imports. In an adverse international economic environment, that form of import substitution—especially for countries on the scale of China and India—had an inescapable logic.

It is a well-worn point in international discussions of development policy that a higher degree of export orientation raises economic growth. This was also found to be the case in the UN sample of countries, but even more important was the composition of exports. Two types of exports did especially well in the first half of the 1980s, namely manufactures and oil from small producers that were not bound by the ceilings on production agreed to by members of OPEC.

Development specialists have argued for decades about what poor countries should produce and export, very often invoking static efficiency (comparative advantage) arguments. The experience of the 1980s suggests tempering such considerations with three others. First, the ability to export a wide range of products seems essential in a volatile world economy, and some significant portion of these should probably be manufactures (as the case of Malaysia attests, where highly diversified exports of primary commodities did not provide protection from external strains when virtually all commodity prices sank). Second, something is wrong if development financing agencies promote the same commodity in a string of countries. The implicit "small-country" assumption that the international market will not be affected by the increment to supply does not hold for many countries added together. Third, a reallocation

---

18. The Asian economies included in the study were Burma, China, Hong Kong, India, the Republic of Korea, Malaysia, Oman, Pakistan, Singapore, Sri Lanka, Thailand, and Turkey. See United Nations (1987b: 155-167).

of resources toward tradeable goods is the wrong metaphor for what is involved. More accurate is intensive investment in the tradeable goods sectors.

A final domestic factor that distinguished the faster-growing countries was that they had substantially lower rates of inflation. Their rate of inflation averaged 11 percent during 1981 to 1985 among the energy importers in the sample, compared to 35 percent in the same period for other energy importers, with a comparable difference among the energy exporters. Coupled with faster growth of output, a relatively more stable economic environment must have helped to raise the savings rates, which were on average higher than in other developing countries. While maintaining a high investment rate, these countries had a smaller "savings gap," and thus needed to rely less heavily than other countries on external resources.

The faster-growing countries seemed, all in all, to partake more heavily of the factors that were claimed above to be central to economic development, including a long-run rise in per capita output and income, a high savings and investment rate, and a policy environment that encourages production of an increasing variety of commodities. But whether other countries can fit such results into their own political and economic environment is not a question easily answered, and neither is whether the conducive conditions in the countries actually developing will persist indefinitely.

So far only one country has graduated from being a troubled high-debt country to a more rapidly growing country with access to private international finance—Turkey. This is not to say that Turkey has solved all its macroeconomic problems, as it still registers high inflation and high unemployment. After having undergone a series of debt reschedulings and macroeconomic adjustment programs starting in the latter years of the 1970s, Turkey was able to return to the private credit markets in 1985. Several things happened along the way, including a large growth in exports, both to the Middle East and Europe. Significantly, the composition of exports also changed: manufactures rose from 36 percent of exports in 1980 to 75 percent in 1985. Output has grown substantially, averaging 5 percent per year thus far in the decade, which has undoubtedly eased the burden of exchange rate devaluations and other adjustment measures. Investment has also been strong, led in 1980—and this is important—by a recovery of public sector investment supported by large-scale net financial transfers from abroad in the form of official assistance.[19]

---

19. The net financial transfer rose from 1.2 percent of GNP in 1978-1979 to 4.9 percent in 1980, which also considerably helped ease the burden of a 23 percent real effective exchange rate devaluation, not to mention an 18 percent terms-of-trade loss largely from the increase in oil prices (United Nations 1987c: 90-91). The IMF and the World Bank alone have provided Turkey with

Aid on a comparable scale for all the heavily indebted developing countries is not now on the horizon. A continuing negative net resource transfer is. And should the world's central banks of the Group of Seven industrialized countries tire of supporting the dollar as much as they have been doing recently,[20] interest rates in the United States would have to rise. If that in turn led to the onset of the next recession—and recessions have not been outlawed—developing countries could find themselves in another financial squeeze of rising interest charges and falling commodity export prices. The shadow that this scenario casts on the outlook for development is a long one.

about $4.5 billion in eight World Bank adjustment loans and three IMF standby arrangements since 1980. See World Bank (1988).

20. Although estimates of the net amount of official financing of the $161 billion current account deficit of the United States in 1987 are necessarily imprecise, it seems to have accounted for two-thirds of the total. See United Nations (1988c: 72-73).

2 EXTERNAL SHOCKS, ADJUSTMENT, AND INCOME DISTRIBUTION

Rolph van der Hoeven

For more than a decade developing countries have undergone a number of external shocks. Depending on their intensity and the characteristics of the economic structure in place, these shocks had direct consequences on developing countries' capacity to pursue domestic economic and social policies; employment and income levels in many countries have been negatively affected in many countries. The various external shocks did not take place simultaneously, but rather overlapped (Table 2-1). After the commodity price boom in 1977, the terms of trade for developing countries deteriorated for five consecutive years, improving slightly in 1983 and 1984, and declining again in 1985 and 1986. Some years of continuous improvement will be needed to wipe out losses accrued during 1978 to 1982. The growth rate in industrialized countries began to decline seriously in 1980, resulting in decreased demand for developing country exports.

Until 1980, foreign real interest rates (measured in terms of nonfuel developing country export prices) were low or even negative. Many developing countries made ample use of the availability of commercial bank capital to finance the losses caused by changes in terms of trade and the shrinking markets, and thus try to preserve consumption and investment patterns of the

The views expressed in this paper are those of the author and do not necessarily reflect those of UNICEF. Parts of this paper draw upon van der Hoeven (1987and 1988) and van der Hoeven and Vandemoortele (1987).

21

Table 2-1. Nonfuel-Exporting Developing Countries:
External Shocks, 1978-1987[a]

(Percent)

	78	79	80	81	82	83	84	85	86	87
Change in Terms of Trade	-3.9	-1.2	-5.8	-4.-0	-2.0	0.6	2.6	-2.3	-2.9	0.6
Real GNP Growth of Industrial Countries	4.2	3.3	1.3	1.5	-0.3	2.7	4.9	3.2	2.7	3.1
Foreign Real Interest Rates[b]	2.7	-6.8	-2.0	16.1	19.4	16.0	10.5	13.6	6.8	n.a.
Capital Flows ($000 mil)[c]	28.4	26.0	59.2	57.3	31.3	19.2	14.7	16.4	5.2	4.9
Latin America[d]	25.8	27.1	33.0	51.3	25.8	5.8	2.3	-1.5	-4.6	-1.8
Sub-Saharan Africa	1.6	0.2	4.0	1.9	0.3	1.4	-2.0	-1.9	-0.9	-1.3
Current Account Deficit[e]	-11.9	-14.2	-16.5	-20.1	-17.2	-10.9	-6.5	-6.1	-1.8	1.0

a. The following developing countries are fuel exporters: Algeria, Bahrain, Congo, Ecuador, Gabon, Indonesia, Islamic Republic of Iran, Iraq, Kuwait, Libyan Arab Jamahiriya, Mexico, Nigeria, Oman, Qatar, Saudi Arabia, Syrian Arab Republic, Trinidad and Tobago, Tunisia, United Arab Emirates, and Venezuela.

b. Long-term rates of seven major OECD countries, adjusted for percentage changes in export prices of nonfuel-exporting developing countries.

c. Net external borrowing excluding borrowing from official creditors and reserve-related liabilities.

d. Data for Latin America include Ecuador, Mexico, Venezuela, and Trinidad and Tobago.

e. As percentage of exports and goods and services.

Source: IMF (1988, and earlier issues).

1970s. However, deflationary policies in industrialized countries pushed interest rates to all-time levels after 1980, making it difficult for many indebted countries, already struggling with low prices and low volume of exports, to service their debts. The debt service problem, especially the dramatic Mexican crisis, and the need to finance the increasing current account deficit of the United States led to a sizable reduction in capital flows to developing countries after 1982,[1] making it difficult for countries to finance their current account deficits through additional borrowing, especially because fuel-exporting countries have ceased to produce current account surpluses.

As a consequence, most developing countries were forced in a rather short time to reduce their current account deficits quickly and drastically either as part of an agreed stabilization and adjustment package or through emergency

1. See Chapter 4 by Lissakers and Chapter 5 by Sacks and Canavan on factors influencing commercial bank lending to developing countries.

measures. Current account deficits expressed as a percentage of exports of goods and services returned in 1983 to the pre-1978 level, declined even further in 1984, 1985, and 1986, and turned into a surplus in 1987. Because these deficits are expressed as a percentage of exports of goods and services, which hardly increased, a lower percentage implies a considerable reduction in imports. This is especially true for Africa and Latin America, where imports dropped 19 percent and 36 percent respectively over the brief period from 1981 to 1983.

In this limited sense developing countries were able to adjust to the effects of these shocks. But three qualifications are in order. First, although as a group developing countries have managed to adjust their balance of payments deficits, such an adjustment is not the most appropriate response on a global level. The contraction inevitably had second-round negative effects on the industrialized countries. It has been estimated, for example, that the economic recession in the Third World cost the United States alone more than $60 billion in exports and 1.7 million jobs from 1980 to 1986 (Sewell et al. 1988). Second, as we have seen, capital inflows decreased and the terms of borrowing worsened, which narrows the margin for a viable balance of payments considerably.[2] This, of course, struck at the roots of growth and employment creation. A less abrupt change and more room to maneuver would have reduced costs of adjustment. Third, as stabilization and adjustment were forced upon developing countries primarily by external events, it seemed difficult for many to adjust in an orderly manner. Adjustment to changed international circumstances could not and cannot be brought about overnight. Adjustment involves a restructuring of many aspects of the economic framework through policies such as changing income distribution, asset distribution, and prices of products and factors, perhaps through direct intervention in some markets. Such policies generally need time to be fully effective. Furthermore, abrupt changes in government policies may meet with so much resistance that implementing them becomes extremely difficult, resulting in popular unrest that prompts abandonment or reversal of policy changes.

Although the macro figures, especially the balance of payments gap, show a favorable trend, this should not be a reason for optimism. On the contrary, it is more important to see how and under what circumstances countries have adjusted. After considering this, one should investigate the consequences for employment levels and poverty, and the future prospects for growth and alleviating poverty. From the ensuing discussion it will become clear that all

2. The concept of a viable balance of payments typically means, especially for many developing countries, a current account deficit that can be financed on a sustainable basis by net capital inflows on terms that are compatible with the development and growth prospects of the economy (Guitian 1980).

adjustment policies and measures have direct and indirect consequences for the distribution of income among various groups in the society. Neglecting these distributional aspects will not only upset any social balance, but will also affect the potential welfare of various groups in the long run.

I examine the effects of the shocks and consequent policies by focusing on two country groups, Latin American and Sub-Saharan Africa (followed specifically by Kenya). Both regions have suffered a drop in per capita income since 1980; in Latin America the 1985 per capita income was about 9 percent lower than in 1980, while the per capita income in Africa was 10 percent lower.

ADJUSTMENT POLICIES IN LATIN AMERICA

Many Latin American countries have known a long tradition of inflation and associated adjustment programs. Persistent inflationary pressure is often explained by prevailing social and economic conflicts on the distribution of surplus (Hirschman 1981, especially chapter 8). More recently, excess liquidity of the international capital market allowed many Latin American countries to finance current account deficits through external borrowing. This was especially relevant from the late 1970s to the early 1980s, when Latin America to a large extent played the role of absorber of the current account surpluses of the oil-exporting countries. External borrowing was used to finance both government deficits as well as investment in private and public enterprises. Investment demand and the financing of the public-sector deficit had an expansionary impact on the economy because domestic savings were not crowded out. With high import coefficients for intermediate and capital goods, imports rose more quickly than exports and current account deficits were financed with yet new inflow of loans and capital.

However, after contractionary policies in the industrialized countries (beginning in 1980), real costs of capital skyrocketed. Most loans were provided on floating rates, so room had to be made to finance increasing amounts of debt service payments, a situation aggravated by a sizable capital flight, especially significant in Venezuela, Argentina, and Mexico.[3] Many countries embarked on a set of adjustment and stabilization measures, which became increasingly necessary after 1982, when capital flows to Latin America virtually dried up.

Policies regarding the external balance succeeded. Latin American current account deficits were reduced from $42,400 million in 1982 to $2,600 million

3. For these countries capital flight as a percentage of gross capital inflows over the period 1979-1982 was respectively 137 percent, 65 percent, and 48 percent, compared to only 8 percent in Brazil (IBRD 1985).

in 1984, and $4,700 in 1985, while the balance in trade account reached a surplus of $37,600 million in 1984 and $32,700 million in 1985 (IMF 1987). But stabilization and adjustment policies were not without costs. Latin American exports did not grow, terms of trade remained unfavorable, and interest rates stayed high. Adjustment was reached through a large contraction of imports, which by 1985 were 43 percent below 1980 levels (Geller and Tokman 1986).

Because of the structure of industry in most Latin American economies such a fall in imports primarily resulted from a contractionary policy. Real per capita GNP fell by 9 percent between 1980 and 1985. Such internal contraction resulted in increases in unemployment: open unemployment in the region increased from 7 to 11 percent from 1980 to 1984. The later figure is still an underestimation, for participation rates were falling and hours worked decreased. A comparable figure would be in the order of 13 percent (Geller and Tokman 1986). Unemployment increased particularly in Chile, Colombia, Peru, and Venezuela. In addition to unemployment rising, real wages fell in most cases. Table 2-2 indicates severe decreases in Mexico and Peru of 35 and 22 percent respectively, and sizable decreases in Chile and Venezuela.

Because most Latin American economies have low shares of agriculture in their GDP, almost all adjustment and stabilization policies carried out relate to urban formal-sector activities. The more important adjustment policies involved reduction of government deficits, devaluation, liberalization, and wage restraint. Reduction of the government deficit has contractionary effects. While devaluation is supposed to have initial contractionary effects, its longer-term impact is allegedly expansionary. Effects of liberalization are both short- and long-term, with the principal aim to stimulate a smoother transfer of resources from one sector to another, as well as to attract foreign finance. Decreases in real wages are aimed at increasing employment opportunities (assuming a high elasticity of substitution), regaining international competitiveness, and diminishing production cost and consequently inflation. But as I will argue, many of the assumptions did not hold and the outcome was often radically different.

As noted elsewhere, hardly any new foreign finance is available to most Latin American countries, so the public-sector deficit can no longer be financed through external loans.[4] Yet the government budget has come under severe pressure at the same time. Budget deficits were partly the result of decreasing revenues (import and export taxes), increased transfer payments because of recession, and increased interest payments on public debt (and private debt that

---

4. See the discussion in Chapter 14 by Dornbusch.

Table 2-2. Cumulative Change in Real Industrial Wages (W)
and Open Unemployment Rates (E) in Selected Countries, 1981-1985

Country		1981	1982	1983	1984	1985
Argentina	W	-10.7	-21.2	8.1	28.9	-
	E	4.7	5.3	4.6	4.6	6.3
Brazil	W	6.5	13.9	3.8	-2.9	-
	E	7.9	6.3	6.7	7.1	5.3
Chile	W	11.7	8.8	-2.4	-3.1	-
	E	9.0	20.0	19.0	18.5	17.0
Colombia	W	0.4	4.3	7.9	16.8	-
	E	8.2	9.3	11.8	13.4	14.1
Mexico	W	3.1	1.7	-23.4	-35.5	-
	E	4.2	4.2	6.7	6.0	4.8
Peru	W	-1.9	-1.0	-22.2	-22.2	-
	E	10.4	10.6	13.9	16.4	17.6
Venezuela	W	-3.0	0.0	-3.1	-10.0	-
	E	6.8	7.8	10.5	14.3	14.3

Source for wages: ILO (1986).
Source for unemployment: ILO/PREALC (1986).

has been taken over by the central government).[5] As a consequence, recourse
had been sought, much more than in the past, to monetary financing of the
public-sector deficit, which contributed to inflation. Still, sizable efforts were
made to cut expenditure, primarily through reduced capital expenditure.
Investment in social infrastructure suffered most (IDB 1985: 63).

To boost production of tradeables, devaluation of the currency has often been
used. Unfortunately, the international situation, as well as the structure of
industry in Latin America, has made devaluation less than effective. The
international recession, mounting protectionism, and application of devaluation
by virtually all Latin American countries reduced expected benefits. Moreover,
a sizable portion of Latin America's export products still consists of raw
materials and minerals that have a low price elasticity. Perhaps more important
is that imports mainly consist of intermediate products and capital goods and
relatively few final consumer goods. The first two categories are much less
sensitive to price changes than the third. The major consequence of devaluation
is the increase in production costs, which is compensated for either by

5. Weeks discusses the socialization of private debt in Chapter 3.

increasing prices of final products or by decreasing wages.[6] To deal with these phenomena firms must either increase productivity or shift production to more profitable activities. The latter, however, requires much more time than is conventionally allowed in stabilization policies. Real wages are often the cost category par excellence to be reduced to compensate for other cost increases. Because the short-term structure of production is fixed, decreases in wages do not immediately lead to increased employment. It has been observed that after implementation of stabilization policies the wage share in national income has decreased (Pastor 1985). Because costs have been reduced, or rather not increased, international competitiveness could increase. But, again, time lags involved could be too long for any program (or the government implementing the program) to survive. An immediate effect of decreased real wages is a drop in demand by wage earners, which adds to the contractionary climate.

Although country experiences vary, most adjustment programs include elements of liberalization and deregulation. The latter is often applied through dismantling public-sector enterprises and reducing government direction of investable funds. The former usually means reducing state intervention on the domestic capital market (mobility of foreign capital) and in the trade sphere (removal of restrictions and taxes or subsidies on imports and exports). However, because the public sector has played an historically important role in establishing enterprises in Latin America, it is difficult to reform this role away. It is indeed questionable whether the private sector in most countries is able and willing in the present economic climate to take over the role of the public sector (PREALC 1985).

Liberalizing factor and product markets in neoclassical theory will have positive results. Unfortunately, the theory starts from a hypothetical situation of equilibrium in which distortions are introduced, and then shown to decrease welfare (Addison and Demery 1986). However, the more relevant situation to start from (a highly distorted economy out of equilibrium in which distortions are dismantled one by one) is much more difficult to analyze, as the experience of liberalization attempts in the Southern Cone of Latin America indicates. Problems encountered arose from two main sources: the opening up of economies during world recession and the method of implementing the liberalization strategy, which went too fast, lacked adequate coordination between liberalization in each market, and was not supported by appropriate macroeconomic policy (Corbo 1985).

The example given at present of the country having most successfully undergone structural transformation and able to reduce current account deficits in

6. See Solimano (1986) for the example of Chile.

a rather short time is that of Brazil. Structural adjustment in Brazil was achieved through very heterodox policies relying on massive public investment and control of various markets rather than on more conventional or orthodox policy instruments. Although not all projects have borne fruit (some projects in Brazil can be quoted as perfect examples of white elephants), the heterodox policies allowed Brazil to undergo a process of structural change that enables it now to react better to external shocks. Had Brazil applied more restrictive policies, as Chile did, it would not be in as good a position to respond positively to the external environment (Cortazar 1986).

Recent experience in Latin American countries has shown that quick turnarounds in balance of payments deficits can be arrived at in a rather short period of time. But such a turnaround is often at the risk of unduly large contraction, which severely affects vulnerable groups of the population. Fundamental structural changes are needed for countries to better weather the shocks in the future. What should be the characteristics of adjustment programs accompanying such structural changes? This obviously depends on the long-term objectives of development policies and the effectiveness of the instruments used. Development objectives should form the major guidance for any adjustment program. If the objectives are not clearly spelled out and translated into effective instruments, any adjustment program will fail to contribute to meaningful development. It should go without saying that setting objectives and choosing the development path is a national prerogative depending on the specific situation in each country. However, a number of general observations can certainly be made.

Two conclusions emerge from studying the problems Latin America has encountered: (1) producing foreign exchange in an interdependent world has to remain (or become) an important priority, and (2) protection has led in the past to decreased incentives and sometimes to prestige projects with little future earning capacities. On the other hand, across-the-board measures like devaluation and sudden liberalization of markets have not led to desired and expected results because of the characteristics of the economic and production system in Latin America. Thus, selectivity in instruments and the recognition that non-market instruments are important should be explicitly built into any adjustment package, which would allow the adjustment program to be more target-oriented and to take into account concerns for employment and poverty (PREALC 1985).

An important element in this would be the selective use of trade policy instruments. Activities that create more employment and cater to production of essential services could be subjected to higher import tariffs. However, to avoid a situation in which too little attention is given to exports, certain export activities, those in which the prospects are more buoyant, should receive subsidies to be paid out of proceeds from increased import tariffs. A more selective application of trade tariff policies should, however, not lead to a neglect of exchange rate policies, which keep the rate at a stable and adjusting level to avoid large fluctuations.[7]

The public sector in Latin America has often acted to protect interests of poorer groups, through low-cost housing and infrastructure construction, for example. It should certainly continue to fulfill this important role, as well as regulating a considerable share of investment in productive sectors. A further element of an adjustment package should be a coordinated set of incomes and price policies acceptable to all parties. Some countries have established complicated indexation systems that tend to perpetuate inflation. If these are to be given up, workers can justifiably expect a period of price control, or at least intervention to secure price moderation for basic goods. Furthermore, to achieve more equitable burden-sharing, reduction should not only be restricted to wage income but also to income from other sources, such as profit and rental income. Equity in this regard could be achieved through direct taxes and selective consumption taxes on luxury goods. By dealing with wages, profits, conspicuous consumption, and prices simultaneously, organized labor's fear of bearing most of the adjustment burden may be removed.

The social climate can improve even further if wage policies that reduce wages of poorer workers less than those of more highly paid workers (or perhaps not at all) are adopted. Furthermore, for some groups of workers profit-sharing could be an acceptable trade-off for wage restraint in times of austerity. Temporary increases in social security benefits represent still another equity option. Wage restraint could in some instances be accompanied by non-economic benefits such as a more complete respect for trade union rights, collective bargaining, participation in certain types of enterprise management, or in the preparation of certain government measures affecting workers and their organizations (Zoeteweij 1985).

The main conclusion is that too much emphasis has been placed on the effectiveness of a restricted number of policy instruments in restoring a viable balance of payments situation in Latin America. The exercise of adjustment needs to be placed in a broader developmental framework. To this we should add that slow growth in the OECD countries had been a major (but not the only) reason for disappointing Latin American export performance. Interest payment and amortization of Latin American debt has taken on such proportions that increases in exports will not lead to increased imports,

---

7. In Chapter 8, Fletcher discusses exchange rate policy with emphasis on manufactured exports.

portending problems especially for the U.S. economy. The drop in demand for U.S. exports has affected manufacturing industries and agricultural exporters, sectors in which unemployment is on the rise in the United States, and in which real incomes have been declining for a number of years. From a political economy's point of view, it is not surprising that proposals are emerging from these affected groups to grant Latin American countries debt and interest relief to make room for increased imports from the United States (Joint Economic Committee 1986).

The costs of such relief proposals are at the expense of the banking community, which has resisted such suggestions. However, the banking community did react enthusiastically to another proposal, the Baker Plan, which sought to restore some of the capital flow to developing countries and especially Latin America, and attempted to stimulate economic growth to allow for full repayments at a late date. The speed with which banks are writing off their loans to Latin America indicates, however, that most have made an implicit choice on practical grounds. If the countries in Latin America could also profit from these changes by seeing the value of their debt reduced, benefits and costs would be more equitably distributed.

ADJUSTMENT POLICIES IN SUB-SAHARAN AFRICA

Economic decline in Africa has forced many countries to undertake stabilization and adjustment policies. In 1987, no less than twenty African countries had concluded standby arrangements with the International Monetary Fund. Balance of payments deficits have been reduced, but the turnaround in economic activity has yet to come. Real wages—in modern nonagricultural activities, for example—have dropped considerably (Table 2-3). Furthermore, the growth of modern nonagricultural employment is lower, often much lower, than that of the labor force, indicating an increase in either open unemployment or underemployment (Table 2-3; see also van der Hoeven, forthcoming).

Why has the situation in Africa not improved? Why were objectives of adjustment policies so difficult to obtain, let alone able to bring about a reversal of the declining trend in real wages and in employment growth opportunities? Although situations differ in many countries, a common denominator is that the structure of African economies renders conventional policies less effective than elsewhere, and in certain cases countereffective. The main elements of adjustment and stabilization policies in Africa are common,

Table 2-3. Index of Nonagricultural Real Wages, Employment and Labor Force
(1980 = 100)

Country	Year Latest Figure Available	Nonag. Wages	Year Latest Figure Available	Nonag. Employment Modern Sector	Nonag. Labor Force
Kenya	1985	78	1983	111	120
Zambia	1984	67	1983	95	114
Tanzania	1983	60	1984	123	124
Malawi	1984	76	1983	103	136
Mauritius	1985	90	1984	102	118
Swaziland	1983	95	1983	119	117
Zimbabwe	1984	89	1983	113	116

Source: Unpublished ILO data.

one of the most important of which is a reduction in the public deficit, usually achieved by decreasing public activities. However, public-sector deficits have often increased because of external causes. Lower imports and exports mean less tax revenue. Taxes on international trade as a percentage of total government revenue dropped in Zaire during 1972 to 1982 from 58 percent to 25 percent, in Tanzania from 51 to 22 percent, in Madagascar from 42 to 35 percent, in Kenya from 38 to 24 percent, and in Zambia from 48 to 14 percent. At the same time, because of the recession increased claims are put on the government to cushion effects through price subsidies and alternative provision of employment. Cutting expenditure is made more difficult by pressure for recurrent costs of development projects financed with bilateral or multilateral aid.

Because most African countries have low credit ratings in international capital markets, borrowing to finance budget deficits is primarily domestic. Moreover, in the absence of sizable domestic capital markets, resort is mostly sought directly from the banking system, which generates a direct inflationary impact. However, as imports are usually rationed or otherwise limited, the inflationary impact does not translate itself directly into increased imports, but into excess liquidity in the domestic market. This excess liquidity finds its way into urban and rural informal activities and into black markets for foreign exchange, where rates are pushed up by great pressure to transfer wealth, at almost any cost, out of the country.

No country would admit that an excessive budget deficit is a healthy cause, and various attempts have already been made to trim down budgets. Central government fiscal imbalances in Sub-Saharan Africa have been considerably reduced since 1982. In 1985, governments of Sub-Saharan countries had lower fiscal imbalances than in the United States and other large industrial countries (Table 2-4). Rather than desperately cutting down fiscal deficit in a very short period, it is more appropriate to remove the underlying causes of the budget deficit, on both income and expenditure, and to spread out fiscal reforms over a longer period of time. This would avoid the frustration for many countries of not regularly meeting targets of lowering public deficits. It is worthwhile to note that African countries with a poor administrative structure are asked to trim budgets at a pace that none of the industrial countries has been able to reach despite official commitment to such a course of action. Spreading deficit reduction over time would allow for planning and discussion of future directions of public spending. Planning could include contingency programs to safeguard essential basic services, a point discussed later. Trimming expenditure too drastically can easily have negative consequences for investment, precisely the category of final demand that needs to expand.[8]

Finally, the effects of reducing government expenditure do not have a large direct effect on imports. The balance of payments effect of reduced public deficits has to come from general deflation which, because of indirect effects, may require rather large expenditure cuts to be effective.

Because of faster inflation as compared to their trading partners, many African countries have seen their effective exchange rates increase, indicating overvaluation. However, most African countries are price-takers at the world market, and a devaluation of the currency will not result in an expansion of their export share. Any positive effect has to come from an expansion of supply, which is supposed to take place after devaluation through an increase in incomes in domestic currency to those sectors of the economy that produce exportables. Imports are supposed to fall as they become more expensive, though the immediate effect of this is to add to inflation. The major effect of devaluation is thus a change in income distribution. Incomes of producers of exportables are increased while others will see their real incomes diminished because of increased prices. To support this change in income distribution, additional increases in producer prices for agricultural crops are often proposed, both for exportables and domestic food crops. As the devaluation will make the cost of imported food products more expensive, prices for locally produced

---

8. Helleiner (1985) argues that reactions to the second oil shock had more drastic effects on investment than the reactions to the first oil shock.

Table 2-4. Central Government Fiscal Balances

	1981	1982	1983	1984	1985	1986
Sub-Saharan Africa	-6.6	-6.9	-5.8	-4.8	-5.0	-5.5
United States	-2.4	-4.1	-5.6	-4.9	-5.1	-5.0
Six Largest Industrialized Countries Excluding U.S.[a]	-4.5	-5.0	-5.3	-5.1	-4.7	-4.3

a. Canada, Japan, France, the Federal Republic of Germany, Italy, and the United Kingdom.
Source: IMF (1987).

crops are often set at a slightly higher level to boost domestic production.

The problem in many primary product countries is that such measures will, for a variety of reasons, not immediately provide the desired effect. First of all, some exportable crops, such as coffee, tea, and rubber, have a long gestation lag from planting to harvesting. Second, because of the continued recession, existing infrastructure to support increases in exports has often deteriorated, to a large extent constraining quick increases in export production. Moreover, in such a situation increased export proceeds from devaluation and/or price increases may merely inflate monetary demand for goods that are unavailable because of the pitiful state of the production of domestic products or import restrictions. This results in inflationary pushes, backward-bending supply-curve reactions, or illicit trading of agricultural goods for consumer goods with neighboring countries.[9]

It is consequently questionable whether the reactions of producers on the export side will be as expected by theory. Equally important is what happens in the urban environment. Poverty in Africa is becoming an increasingly urban phenomenon, as the gap between rural and urban incomes has narrowed (Jamal and Weeks, forthcoming a; Ghai 1987). Although this may mark a reversal of earlier and unwanted trends, some aspects are a cause for concern. First, the decrease in the rural-urban earnings gap has come less from a sizable increase in rural incomes than from large cuts in real wages. In Tanzania and Zambia, for example, real wages have halved in a time span as short as five to six years. Second, real wages have decreased largely because of sizable increases in the price of basic staples, either because subsidies were abolished or through the

9. In Chapter 12, Jamal discusses these "perverse" reactions in some detail in his analysis of Tanzania under structural adjustment.

combined effects of adjusting producer prices to border prices at a time of currency devaluation. The price of food traditionally plays an important psychological role in African societies, and although price increases may have been warranted, their extent has often met with strong reactions.

The measures indicated above aim at a shift of factors of production toward producing exportables. But the question is whether such a shift can take place quickly to relieve the pressure on the balance of payments and whether such a shift is always in the long-term interest of the country involved. For most primary producing countries the shift will mean for some time to come a process of deindustrialization. One may wonder whether measures to adjust and stabilize will not overshoot their objective by diverting the long-term development paths of primary product producing countries. Stabilization and adjustment measures, if they were better able to serve the aim of increased growth and employment, should take into account the economic structure and the long-term development goals of the country. This will mean that programs should be more country-specific and take into account the particular problems African countries are facing (Loxley 1986a).

One of the most serious problems most African countries face is that of import strangulation. Imports have been reduced to the bare necessities. Per capita import volume in Sub-Saharan Africa in 1984 was 82 percent of that in 1981, the level for the latter year being 25 percent lower than in 1970. This decline resulted in increases in excess capacity (ILO 1988) and caused a slow-down in economic growth. Adjustment programs aimed at reviving growth will not succeed unless a sufficient amount of imports can enter the country right from the beginning of the program in the form of intermediate products or consumption goods, which would imply allocating funds at the beginning rather than during the program.[10]

Because of the structure of many African countries, policies need to be more selective rather than rely on across-the-board effects of changes in prices. Not all Africa's export products will be able to rapidly expand; selective incentives will need to be given to those products that show more prospects. Furthermore, imports should be (or continue to be) allocated to the most dynamic sectors in the economy, and imports of basic consumer goods may be

10. Such "front-loading" of imports would, of course, reduce the amount of control financial agencies have by means of checking against performance indicators during the course of the program. However, as most countries are on an almost permanent basis engaged in activities with the IMF and the World Bank, the question of control becomes less urgent. Performances and assessment of programs can be made from one program to the other, allowing for a greater time period of the program to materialize. Moreover, regular discussion on performance can still be held because the threat of discontinuing financing of a program has often been more theoretical than practical.

required at the same time. Imports should thus form part of a preconceived investment and spending plan in which more funds are to be allocated to intermediate products and to maintenance in order to arrive at a rapid increase in output. As a sizable portion of imports enters in the form of goods and products of projects financed with foreign aid, coordination of donor activities should form an integral part of selective import and export measures.[11] Regarding the agricultural sector, emphasis in adjustment programs is overwhelmingly on export crops (although farm and consumer prices of food crops are usually taken into account). Given the poor state of food production in Africa, more emphasis ought to be given to domestic food production. Here a fresh look could be given to the various institutions involved in transporting and marketing foodstuffs, cutting waste and overheads, and transferring some activities to the private sector (Green 1986).

Adjustment policies often change the distribution of income considerably; special consideration should be given to the social effects of income distribution. Large decreases in real wages and reduction of essential services, including education and health, will have not only social effects, but effects on labor productivity, especially for low-income workers. If wages drop quickly and reach extremely low levels, worker morale suffers, productivity falls, and second-job activities increase to complement falling incomes, a scenario that sets into motion a downward spiral of lower wages and lower productivity. In cases where a decrease in real wages in some industries and public services appears unavoidable, alternatives to cushion the effects of falling wages should be introduced from the outset of the program. These could include traditional measures such as increased social security and workers' participation in the capital of the industry in exchange for cost of living adjustment, but also allocation of plots of land to grow one's own foodstuffs and set times of the day or week to cultivate these plots to avoid high and random absenteeism. Low and falling wages also add to a reduction in final demand, with adverse consequences for economic growth, as the production can often not be geared to exports. In many African countries, domestically manufactured consumer products should be regarded as quasi-nontradeables. The reason for this is twofold: the product specification is often not suited for industrialized markets, and the possibilities for exports to neighboring countries are usually limited.

Equally important are the consequences of macroeconomic measures for the welfare of poverty groups, which must be scrutinized closely in the design of any adjustment program. Instead of simply advocating an increase in tax

11. See Morss (1984), where demands of donors on local administration capacity is shown to hamper domestic institution-building and, as a consequence, economic growth.

revenue, the type of tax to be raised could be made more specific to exclude the incomes of poorer groups or the products they consume (Stewart 1987). Similarly, rather than apply credit restrictions in general, exemptions could be given to small-scale enterprises and farmers.[12] As to the essential services for education and health, the financial stringency that is often unavoidable should be seen as an impetus to developing cost-saving measures and better targeting expenditure to those groups most in need by focusing on special programs (Cornia et al. 1987). For most countries this often means a departure from existing practice; such changes in policies could be discussed and supported in donor coordination activities referred to earlier.

ADJUSTMENT AND STABILIZATION IN KENYA

The general points made in the previous section can be applied to the Kenya situation. During 1979 to 1985, Kenya stabilized its economy and reduced its current account deficit, but did not succeed in increasing nonagricultural exports or in restructuring the economy in response to changed external conditions. Growth suffered and employment creation slowed. Stabilization measures included the restriction of imports, a fall in real minimum wages, an increase in real interest rates, control of government expenditure, and devaluation. The latter resulted in a shift in income distribution to producers of tradeables (agricultural exporters) from nontradeables, but the supply response was limited. Similarly, increases in the real rate of interest in 1983 and 1984 came after, rather than before, the large increases in savings that occurred in 1981 and 1982. Thus, the rise in the interest rate benefited those who had been able to accumulate assets in the past. Because in all sectors real wage costs increased less than sectoral GDP and employment lagged behind in most cases, income distribution changed in favor of nonwage earners.

Due to the fall in urban real wages, rural-urban differences decreased, but overall income inequality has probably increased. First, in urban areas the position of wage earners has deteriorated in relation to that of nonwage earners. Second, in the agricultural sector exporters of tradeables profited from devaluation and price increases in 1983 and 1984. Export crops are now grown by large farms and by a minority of prosperous farmers (less than 20 percent) who have large plots of land. Increased attention to export crops would probably increase inequality within the rural areas. Plantations, which had

12. In Zambia, for example, it is argued that more credit to farmers in 1980 would have increased food production and saved the country foreign exchange going into food imports (van der Hoeven 1982).

difficulty hiring labor in 1980 and thus recruited foreign workers, appear to have had no difficulty in hiring since 1984. Also, the lower real urban wages tend to lower supply price of rural labor. During 1979 to 1984, funds available for investment shot up, initially because of increased foreign borrowing and later because import restrictions limited domestic output. In 1983 and 1984, investment rates returned to "normal" Kenyan values of around 25 percent. It remains puzzling why Kenya is unable to grow faster and to create more employment with such a high investment rate.

In 1985 and 1986, the economy benefited greatly from the increase in coffee prices. Because of the increase, the International Coffee Organization lifted quotas, and Kenya was able, on top of normal exports, to sell off coffee stock from 1985, resulting in a doubling of proceeds from coffee in 1986 compared to 1985. In contrast to the coffee boom of 1976-1977 and the tea boom of 1984, the government does not intend to pass on all price increases to coffee exporters in 1986, but rather plans to use part of the increased revenue to pay off external public debts. However, because exporters form an important political group, it is too early to say how much of the windfall gain will in fact be used to reduce external public debt. Current projections of coffee and tea prices are not encouraging. Kenyan authorities have begun to make the case for an increased quota, arguing that when present trends in production continue Kenya will be able at the end of the decade to sell only 50 percent of its production through its quota on the world market.

Another serious problem is that the volume of Kenya's exports of agricultural products has kept up better than the volume of nonagricultural exports, though the latter have better price prospects. Although lower real wages could be a comparative advantage for Kenya, this has not manifested itself as yet, primarily because of restrictions in surrounding countries and difficulties confronting Kenyan products in competing in industrial country markets. This suggests that, excluding some positive shocks, such as bad harvests in other parts of the world, its trade prospects are not favorable.

The important policy question is whether stimulus of export crops (tea and coffee) can be achieved without detriment to food production. Evidence on this is mixed. This question is compounded by the fact that Kenya is quickly reaching its limit of arable land, and increased production has to come from intensification, which means inputs and improved technologies. In the medium term increased output could also be promoted by land redistribution, because small farmers have higher yields than large-scale farmers. The World Bank estimates that a 10 percent reduction in the holding size raises output per hectare by 7 percent and employment by over 8 percent. A recent government paper, "Economic Management for Renewed Growth," is much less outspoken and puts the emphasis on intensification.

The formulation of a strategy or set of scenarios for future development should take into account the basic characteristics of the economy: namely its large and dynamic small-scale agricultural sector, high savings rates, high population growth, and the land shortage, all of which suggest increased attention to small-scale agriculture. Such attention should go beyond the present emphasis on domestic and foreign pricing policies to include a much larger transfer of national savings to the agricultural sector as a whole. This transfer should be accompanied by policies for land redistribution to increase output and provide income opportunities to the fast-growing population. These policies would be facilitated by an increased inflow of foreign aid and capital, but initiatives are not blocked by lack of funds. Increased investment in agriculture can be stimulated by offering special benefits or be financed from increased taxes on nonwage income, which has increased in several urban sectors, as indicated earlier. This taxation would mean a lowering of the investment rate in urban areas, which would not necessarily decrease growth, as ICORs have been rather high and could be lowered through better capacity utilization and improved efficiency.

In the modern sector, lack of investable capital is less relevant than lack of foreign exchange, resulting in low-capacity utilization ratios. Another reason for low-capacity utilization is the stand-still in real consumer demand by workers who have seen their incomes reduced by up to 20 percent from 1979 to 1984. Increasing private consumer demand should be stimulated, not necessarily by wage regulation but rather by changes in the fiscal regime, where the wage tax on lower income groups could be reduced and that on higher income groups and accumulated wealth and assets increased. Another, not necessarily opposed, variant would be to stimulate public consumption rather than private consumption (noninflationary if financed by fiscal reforms) to maintain provision of basic services, such as education and health, at present or slightly higher levels. Although the direct productivity effects of the provision of such services are difficult to measure, indirect effects in the form of increased social mobility have been noted by several authors.

The policies discussed above would of course have implications for the balance of payments. An expansion of final demand to reduce excess capacity may cause imports to increase above sustainable levels, because access to foreign exchange remains constrained. However, in such cases import restrictions or prohibitive tariff structures could be imposed, coupled with policies to expand supply by allowing a greater role for the informal sector, which has already shown signs of increased dynamism during the stabilization period and is meeting the demands of many low-income consumers. The import problem would be less if public consumption (noninflationary-financed) is increased rather than private consumption, but a combination of the two seems likely to be most acceptable socially.

CONCLUSION

I have described briefly how several external shocks have affected developing countries rather drastically, especially primary commodity exporters and exporters of more traditional manufactures. Although response to the crisis was different, a large number of countries ended up in the early 1980s with large and unsustainable deficits on their current account. Through formal adjustment and stabilization programs, or through more haphazard activities, most countries managed in the middle of the decade to reduce considerably their current account deficits. However, social costs were high. In the two cases examined in detail in this chapter, Latin America and Sub-Saharan Africa, real wages in modern-sector undertakings dropped substantially and unemployment increased, leading to increased urban poverty.

These negative effects occurred because in most adjustment programs any form of buffer mechanism or protection of the poor was absent. Policies were usually defined as to their effect on macroeconomic indicators, such as size of government expenditure and credit expansion, with no explicit concern for income distribution and poverty effects. Special schemes to deal with the poor were for budgetary reasons often not even considered. Furthermore, adjustment and stabilization policies were of a deflationary nature (at least in the short run), and most poor people suffered already through sheer element of contraction.

Alternative adjustment strategies are necessary. In general, policies should be carried out over a much longer period and be part of a long-term growth and development policy. The latter would call for more selective economic instruments rather than rely solely on broad macroeconomic indicators. For a development strategy to become successful, any adjustment policy should also set the basis for equity-oriented growth to satisfy the basic needs of the population. Although this would require country-specific analysis, a general set of policies needs to be developed. It is necessary to reassess macroeconomic instruments for their growth potential as well as for their direct effect on poorer groups. Rather than relying on across-the-board tax increases, for example, taxes can be targeted with respect to specific groups. To redistribute productive assets, such as land and education, as well as to increase the productivity of the poor, various interventions aimed at increasing the satisfaction of basic needs, as well as at structural changes in the sociopolitical setting, are required.

Because adjustment policies often involve difficult policy choices such as how to distribute the burden of adjusting to adverse external shocks, any meaningful program should be based on social consensus if it is to be successfully implemented. This would imply designing programs together with all affected social groups. This could lead, for example, to the formulation of incomes and price policies that affect wages and include other incomes such as profit and rental. As part of a broader developmental policy, social consensus could be sought to exempt the poorer wage groups from declines in their incomes in times of contraction by setting a floor to minimum wages and guaranteeing access to essential services to safeguard a minimum level of living.

3 LOSERS PAY REPARATIONS, OR HOW THE THIRD WORLD LOST THE LENDING WAR

John F. Weeks

In the late 1970s, the economies of Latin America and Africa entered into an economic depression worse than that of the 1930s, plunging the populations of these countries to levels of poverty and unemployment of a decade before. A disturbing aspect of this profound economic and social crisis is that most of the concern of the international community has focused on what in human terms is a minor side effect of this catastrophic depression—the inability of governments to service their foreign debts. In any rational world, the financial side of the crisis would be the least of our worries, a problem easily dealt with through a moratorium on payments, "forgiving" part of the debt, or general default, as in Latin America in the 1930s.[1] But on the contrary, the solution to the narrow financial issue, whose resolution directly affects relatively few people and to an extent merely involves manipulation of accounting categories in a world of ledger entries and reserve ratios, has become the prior condition

---

1. "Those who tremble at the prospect of widespread fault will find their fears reinforced by the World Bank. The biggest and most lasting casualty of a conflictual breakdown of loan agreements would be the confidence indispensable to future economic and financial relations and the broad perception of a shared common interest in making the international economy work. At stake may be not only future financial flows to developing countries, *but the preservation of the whole international framework*" (World Bank 1987b: x). Emphasis added.

On the Richter scale of apocalyptic polemics, the last phrase must register quite high, and one can perhaps speculate on the discretion involved in invoking such visions of doom.

for amelioration of starvation, deprivation, and the general degradation of human existence that accompanies a sudden descent into abject poverty.[2]

We are indeed in a world turned upside down, a world in which those who stress the urgency of material problems such as poverty and unemployment are considered hopeless romantics, and those who restrict themselves to the rarefied world of high finance are hard-headed realists. There is good reason for this inversion of reality. At one level, we live in a world in which finance does in fact take priority over material life. The representatives of the international financial system speak with a certain truth when they say that default on debt, particularly by the Latin American governments, could destabilize the world monetary system, though the long-term cost of this for the peasants and wage earners of the Third World might be less than that of orderly debt servicing.[3]

While at one level we can grasp the irrationality of a world gone mad in which finance counts for all and the human condition for little, we necessarily must enter into that world lest we ourselves be judged as unbalanced, and our suggestions discarded as the ravings of deranged romantics. It is the purpose of this paper first to review the process by which Third World countries accumulated large external debts over the last fifteen years. Second, I consider why the accumulation of debt has resulted in a protracted crisis. Finally, I critique structural adjustment programs in light of the preceding discussion.

THIRD WORLD DEBT AND RESERVE CURRENCIES

It is obvious that the great impetus to developing country debt was the dramatic increase in petroleum prices during 1973-1979, which redistributed world income from oil importers to oil producers. But before considering why governments of underdeveloped countries reached a point of over-indebtedness, one must ask a prior question: Why is it underdeveloped countries that are in this situation and not developed ones? A quite plausible argument can be made that a number of advanced industrial countries were more sensitive to the increase in oil prices than were underdeveloped countries.[4] Japan and the Federal Republic of Germany, the second and third industrial powers in the

2. On human suffering, see Jolly and Cornia (1984).

3. Commenting on default as a policy alternative to full debt service, Robert Devlin writes: "It is not at all obvious that the debtor countries [in Latin America] would have been worse off with full or partial conciliatory defaults and acceptance of the risk of costly sanctions . . ." (Devlin 1987: 93). In an insufficiently noted paper, Carlos Diaz-Alejandro demonstrates that debt default in the 1930s had a net positive effect on Latin American economic development (Diaz-Alejandro 1985).

4. Certainly the decline in oil prices in recent years has benefited industrial countries more (World Bank 1987b: xi).

western world, produce no oil, and because their economies are so industrialized they are much more dependent upon oil than even Brazil and Korea. Yet Brazil and Korea have huge absolute and per capita foreign debts, while the FRG and Japan do not. Clearly something more than a rise in oil prices was involved.

First and most important, the monies of the western industrial countries serve as de facto reserve currencies, the currencies in which other countries, namely underdeveloped countries, must conduct their trade (even among themselves) and hold in hoards to clear trade imbalances. This has a profound effect on the balance of payments of the western industrial countries. If Brazil runs a persistent deficit in its international payments, it must sooner or later seek private bank financing or go to the IMF in hopes of striking a bargain on a standby agreement. Further, when borrowing from private banks the government is partly financing its deficit via the deficits run by reserve currency countries. The "hard currencies" that banks lend to Brazil do not accumulate in those banks by magic.

This interactive relationship, in which the currencies of western countries are sustained in part by the borrowing of governments of underdeveloped countries, was quite obvious during the boom in petroleum prices. During the 1970s, the major oil-producing countries ran enormous surpluses on their trade accounts. These were matched by deficits suffered by oil importers, both developed and underdeveloped. The so-called "recycling" of petrodollars involved in part the financing of western economy deficits by Third World governments' borrowing.[5] Far from facing a situation in which they had to borrow to finance their trade deficits, the governments of the western countries found themselves in the enviable position that their financial systems were net lenders. Their currencies returned to them as hoards held by oil exporters and, to a lesser extent, direct investments in physical assets. Rather than creating a financial squeeze in the western economies, the worldwide trade deficits of non-oil producing countries stimulated a financial boom.

For those romantics who might question a monetary system in which a major shock (oil prices, for example) hits underdeveloped and developed countries alike, but stimulates potential crisis in the former and a boom (financial at least) in the latter, an apologetic answer is at hand. Were it not for stable reserve currencies (of individual countries or in the form of Special Drawing Rights from the IMF), world trade would be chaotic, we are told. While the arrangement may not be precisely to the liking of the government of each country, it is hardly realistic to think that international payments could be

---

5. See Chapter 13 by Representative Bruce Morrison for a discussion of the public policy implications of the recycling of petrodollars.

cleared with currencies as unstable and legally restricted as those of, say, Latin American countries.

This, however, is a transparently fallacious argument. To the extent that the dollar, mark, pound, et cetera, are more stable than the currencies of Latin American countries, this is in part *because* they have a reserve status, not vice-versa. If in Bretton Woods at the end of World War II the criterion for reserve status had been stability, no rational person would have selected the pound sterling as a medium of international payments. Not only was it severely devalued after the war, it was sharply restricted as to the conditions for its convertibility (though most of these restrictions were later dropped). The pound was selected for geopolitical reasons, not the least of which was the existence of Britain's colonial empire, in which the pound played a central role. The role of the dollar in clearing trade accounts in Latin America has an analogous origin. Specifically with respect to the U.S. dollar, little claim can be made for its stability in recent years. Indeed, a significant part of the instability of Latin American currencies can be traced directly or indirectly to the instability of the dollar, a point I consider below when treating interest rates.

Thus, we can conclude that a major reason the oil price boom manifested itself in developing countries in the form of heavy debt burdens, but did not do so in the western economies, is because of the organization for the international monetary system. It should come as no surprise that from 1976 to 1982, 108 of the 114 standby agreements reached with the IMF involved governments of underdeveloped countries (Killick 1984a).[6] But there is a further reason that the western industrial economies fared better with regard to the oil price increases, namely the flexibility of these economies.

After the first rise in oil prices, many commentators predicted that the debilitating effects would be overcome by conservation measures in response to relative price changes, both through lower use of petroleum due to income effects and the substitution of alternative fuels for oil. In the industrial countries these predictions have largely been fulfilled, but not in the countries of the Third World. While there are notable examples of development of alternative fuels, such as the production of combustible fuels from sugar, "conservation" in the Third World was primarily achieved by lowering the level of economic activity, or not at all. There is a good reason for this: the development of alternative energy sources requires investment. Foreign investment flows to developing countries declined substantially over the last ten years, and

---

6. For an analysis of the 1947-1979 period, when borrowing by developed countries was more important relatively, see Officer (1982).

government investment has been constrained by the same balance of payments pressure that was the impetus for conservation. The possibility that existing plant and equipment could be used for alternative energy sources was virtually nil.

Further, in the industrial countries reduction in use of petroleum came not only in use of fuel but also in use of petroleum-based inputs, as natural fibers and nonmetallic minerals became relatively cheaper. Such substitution requires a developed production structure, which most developing economies do not have. For example, Nicaragua was an exporter of raw cotton; the increase in petroleum prices made cotton a cheaper input for clothing than synthetic fibers, yet there was not a single plant in Nicaragua in the 1970s to render raw cotton into thread (Weeks 1985a: chapter 7). Adjustment to the rise in petroleum prices required new investments at every level of production in developing countries, new investment which for the most part was not forthcoming.

The answer to the question of why underdeveloped countries in particular accumulated large debts: It was the necessary consequence of their relationship to the international monetary system and the underdeveloped nature of their economies. Given this, is it nonetheless the case that governments borrowed beyond their means and banks lent beyond the point of financial responsibility? One can only pose that question by ignoring the events that followed the increase in oil prices, or by treating those events as predictable. If there has been any event since the end of WWII that can be described as a transitory, "once-and-for-all" change, it was the increase in oil prices. Given the tremendous price increases in 1973 and 1974, it was only reasonable to assume that at some point in the not too distant future an oil glut would result. Many observers predicted this and, notwithstanding the sharp price rise in 1979, these predictions proved correct, perhaps beyond the dreams of those who had made them. In the mid 1970s, it was reasonable that both governments of under-developed countries and private bankers would view the large trade deficits of Latin American countries as transitory, which with respect to oil prices they were. Further, many developing countries of the region had experienced rapid growth just prior to the price increases, and there seemed no reason to think that such would not be the case once the effect of the oil shock had run its course.

Three other factors indicated reason for optimism. First, the prices of many nonoil primary product prices experienced a moderate boom, so even the short-run repayment situation seemed favorable. Second, increased oil prices had a depressing effect on the rate of growth of the western industrial economies (particularly in the United States), and a reasonable prediction was that once adjustment had occurred, their rate of expansion would be rapid. This in turn would presumably increase the demand for primary products, facilitating the repayment of the debts that were being contracted. And third, the debts were negotiated in a period of inflationary pressure at real interest rates that were quite low.[7] Few experts seriously believed that international inflation would fall dramatically within the space of a decade, particularly if the recovery of the western industrial countries occurred as anticipated. Therefore, the future interest burden appeared manageable. In light of these reasonable expectations, a Third World government would have been foolish *not* to borrow, for not to do so would have implied as an alternative a program of domestic deflation that prevailing expectations predicted to be unnecessary. After all, one of the major functions of credit, for individuals, firms, and governments, is to "smooth out" short-period fluctuations along a long-term trend.

Some of these expectations were fulfilled, namely a dramatic shift to a petroleum market characterized by excess supply. However, the other expectations—buoyant primary product prices, continued inflationary pressures, and economic growth of developing countries with a strong export record—all derived from the anticipation of economic growth in the western industrial countries. Instead of growing as projected, the U.S. economy entered into its worst depression in half a century, with its performance in 1981 to 1983 nothing short of disastrous in terms of unemployment and falling real wages. Instead of rising, primary product prices fell, and petroleum-importing developing countries began to run deficits even on their nonoil imports. Worse still, while the sharp decline of the U.S. economy had the effect that any Keynesian would predict—lowering the rate of domestic inflation—nominal interest rates rose to historically unprecedented levels.[8] Why real interest rates rose I consider below.

Were these problems not enough, the glut on the petroleum market proved a mixed blessing indeed to the developing countries, if it was a blessing at all. While high oil prices had generated trade deficits, they had also generated the liquidity by which those deficits could be financed in the short run—the "recycling" of petrodollars discussed above. But the new trade deficits, created by the depression in the U.S. economy, had no such benevolent side effect. Once oil-producing countries no longer enjoyed large trade surpluses, the supply of world liquidity contracted dramatically. In retrospect, the years of high petroleum prices made for an environment considerably more favorable for

---

7. For example, Devlin calculates that interest rates deflated by changes in the world price of Latin America's exports averaged -4.8 percent for 1973 to 1979 (Devlin 1987: 91).

8. Devlin calculates an average real interest rate for Latin American debtor countries of 17.4 percent for 1981 to 1986 (Devlin 1987: 91). The World Bank calculation for all developing countries for the same period is about 15 percent (World Bank 1987b: xii).

the growth of developing economies than do present circumstances. For oil-producing countries, it was obviously a time of boom. For nonoil producers, the higher cost of petroleum was partly offset by easy access to liquidity and the concessionary oil sales by Mexico, Venezuela, and the Gulf States.

Less tangibly, but of great importance, during the 1970s the relationship of developing country governments to the world financial community was quite different from what it had been before or is likely to be in the foreseeable future. From the end of WWII until the oil boom, short-term balance of payments support was usually obtained only from the IMF or bilaterally. Both sources involved governments entering into economic and/or political commitments that they might otherwise not have chosen. With liquidity in effect no longer scarce during the years after 1973, private banks with money to lend lacked the market power to impose conditions on the borrowing governments, due to the competition among banks.

By contrast, the developing country governments found themselves in the worst of possible worlds in the 1980s—low export prices, tight liquidity, unprecedented real interest rates, and a staggering debt burden carried forward from the previous decade. And the situation has proved worse still. In the past, the recovery of the U.S. economy has been associated with an improvement in primary product prices. In 1983, the United States economy began to revive, growing rapidly in 1984 and early 1985 (via enormous depression-induced idle capacity and excess demand stimulated by massive budget deficits, as any Keynesian would predict). However, the response of primary product prices has been sluggish at best, suggesting support for the famous Prebisch-Singer hypothesis that primary product prices tend to fall relative to prices of manufactures in the long run.

The recovery of the U.S. economy has brought no relief for hard-pressed Third World governments. The export demand was sluggish for Latin American countries, whose economies were particularly dependent on the U.S. markets.[9] Given the contrast between the medium-term expectations by governments and bankers in the 1970s and subsequent economic events, attributing an unmanageable debt burden to the irresponsibility of the contracting parties is absurd. In effect, it seeks to cast blame and divert attention from the institutional and economic context in which the debts were contracted and the market interventions by creditor governments and multilateral agencies to force payment.

9. Mexico and Brazil increased their exports to the United States by about US$5 billion on an annual average, 1982-1985 compared to 1980-1981. However, for the rest of the hemisphere the increase was barely US$1.5 billion. In the case of Central America, half the increased exports to the United States represented trade diversion (Weeks 1988).

One of the most debilitating aspects of the economic environment of the 1980s for debtor governments has been the extraordinarily high real interest rates, which, it is generally agreed, are the result of the policies of the government of the United States. In the last four years, developing country governments have faced interest rates in relation to export prices (the relevant comparison) that were multiples of what was experienced from 1950 to 1980. The usual explanation of these high interest rates is the astounding size of the operating deficit of the federal government budget in the United States—more federal debt accumulated in the first four Reagan budgets than in the 200 years since the American Revolution. There is a certain bitter irony about these deficits, which no doubt is not lost on Latin American politicians and policymakers. As we shall see in a subsequent section, the policy packages being pressed upon Latin American governments by the multilateral agencies with the enthusiastic encouragement of the current U.S. administration place heavy emphasis on "fiscal responsibility," reducing state expenditures to cut the gap between those expenditures and state revenues. Were the IMF to impose the same discipline on the most profligate government in the world, one might take the commitment to fiscal austerity a bit more seriously.

However, the hypothesis that interest rates are high because of the size of the federal deficit ("crowding-out") is based on dubious application of closed economy monetary theory. It obscures a much more fundamental difficulty of the U.S. economy that will not be eliminated by cutting the deficits. Over the last two decades, the U.S. economy has become increasingly import-using, with the share of imports in GNP more than doubling since the 1950s and early 1960s. On the other hand, export performance has been quite poor, resulting in enormous annual trade deficits. In most developing countries, as local policymakers know to their chagrin, the result of a huge trade deficit would be to force a program of severe austerity on the population. In contrast, the U.S. economy enjoyed a recovery beginning in 1983, though trade deficits continued to grow. This was possible because of high interest rates, which drew in short-term capital from abroad to finance the excess demand for imports. Thus, far from being a factor restraining economic expansion in the United States, as some argue, the high interest rates are the necessary condition for economic expansion. Lower interest rates would make the trade deficit unmanageable (even though the dollar is a reserve currency), forcing deflationary policies on the current administration to reduce the import bill.

In other words, the growth of the United States economy in the 1980s was based on attracting short-term capital, which intensified the international liquidity shortage for Third World governments. It was largely circumstantial that the capital inflow served to finance a government deficit. Were the United

States fiscal deficit to be substantially reduced, high interest rates would still be necessary to finance the large import bill, whose basic cause is the lack of competitiveness of domestic production compared to production in Western Europe and Japan. To the extent that there is a "crowding-out" phenomenon, it is borrowers in Latin America and other parts of the underdeveloped world that are being "crowded," not the private sector in the United States.

BANK MARKET POWER AND THIRD WORLD DEBT

During the 1970s and early 1980s, developing countries accumulated external debts to a previously unprecedented level. However, this accumulation need not have resulted in a prolonged crisis of debt management. Given the economic environment, a payments crisis was inevitable for governments of developing countries, but properly functioning financial markets provide a variety of means to resolve even the most severe payments difficulties. The accumulation of unmanageable debt in the private sector is hardly uncommon, and the response in financial markets is bankruptcy or some form of devaluation of debt paper. The purpose of this section is to consider why world financial markets did not respond quickly and smoothly to eliminate the payments crisis.

It is useful to begin with a thought experiment that demonstrates the efficient response of financial markets to a payments crisis. Following common practice, let it be assumed that private banks in the 1970s carried out their lending on the basis of rational calculations of costs and benefits. Further, as is the current vogue, let it be assumed that economic agents made their predictions of the future on the basis of rational expectations. That is, they formulated their lending policy on the basis of a correct and complete model of the world economy, such that those predictions corresponded to the mean outcome of a set of alternatives each characterized by random shocks. In formulating policy, banks presumably set the lending rate to incorporate the probability of varying degrees of default and rescheduling. On the reasonable assumption that banks treated the world economy as characterized by uncertainty and risk, the lending rate and terms of loans were set above what would have prevailed in a world of perfect foresight. It should be added that market power on the part of banks, an issue that looms large below, would not affect the evaluation of probable outcomes. If capital markets are efficient, then at a minimum the average terms of loans incorporated the possibility of outcomes unfavorable to creditors even had expectations not been rational. To assume otherwise requires one to justify systematically irrational behavior, which among other things would imply a general lack of faith in the efficiency of market outcomes.[10]

The implication of this thought experiment is that while the economic environment of the 1980s was radically different from that of the 1970s, the new conditions were ones that rational agents would have anticipated and that efficient markets would accommodate. Once the payments crisis began, one would expect that competitive financial markets would produce secondary trading in Third World debt paper, with bond values falling to a level that would adjust the actual debt service toward the long-term equilibrium level. If private trading was efficient there would be no reason to expect the competitive market outcome to be disruptive to the international financial system. This unfortunate occurrence (from the point of view of banks) would be read as but one of many possible outcomes, to be balanced against past and future outcomes when banks benefited from favorable random shocks. To assume that banks and the international community would be thrown into shock by the commonplace and mundane vehicles of secondary trading in debt paper and loan default is to attribute an irrationality to economic agents in this case that economic theory refuses to entertain in any other line of inquiry.

Economic theory tells one that secondary trading in debt paper would be stabilizing. While the devaluation of loans might result in bankruptcy of lenders, there is nothing in the theory of the firm that suggests that bankruptcy is anything more than an aspect of the efficient working of markets. On the debtor side of the ledger, default and discount sales of debt would reduce debt service to a manageable level, which as a side effect would strengthen the balance sheets of remaining international banks.[11] Once debt had been discounted and defaulted to a manageable level, debtors would again be creditworthy and competition among lenders would bring forth new loans if such were required. If one is skeptical about this sanguine scenario, then one is in effect rejecting the general conclusion of mainstream economics that markets produce efficient outcomes, with the implication that policy should be based on political and power considerations rather than criteria of economic efficiency.

In light of what theory suggests as the obvious market solution to the payments crisis, this question necessarily arises: Why did not efficient secondary markets in Third World debt paper develop? The answer to the question is that the monopoly power of the primer international banks prevented the emergence of such a solution. A brief comparison to the 1930s is

---

10. In Chapter 16, Darity argues that banks in fact may not have incorporated a risk premium.

11. During the lending boom it was common practice for borrowing governments to contract not to repurchase their debt on a secondary market. Such a pledge could easily be circumvented.

relevant here. In the 1930s, the governments of Latin America escaped from an unmanageable debt burden through default and secondary market discounts of their debts. The decentralized character of debt-holding meant that creditors could neither combine to distort the operation of the market mechanism nor combine and conspire to enforce punitive sanctions against debtor governments.[12] The experience of the 1930s, along with economic theory, suggests that the fear that "the whole international economic framework" (to use the World Bank phrase) might crumble in response to the efficient operation of financial markets is not inherent in default and discounting, but the result of the monopoly power of international banks. That the market distortions preventing the spread of secondary trading in debt are the result of a cartel of banking interests is generally recognized, and World Bank authority can be cited:

> . . . [M]any banks remain concerned that an expanding secondary market in developing country debt will call into question the valuation of loans. . . .U.S banks, in particular, have been reluctant to trade in the secondary market for this reason, and have thus restrained its growth.[13]

It is hardly surprising that banks would be reluctant to encourage the development of secondary markets, because their efficient operation would be precisely to discount debt ("call into question the valuation of loans"). It remains the case that action by banks to prevent the emergence of such trading represents perhaps the most serious market distortion associated with the debt crisis. One can identify several inefficient consequences of this market distortion. First, it has prolonged the payments crisis, which might well have been several years behind us had secondary markets operated efficiently. As a consequence, inefficiencies in the banking systems of the developed countries have been perpetuated, the growth of world income has slowed, and there has been a substantial increase in the tension between governments of developed and developing countries.[14] Second, the exercise of monopoly power has effected an arbitrary redistribution of income from debtors to creditors. The redistribution is arbitrary in that it bears no strict relationship to efficient market outcomes. As argued at the outset of this section, either the lending policy of banks reflected a rational expectations prediction of probable outcomes or borrowing costs incorporated the risk of default and discounted

12. For a brief but illuminating discussion of the 1930s, see Devlin (1987: 92-93); and also Diaz-Alejandro (1985).

13. World Bank (1987b: xxxiii).

14. One might also speculate about the Third World governments that have fallen, the increase in the incidence of malnutrition, the children that have gone uneducated, and the public investment in social infrastructure that has been cancelled.

refunding of debt. In either case, the distorted management of financial markets to achieve full repayment under original conditions represents an attempt by banks to recover not only the normal rate of return, but also a monopoly rent. This can be demonstrated by way of a hypothetical example. Assume over n time periods competition among lenders sets normal loan conditions. In some time periods the lenders will do abnormally well (for example, full repayment at a real interest rate above what was predicted); in other time periods the lenders will do abnormally poorly (high default rates or real interest rates well below predicted levels). However, if shocks are random and expectations rational, the mean outcome will correspond to the normal rate of return under conditions of long-run equilibrium. When lenders seek to avoid losses during the unfavorable periods they are in effect violating the operation of competitive markets and unilaterally altering the rules of the game.

The foregoing analysis suggests a major item for the agenda of public policymakers in developed countries and multilateral agencies: If one adheres to the principle that market outcomes are efficient, then the distorting effect of the bankers' cartel should be eliminated;[15] and at the very least responsible agencies and governments should not aid and abet the distortions. The issue can be put another way: Secondary trading in debt paper might not have solved the payments crisis, but it is a solution offered by the market mechanism. Given that representatives of creditor governments and multilateral agencies have professed great faith in the magic of the market, why was this possible solution not seriously pursued?

THE ALLIANCE OF THE INTERNATIONAL BANKS AND THE "BRETTON WOODS TWINS"

Anyone who has followed World Bank publications in recent years will know that the Bank has come to place increasing stress upon the importance of the private sector in the process of growth and development in the Third World, to the extent of recommending privatization of state property. The IMF can of course be commended for its consistency on this issue throughout its existence. One can presume that such emphasis reflects a theoretical and empirical judgment that market outcomes are generally efficient. Therefore, it is rather puzzling that with regard to Third World debt both of these institutions have discouraged policies that would allow market processes to operate effectively.

---

15. Combination and conspiracy to restrict the size of the secondary market is not inconsistent with disarray among the banks on other issues, as described by Sacks and Canavan in Chapter 5.

Creditors have used monopoly power to insulate themselves against market discipline in a number of important ways, none of which the Bretton Woods multilaterals have shown disposition to criticize. Indeed, cooperation of the multilaterals was probably a key element in the success of monopoly intervention in the financial market. First and perhaps most important, the international banks have been impressively successful in maintaining discipline in their own ranks against the pressure of market forces while preventing any symmetric solidarity among debtor governments. In a strategy any general would envy for an armed conflict, the banks have managed to concentrate their forces in a protracted series of case by case battles against scattered and disorganized debtors. More than incidental to this strategy of avoiding a pitched battle against the combined opposition has been the role of the IMF as an advance force to define the scope of conflict. The combination of the case by case review of debtor government financial needs and serving to confirm creditworthy status has made the IMF central to the exercise of bank monopoly power. This role of the IMF as the broker for the bank cartel began on an ad hoc basis, and its impressive success in preventing official default led to its emergence as official Fund policy in mid 1982, when Managing Director J. deLarosiere announced that the multilateral would serve as a catalyst for organizing debt rescheduling on a case by case basis.[16]

Second, the multilaterals have been instrumental (or at least acquiescent) in bank pressure to force debtor country market intervention to nationalize (socialize) private sector debt, a policy most important in Latin America. A substantial proportion of the money owed by the most indebted countries was contracted by private economic agents. One can presume that this portion of the debt was agreed upon with rational calculations of profit and loss by both sides of the exchange under the rules of governance of market trading. Therefore, it is a quite brazen exercise of monopoly power by international banks to demand debtor government intervention to "guarantee" private debt.

"Guarantee" in this case is a misnomer, for what is involved is state intervention to protect private agents from the judgment of market outcomes. Clearly there can be extenuating circumstances. If a private debtor operates in a country with severe exchange controls such that hard currency is available only through an administrative process, then the state has de facto socialized private debt and should do so officially. However, the most celebrated case of cartel pressure to force socialization of foreign debt, that of Chile, involved no such

---

16. It is difficult to find neutral observers with regard to the payments crisis, but a quite balanced discussion of the role of the IMF is contained in ECLAC (1985). An excellent analytical treatment is found in Darity and Horn (1988: chapter 9).

extenuating circumstances. When the government of Chile announced that the private sector's foreign debt was the responsibility of those who contracted it, capital controls were sufficiently lenient to leave little complaint about the convertibility of the national currency.[17] Yet the government of Chile immediately came under tremendous pressure from the international financial community, including threats of sanctions. Both the IMF and the World Bank were at that time counseling governments throughout the Third World to limit the scope of government intervention and rely more on private initiative in resource allocation. Therefore, it is surprising that these two multilaterals did not use their great influence to support this privatization move by the Chilean government. What seems to be involved here is a double standard. In as far as privatization and deregulation facilitate private profitability, governments should limit their intervention in markets. However, when market outcomes dictate private losses, government intervention is not only tolerated but forced upon debtor countries. This asymmetric position—for example, enthusiasm for privatization of virtually any state activity but pressure to socialize the foreign debt—casts doubt upon the allocative efficiency arguments offered by the World Bank and the IMF.[18] Markets achieve their allocative magic through penalizing losers with losses as well as rewarding winners with profits. Deregulating to stimulate the latter while socializing to discourage the former generates major market distortions. The "practical" argument one hears to justify socializing developing country foreign debt is that not to do so would result in a serious loss of confidence on the part of the international banks. This may well be so. If it is, it implies that market processes are destabilizing and not to be trusted for resource allocation. To continue with the present example, if the Chilean private sector cannot be trusted with the responsibility of its external debt, should it be entrusted with the over 500 firms denationalized since 1973?

There is a further market distortion created by socialization of the foreign debt. As argued above, presumably the lending conditions of the contracted debt incorporated a risk element to compensate banks for the possibility of default. Once all governments are forced to socialize the debt and repay in full, the risk element has been eliminated. Part of the debt service then represents a

17. For a discussion of controls on capital flows in Chile in the mid 1980s, see Arellano and Ramos (1987).

18. Interestingly enough, when discussing how privatization increases the return on investment in developing countries, Chile is noted as a positive example. "Several countries, notably Chile, have begun to return government-controlled companies to the private sector in order to improve competitive conditions and reduce budgetary outflows" (World Bank 1987b: xii). It is a surprising oversight that the passage does not refer to the government's forced nationalization of approximately 2 percent of GDP (the relative size of private debt servicing).

pure monopoly rent and a misallocation of national resources to unrequited foreign transfers. One looks in vain in the reports of the multilaterals for reference to this major market distortion. A third source of market distortion regarding the payments crisis should be mentioned: capital flight. There seems to be a consensus that the international banks, aided by creditor government policies, have actively sought to attract private deposits from wealthholders in Third World countries.[19] Rodriguez characterizes this process as "criminal":

> . . . [F]oreign banks and governments have created various incentives to stimulate capital flight, and thus tax evasion from Latin American countries A behavior considered criminal . . . in the advanced countries is actively prompted by the members of the . . . OECD, especially the United States.[20]

Perhaps the most surprising aspect of this inconsistent policy by the multilaterals is the heavy stress placed on the disruptive effect of nonpayment. The emphasis given to apocalyptic consequences of default and debt discounting is a relatively recent phenomenon, one which contrasts sharply with previous views. For example, in the influential Pearson Commission Report, one is told "debt relief should be recognized as a legitimate form of aid," and the contemporary Rockefeller Report took a similar view (Pearson 1969: 18; Rockefeller 1969).[21] One should entertain the possibility that the predictions of catastrophe emanate more from the boardrooms of the international bank cartel than from the inherent workings of the international financial system.

STRUCTURAL ADJUSTMENT: THE LENDING WAR ON THE DOMESTIC FRONT

Since its creation, the International Monetary Fund has functioned as an institution concerned with short- and medium-term monetary and balance of payments adjustment. As such, its role has not been to promote economic development, though its defenders might argue that the policies of the Fund have a favorable effect on development. The task of promoting development was assigned to the International Bank for Reconstruction and Development (World Bank), and the Inter-American Development Bank was established to

---

19. "[M]any foreign private banks and financial institutions were accomplices of capital flight a: competitive pressures induced them to actively solicit deposits from private economic agents in [Latin America]" (Devlin 1987: 90). The word "competitive" should be interpreted in the context of oligopolistic competition.

20. Rodriguez F. (1987: 139).

21. A detailed treatment for debt refunding in this century is found in Bitterman (1973).

play the same role on a regional level. Until recently, the approach to lending by the Fund on one hand and the World Bank and the IDB on the other reflected the two different roles. The Fund provided balance of payments support, and in doing so felt justified in the dubious practice of imposing conditions on its loans that involved policy decisions we normally take to be the responsibility of governments.[22]

This role of the IMF—laying down macroeconomic conditionality—has always been controversial, and is generally avoided by the World Bank and the IDB. Restricting themselves primarily to program and project lending, these two institutions did not in the past tend to set macroeconomic conditions, though continued lending to a government was always conditional upon "creditworthiness." Creditworthiness basically referred to the likelihood of a government's being able to repay a loan, but the criterion was applied with considerable flexibility, consistent with its vagueness. Country reports by these two institutions included macroeconomic policy suggestions, but an official of a Latin American country who went to Washington to negotiate a loan with the World Bank or the IDB would not anticipate being presented with a shopping list of policy changes that would be the precondition for financing of a highway, rural development project, or social development scheme. The technicians of the World Bank and the IDB were primarily concerned for it to be demonstrated that the money would be used for the stated purpose and reach the proposed beneficiaries. Such an approach was particularly the case with the IDB, whose executive officers took the view that their institution had been created by the governments of the hemisphere, after all, and it would be inappropriate to dictate policy to the organization's ultimate constituency.

Given this orientation of the World Bank and the IDB, it is not surprising that the two organizations took a considerably more eclectic view than the IMF of the possible economic policy regimes that might be consistent with successful economic development. Within the halls of these institutions one found a response to the shifts in current thinking about the nature and goals of development that was notably absent in the IMF. For example, a considerable amount of theoretical and empirical work was done in the World Bank on what came to be called the "basic needs approach" to economic development (though official World Bank policy never endorsed such an approach). The eclecticism of these institutions gave a degree of freedom to borrowing governments that they would not have enjoyed a few hundred yards away at the IMF. In

---

22. By custom, governments are considered to some degree to represent their populations, so it is appropriate that they alone should take the momentous decisions that affect the welfare of their populations and be held responsible for taking them.

particular, the fact that a government might be unwilling to agree to conditions set down by the IMF for a standby loan did not necessarily prejudice its chances of obtaining project or program funding from the World Bank and the IDB.

This situation has undergone rapid change in the last five years, to a point that soon the division of labor between the Fund and the Bank may be more apparent than real. The vehicle for this shift in World Bank basic policy is the structural adjustment loan (Wright 1980; Landell-Mills 1981).[23] Structural adjustment loans are very close cousins of the IMF standby lending, with the same type of conditionality. The shift in emphasis from project and program lending to lending based on macroeconomic conditionality would seem to be the wave of the future in the World Bank. The similarity in outlook between the IMF and the World Bank, with the IDB moving in the same direction, is even more clearly demonstrated in the unprecedentedly close cooperation among the three institutions in recent years. This is shown in two developments. More overtly, emergency loan packages have been put together among these institutions for several countries, a notable case being the Costa Rican crisis of 1981-1982. It might be thought that cooperation can only be a good thing in these matters so that efforts are coordinated. This would certainly be the case in a perfect world in which the borrowing government and the lending institutions shared the same goals and assessment of current economic difficulties. But as shown in the previous section, this cooperation has become an integral part of monopoly intervention to block market outcomes.

This is particularly the case with the IMF serving as the international financial system's gatekeeper and watchdog. In case after case in Africa, Latin America, and Asia, reaching a standby agreement with the IMF served as the necessary condition for obtaining World Bank structural adjustment loans as well as progress in renegotiating outstanding debt with private banks. The international financial community has indeed responded forceably to the Latin American debt crisis. It has closed ranks, established a common hard line, and developed a policy package that all governments must accept or face the real prospect of international financial boycott.[24]

Needless to say, the Reagan administration was extremely enthusiastic about this approach to the debt crisis, for the policy measures incorporated in structural adjustment programs are very close to the hearts of conservative politicians. However, there is a more fundamental reason for the return to importance of the pre-Keynesian theoretical and analytical framework. Given

23. See Chapter 9 by Epstein for the history of policy-based lending by the World Bank.
24. It should be stressed again that the cost of noncooperation with the Fund may be exaggerated. As Lissakers and Sacks and Canavan argue in chapters 4 and 5, no new lending would be forthcoming in any case.

the severity of the debt crisis, there is little, if any, possibility of Latin American countries achieving historic growth rates and repaying the debt.[25] Because the financial community in the 1980s ruled out any significant reform that would reduce the debt burden in the foreseeable future, policies for growth must yield to policies to facilitate repayment. This, however, is a difficult argument for the multilateral agencies to make explicitly—that the economic welfare of millions must be sacrificed (at least any significant improvement) to satisfy the welfare of the world's major private banks.

The conservative structural adjustment programs offer a way out of this difficult ideological situation. The central message of the structural adjustment programs is that the present difficulties of the Third World economies are the result of bad policy, and if correct policies are followed growth will result with no change in the present international economic environment. This is a powerful ideological message, an apparent exception to the general rule in economics that there is no such thing as a "free lunch." The argument is that if "distortions" are eliminated—economies opened to the international environment and "government taken off the backs of people"—exports will expand, investment will be forthcoming, and growth will follow. Though some developing country policymakers may have been under the impression that their economic difficulties arose in part from the instability of the world economy, the fact of the matter, we are told, is that the difficulties arose because their economies were insufficiently integrated into the world economy. It is this powerful ideological message, that throwing one's economy into the arms of the unregulated market will be the salvation of the Third World, that I now briefly consider.

While the word "structure" is vague when used in the term "structural adjustment," it suggests changes that involve basic alterations in an economy. "Changing the structure of production," for example, suggests more than just policies; it suggests also investments, technical innovations, and retraining of the workforce. However, in the contemporary context, the term means something quite different and much more limited—deregulation, denationalization, and reducing the size of the government sector. The basic change it suggests is primarily an ideological one—for Third World policymakers to abandon the path of economic nationalism and adopt the doctrine of laissez faire. This is offered as if its benefits are so obvious that only the ignorant would challenge them, despite the fact that no presently developed country developed by following laissez faire policies, with the exception of Great Britain.

25. Chapter 15 by Sunkel addresses this issue.

Let us consider the argument at face value. The basic structural adjustment package includes some or all of the following policy measures. The alleged benefits are given after each policy measure.[26]

1. Devaluation of the exchange rate: to reduce imports and increase exports.
2. Restriction of the growth of money wages (and, implicitly, lower real wages): to increase the rate of growth of employment, dampen inflationary pressures, and increase international competitiveness.
3. Cut government spending: to reduce the growth of the money supply (if there is a fiscal deficit) and "free" resources for private-sector initiative; domestic demand will fall, further releasing resources for export production.
4. Directly reduce the growth of the money supply by central bank action: to reduce inflationary pressures.
5. Deregulate markets, eliminating price controls, interest rate ceilings, and subsidies on commodities and services: to achieve a more efficient allocation of resources.

These policy measures reflect certain assertions of causality that have an almost religious status: "a fall in real wages will increase employment," "inflation results from excessive expansion of the money supply," and "a devaluation of the exchange rate will stimulate exports and discourage imports." These are only a representative sample. It should be noted that none of these are factual statements, nor are they theoretical inferences about which there is general agreement. On the contrary, even at the most theoretical and abstract level each of these apparently simple statements is a victim of intense controversy. If one surveys the literature on macroeconomic theory over the last twenty years, one discovers that none of these statements holds true except under very restrictive theoretical conditions. This cannot be stressed too much. Contrary to what some may argue, these statements do not reflect basic economic laws. They are nothing more than abstract conclusions derived from a highly controversial theoretical model whose internal, logical inconsistencies are well documented.

I shall take each of these statements in turn and demonstrate the theoretical controversy surrounding each. In the case of the first, the means (lower wages) achieves the end (more employment) on the argument that lower wages will induce capitalists to change from their current technique of production to one that is more "labor-intensive." This analysis of technique-switching is

26. The discussion that follows might be compared to the presentation in Chapter 6 by Liebenthal and Nicholas on the World Bank approach to adjustment policies.

theoretically valid only if the economy produces a single product. Thus, even in theory (to say nothing of the real world) it holds in conditions so restrictive as to be absurd.[27] The difficulty with the second statement (money supply/inflation) is that it cannot be established that there exists something called "the money supply" that is under the direct control of government authority (through the central bank) or indirect control (through government expenditure and taxation), except again under very restrictive assumptions.[28] With regard to devaluation, there are at least six separate approaches to its impact on imports and exports, the majority of which conclude that its result is *a priori* indeterminate. The monetarist approach tells us that devaluation has no permanent effect at all except in so far as it reduces the "real money supply."[29] All of this suggests that experts do not agree, to say the least.

Ten years ago this highly restrictive model of economic behavior upon which the structural adjustment medicine is based was in disfavor in the economics profession. In recent years, with the rise of right-wing politics in the United States and Great Britain it has come back into vogue. But its resurgence is not the consequence of finding solutions to its fundamental theoretical difficulties, but rather the result of a change in political climate that has made its ideological implications more functional. There is no compelling theoretical or intellectual reason to adopt the policy package. Nor is there much reason on empirical grounds. The experience of "market-oriented," "outward-looking" macroeconomic regimes in recent years has been mixed.[30]

The theoretical and empirical judgment on the conservative policy package is negative; there is little reason to think that these policies would generate growth any better than protectionist, nationalist-oriented policies. Why, then, is the policy package the new orthodoxy among the multilateral agencies? The answer is quite simple: This is not a growth package; rather, it is a policy package designed to minimize the possibility of loan default. With regard to debt repayment, its strength and appeal lie precisely in it not being a growth package.

27. The debate over whether lower wages induce more employment is part of the "capital controversy" in economic theory, and is treated in the context of short-run macroeconomic models in Weeks (forthcoming).
28. The hypothesis that the availability of money adjusts automatically to its demand has theoretical credentials at least equal to the hypothesis that there is a money supply determined independently of the demand for money.
29. The "monetarist approach to the balance of payments" denies that devaluation can alter domestic relative prices (Ghani 1984: 7-12).
30. See the analyses of Chile, Argentina, and Uruguay in Foxley (1982); see also Fishlow (1985: 133-142). The Fishlow article provides a thorough and balanced critique of the free market orthodoxy prevalent in the IMF.

The structural adjustment/liberalization package is essentially an output-reducing policy. If there is one economic relationship for which there is general agreement among economists and considerable empirical support, it is that if an economy is depressed sufficiently, there will come a point at which exports exceed imports. This remedy, which some critics have called "leeching" after the nineteenth century medical practice of applying leeches to the sick to extract "unhealthy blood," does not always work; and sometimes when it does work it requires a catastrophic decline in production to achieve its desired effect. However, it does work with great regularity, making it a least-risk choice for the financial community. The goal is to ensure that debts are repaid in full. If a balance of payments surplus (the necessary condition for debt repayment) is more likely to be achieved through depression or stagnation of economies than through growth (which is probably correct under present world market conditions), then depression or stagnation it must be.

The stabilization package is directly deflationary through its stress upon cutting government expenditure. Arguments about the inflationary impact of fiscal deficits are purely window dressing. For example, the IMF set for Costa Rica a government deficit target of less than 2 percent of GDP as conditionality at a time when the actual Costa Rican deficit was already one of the lowest in the hemisphere relative to national product.[31] Wage restraint has the same effect. Even more deflationary is the demand that economies be "opened." The consequence of this is to drive out of operation import substitution industries, thus reducing the demand for imported inputs. At this point, devaluation becomes functional. Without devaluation, the collapse of domestic industry might result in a flood of imports to replace commodities previously produced locally. Devaluation generates inflation in the prices of imports, as well as a regressive redistribution of income, which lowers aggregate demand. It might also be noted that liberalization policies have the side-effect of undermining regional economic integration, such as the Andean Pact and the Central American Common Market, a result consistent with preventing Latin American cooperation on debt issues.

The hypothesis that throwing oneself at the tender mercy of world market forces will result in debt repayment *and* prosperity is hardly convincing. Were it so simple, the governments of developing countries would have followed such a policy course long ago. The IMF has been singing the praises of the free market-liberalization strategy for forty years, and a mid 1980s policy paper reports that not only does this medicine work relatively painlessly, it also has

31. For a discussion of the Costa Rican case, see Weeks (1985b).

equitable distributional effects (IMF 1985b).[32] If this is true, one is left to wonder why few governments ever apply it except under duress. Either the patients are exceedingly stupid or the medicine is not the wonder drug it is advertised to be. Perhaps policymakers in Latin America have noted that governments have returned to the IMF for the same treatment up to nineteen times since the end of WWII with no obvious improvement in the health of their economies (Weaver and Wachtel 1984). Finally, one must be skeptical about a policy package that proposes deregulation with regard to one part of the economy (production and distribution), and massive government intervention with regard to another part (private external debt).

CONCLUSION

It has not been uncommon in world history for the victors in wars to demand reparations of the defeated, two notable examples being the Franco-Prussian War and World War I. These reparations represented unrequited transfers forced upon the vanquished, enforced by the threat of punitive sanctions. At the risk of entering into polemics similar to those invoked by the supporters of current international policy (with their visions of financial apocalypse), the current payments crisis can be likened to war reparations. Once the world economic environment turned dramatically unfavorable to creditors and borrowers around 1980, the issue became how losses would be apportioned. Because borrowers and lenders had contracted jointly, a joint sharing of losses would not have been inappropriate; indeed, theory suggests that a competitive market solution would have produced such an outcome. In place of this, the international banks embarked upon a conflict strategy designed to shift as much of the loss to debtors as would be possible. What then ensued was a financial war in which the debtors lost, often ignominiously, and were forced to declare something close to unconditional surrender. If the war analogy seems too farfetched, one might refer to various calculations of the debt service burden of developing countries compared to the reparations paid by France in the 1870s and Germany in the 1920s (Devlin 1987: 81-82; Fishlow 1985: 142). For African countries, one can note that the net flow of IMF funds has been a negative US$2.25 billion from 1985 to 1987 (United Nations 1986b and 1988b: 12). The

32. Recently the IMF seems to have in part accepted the argument of its critics that its programs harm the poor. It was reported in the *Wall Street Journal* on June 1, 1988, (p. 7), "A report from the International Monetary Fund acknowledges that poor people have been hurt by policies it has pressed on Third World countries with the support of the U.S." It was not possible to obtain a copy of this report before this volume went to press.

decision before the international community in the late 1980s is whether to continue to enforce reparations or to declare an end to conflict and pursue an enlightened and magnanimous policy toward the vanquished. Key to ending the conflict would be for the multilaterals to play a neutral role, rather than facilitating the monopoly intervention of international banks.

II THE DEBT CRISIS AND COMMERCIAL BANKS

Among the most stimulating and thought-provoking sessions of the seminar that produced this book were those dealing with the debt crisis and structural adjustment programs from the perspective of the private commercial banks. Both essays in this section demonstrate why this was the case.

In a paper that should be read by all who hope for a renewal of bank lending to developing countries, Karin Lissakers in Chapter 4 carefully traces the institutional and attitudinal changes in the private financial sector over the last decade. Her analysis is both fascinating and profoundly depressing, for it convincingly demonstrates that even before the debt crisis began, private banks were shifting their priorities away from lending to developing countries—indeed, away from traditional lending as such. A clear conclusion can be drawn from her chapter: "Fresh" lending to developing countries will not be forthcoming without strong policy intervention by governments of developed countries (and perhaps not even then).

This view, that banks are incxorably divesting themselves of "sovereign debt," is pursued further by Paul M. Sacks and Chris Canavan in Chapter 5. In their analysis, as in that of Lissakers, it is not a question of whether the commercial banks will abandon the Third World to its fate, but when and whether it will be an "orderly" process. Chapters 4 and 5 set the stage for the proposals in Part IV; particulary relevant is the proposal by Osvaldo Sunkel, outlined in Chapter 15, to convert debt service to development expenditure.

4 BACKGROUND TO THE DEBT CRISIS: STRUCTURAL ADJUSTMENT IN THE FINANCIAL MARKETS

Karin Lissakers

Post-1982 analyses of the debt crisis and the search for a solution have focused on the economic successes and failures of debtor countries. Far less attention has been given to major structural changes in international financial markets in this decade, changes that have come about coincidentally with the debt crisis but not necessarily because of it, changes that will have a direct and profound impact on its resolution.

Beginning in 1979-1980, there was a series of events—of which the Mexican moratorium is only one—that created a set of conditions in world financial markets fundamentally different from the conditions that prevailed in the 1970s. I argue that structural changes in the markets are one of the factors that triggered the debt crisis, and that failure to recognize the long-term implications of these changes has led to the adoption of a debt strategy that was doomed to fail.

THE CRISIS

International economic conditions turned against developing countries in the early 1980s and hit Latin America particularly hard: (1) dollar interest rates went through the roof, (2) the industrial economies suffered recession, and (3) oil prices weakened. The first development increased the cost of servicing outstanding commercial debt, while the second and third conditions made earning foreign exchange through exports much more difficult. Worst of all, banks that in the late 1970s had been willing to finance an ever-increasing proportion of the major borrowers' debt servicing costs stopped lending.

The simple explanation for the banks' sudden disenchantment with sovereign lending is that a large number of sovereign borrowers have gone bust or very nearly done so. However, one can turn this statement on its head: These countries are in financial straits in part because commercial bank funds are no longer flowing. Foreign bank credit has dried up because the underlying macroeconomic, institutional, and regulatory conditions that drove the banks heavily into cross-border lending in the 1970s are no longer present.

The increasing reluctance of financial markets to extend credit was apparent even before August 1982. The Falkland (Malvinas) War is often said to have been the shock that triggered the loss of bank confidence in Latin American borrowers, but Argentina was in fact on the brink of seeking a rescheduling *à la* Poland when it launched the invasion. Former Brazilian Finance Minister Luiz Carlos Bresser-Pereira reports that in late 1980 and early 1981, Brazil had extreme difficulty raising Euromarket loans and seriously considered going to the International Monetary Fund. Ironically, Citibank, as well as other larger creditors, talked Brazil out of doing so, arguing that going to the Fund would further damage Brazil's credit standing (Moreira 1986: 31). And the syndication of a $250 million Eurodollar loan for Mexico in spring 1982 was successful only because Mexican banks in the U.S. picked up part of that loan (Kraft 1984: 37). Overall, international financial markets during this period were expressing their doubts by steadily shortening maturities on large sovereign borrowers.

Since 1982, OECD-based bank lending outside the region, even to non-rescheduling countries, has declined dramatically. Foreign assets are a shrinking part of U.S. banks' total loan portfolio: loans outstanding to Latin America have fallen 10 percent since their 1984 peak, loans to OPEC are down 39 percent from their peak in 1983, and loans to Asia have fallen by 45 percent since 1983 (Merrill Lynch 1988). The reasons for the decline are far more complex than just the economic woes of some major debtor countries.

CHANGES IN FINANCIAL MARKETS

Sovereign lending ebbs and flows with the tide of world finance. That tide now flows in a different direction and through different channels than it did in the 1970s. OPEC, whose financial surpluses fueled the surge in international bank lending in the 1970s, now has too much oil and too little cash. Japan has become the world's largest capital exporter, the United States has become the largest capital importer, and the industrial countries as a group are net takers of funds rather than net suppliers to the rest of the world.

Japanese investors have investment preferences far different from those of the oil sheiks. The oil states placed a substantial part of their savings as short-term deposits with U.S. and European banks, which converted them into long-term claims on other developing countries. The Japanese surplus is being channeled mainly through securities markets into long-term claims on other industrial countries. Seventy-five percent of the long-term capital flow from Japan from 1981 to 1987 was in securities, primarily bonds, and direct investments. The overwhelming amount flowed to the United States and to Europe—and stayed there. The United States alone accounted for 50 percent of the foreign bonds purchased by Japanese investors. The U.S., with large twin budget and trade deficits, cannot afford to intermediate these funds to Latin America (except to the extent our Japanese loans help pay for our imports from Latin America and other debtor countries with whom we have a trade deficit).[1]

Japanese banks have played an important intermediation role, not as lenders of Japanese savings to the rest of the world, but as net *borrowers* of short-term funds abroad which are relent at home. Such loans enable Japanese investors to hedge the currency risk on their long-term foreign investments, particularly dollar investments, by taking on short-term foreign currency liabilities. Recently Japan's capital exports have actually exceeded its current account deficit, which means that Japan is in effect recycling surplus savings from the rest of the world to the United States. But recycling in the 1980s largely leaves the troubled debtor countries out of the circle, and to an extent shuts out the big multinational banks as well.

There are other forces turning financial flows away from developing countries. World financial markets have undergone rapid and dramatic change since 1979. "Global Bang" is what the *Financial Times* calls the sweeping away of geographic, institutional, and regulatory boundaries within the financial services industry that is taking place in every major money center from London (where deregulation of the stock exchange in October 1986 was dubbed "Big Bang") to Tokyo, New York, and Amsterdam. The technology of financial services has undergone an electronic revolution, and governments are for reasons of necessity scrapping, rewriting, or ignoring the rules that controlled the industry since the Depression, regulations which delineated national markets

---

1. Japanese investment from Bank of Japan as reported in Salomon Brothers (1985) and *AMEX Bank Review* (1988).

and distinguished the providers of one type of service from another, insurers from stockbrokers, lenders from underwriters, foreign banks from domestic banks. Every existing or aspiring player is having to reorganize, restaff, and rethink its position in the market in response to these recent and impending changes.

Global deregulation means that banks will increasingly be allowed to do the kind of business at home and in the domestic markets of other industrial countries that was previously permitted only in the special context of cross-border lending, if at all. The regulatory lines of demarcation that distinguished the "international" Eurocurrency markets from national, "domestic" financial markets are becoming blurred or erased altogether and the "regulatory differential" favoring the international credit markets over domestic markets is disappearing.

Among the attractions of overseas markets for American banks in the 1960s and 1970s were the rights to open multiple branches (with the Fed's permission) and engage in certain investment banking activities prohibited at home, plus the absence of reserve requirements and interest rate ceilings on Eurodollar deposits. But in the 1980s, domestic regional interstate banking has become a reality, and national interstate banking is waiting in the wings. The Glass-Steagall Act, which separates commercial from investment and merchant banking in the United States, is under assault. Even as Congress considers scrapping the 1930s reform act, the law is being circumvented with increasing frequency and apparent impunity. In 1980, Congress passed the Depository Institutions Deregulation and Monetary Control Act, which drastically lowered reserve requirements and phased out "Reg Q" interest rate ceilings on domestic deposits. The home market suddenly looks a lot more attractive to the big American banks, and that is reflected in their spate of new activities and acquisitions, from Bankers Trust winning court approval to underwrite commercial paper to Chemical Bank buying Texas Commerce Bank (and all its troubles), which would not have been possible five years ago.

Liberalization is not limited to the United States. Germany, Japan, Britain, Canada, Australia, the Scandinavian countries, and others, began dismantling post-war capital controls in 1979 so that their citizens may more freely borrow and lend outside their borders. Since 1980, Australia, Norway, Sweden, and Portugal have decided to let in foreign banks; Canada has raised the ceiling on domestic bank assets that can be held by foreign banks; and Britain, Germany, and Japan have announced measures that will substantially increase the range of domestic banking activities in which foreign banks may engage and broaden the international role of the mark and the yen. Foreign banks are now allowed to own seats on the Tokyo stock exchange. Foreign banks are for the first time able to deal in Japanese government securities, lead manage bond issues in

Japan and the Euroyen market, do trust banking, and offer Euroyen CDs, among other things.[2] Similarly, Germany now permits foreign banks to lead manage mark denominated bonds and allows new mark instruments such as floating rate and zero coupon bonds (Tagliabue 1985). In early 1985, Bank of America became the first foreign bank to manage a public sterling securities issue for sale to British investors, while Citicorp became the first foreign bank to take control of one of the Bank of England's nine money market agents and the first to function as a clearing bank in Britain (Winkler 1985). The Bank of England has opened the way for foreign banks to acquire building and loan societies, while at the same time expanding the powers of such mortgage finance companies. And U.K. and foreign banks have brought up London's largest stockbrokerages to take advantage of liberalization of the securities market there.

The net effect of all these changes, according to Wall Street economist Henry Kaufman, late of Salomon Brothers:

> The trend of commercial banks, therefore, is taking a strange turn. The regulations prevailing during the sixties and seventies contributed toward an outward search for growth, the massive increase in debt of less developed countries, and the overextension of international credit. In contrast, the deregulation of financial institutions is now turning bank lending inward and limiting the availability of funds internationally, where the need for credit remains urgent.[3]

"Globalization" is a misnomer. So far, international financial integration has been limited to markets in the industrial countries. That is the turf banks and other financial intermediaries are now marshaling their force fight over. LDCs meanwhile are put on the back burner except when some flare-up of the debt issue forces them out front.

FINANCIAL MARKETS AND DEVELOPING COUNTRIES

While market liberalization is making banking in the industrial countries more attractive, a simultaneous tightening of certain regulations is making cross-border lending to developing countries decidedly less so. These changes include

2. See statement of Donald T. Regan, Secretary of the Treasury, before the Committee on Banking, Housing and Urban Affairs, United States Senate, September 26, 1984.

3. H. Kaufman (1986: 101).

new capital requirements, more public disclosure of foreign loan exposure, and changes in tax laws.

U.S. regulations put firm minimum capital requirements on large banks for the first time in 1983. Many banks had to raise equity or long-term debt to slow the accumulation of assets (loans) and to meet the new capital/asset ratio. Then in 1987, U.S., British, Japanese, and other industrial country regulators, presented a joint agreement to impose uniform "risk weighted" capital adequacy requirements that not only tighten the definition of capital but also include many off-balance sheet items in the denominator. The new requirements will be phased in until 1992. Keefe, Bruyette, and Woods, bank stock analysts, estimate that twenty-six large U.S. banks would have to dispose of assets or issue new common stock if these standards were effective immediately (Shaw 1988). British and Japanese banks, among others, will probably also have to add capital relative to assets in order to meet the new requirements. The capital situation is further complicated by last year's large addition to general loan loss reserves against Third World debt. Some of these reserves came out of equity, but under the old rules were still considered primary capital for capital adequacy purposes. Now the central banks have decided that after a transition period general provisions will no longer count as core primary capital.

The price of new bank capital may be quite high as rating agencies and investors have become increasingly skeptical about the viability of Third World loans. Among American money center banks, only Morgan is currently rated AAA, and at least one large bank has slipped so far in the ranks that it is having to pay more than Mexico for long-term funds. The small secondary market for Third World loans that developed as an escape valve for the banking system came back to bite the big banks by setting a price on this paper that all could see, thereby putting a value on the banks' loan portfolios without the banks formally "marking to market." Big bank stocks trailed the run-up in the bull market and have lagged the S&P 500 recovery since the October 19 crash. Worse, stocks of regional banks, which pose increasingly serious competition for the money centers in the era of deregulation and are not as burdened with Third World exposure, have been selling at a far higher price/earnings ratio than the money centers.

Recent changes in tax and accounting rules also affect the banks' cost/benefit analysis of carrying LDC loans. The alternative minimum corporate tax imposed by the 1986 Tax Reform Act and the interruption in interest payments from countries like Brazil may make it difficult for banks to fully realize the tax benefits of LDC loans. At the same time, revised accounting standards are limiting the ability of banks to report anticipated tax benefits on their income statements before tax losses are actually realized. Because the IRS only grants tax deductions for losses actually taken (loan write-offs), the large loan loss reserves taken by U.S. banks last year now yield no tax benefits at all, in either real or accounting terms.[4] U.S. banks are at this point asking themselves: If loan loss reserves will not count as primary capital, will not reassure investors, and will not yield any tax benefits, what is the point of having them?

These changes affect different banks differently, depending on relative loan exposure, capital base, and mix of domestic and international earnings. These differing effects may in turn explain the growing divisiveness in the banking community over how to proceed in managing the international debt problem. Taken together the regulatory, tax, and accounting changes probably make holding the LDC assets to maturity less attractive for many banks than securitization or even write-offs.

And, significantly in the context of the current debate over debt strategy, these changes also dim the prospects for any resumption of large-scale "voluntary" lending by the banks to Third World countries. Thus, the original debt strategy and the Baker modification, which presumed just such a resumption of lending once debtor countries had "adjusted," is based on a false premise. The current debt strategy, which is supposedly "market based," is not that at all. It in fact runs directly contrary to current, strong trends in the financial markets: against balance of payments flows, against capital constraints on the banks, against the negative investor attitude toward banks with large Third World loan exposures, and against the new opportunities and competitive pressures for banks at home.

A very different approach will be needed to solve the debt problem—an approach that takes these "structural adjustments" in financial markets into consideration. Looking beyond the debt issue, a very different approach will have to be taken by developing countries to regain access to international capital. A restoration of the status quo ante is not in the cards.

---

4. Before the accounting rule changes (which the banks are fighting), banks could boost reported post-tax earnings in a given year by "anticipating" future tax loan loss deductions on their income statements, even though the actual loss—and the actual tax deduction—might not be taken until several years later.

5 SAFE PASSAGE THROUGH DIRE STRAITS: MANAGING AN ORDERLY EXIT FROM THE DEBT CRISIS

Paul M. Sacks and Chris Canavan

In the last year, a growing number of experts and participants have concluded that the debt crisis is worsening. They cite militance of debtor countries, some of which have halted interest payments, an event that shook the world's financial system when threatened by Mexico in 1982. Banks have displayed equal drama: Citibank, America's largest bank, took record losses in 1987, claiming that Brazil's moratorium had forced its hand. In the minds of many, these events conjure up images of a process unravelling beyond anyone's control.

Despite this apparent anarchy, the debt crisis has a distinct logic. The market that interlocks commercial banks and Third World debtor countries has changed markedly, but it has become no more unruly. In our opinion, the rules have simply changed, and the new rules must be understood if the debt crisis is to be managed properly. Those who fear a chaotic deterioration may be vindicated in the end, but only if the players in this drama continue to behave as if the market has not changed. We can understand these new rules if we compare them to the earlier phases of the debt crisis, which include the competitive entry phase that began in the early 1970s and the freeze phase brought about by the Mexican crisis of 1982.

THE FIRST PHASE

The first distinctive phase, which we call the competitive entry phase, began in the early 1970s, sparked by an economic shock with which we are all familiar. The first oil price shock drastically shifted the profile of international liquidity, creating huge current account deficits in poorer regions of the world and cash gluts in the banking systems of the richer nations. All at once, the demand for international credit rose in the South and the supply rose in the North. A process we called "petrodollar recycling" began to roll, gathering steam over the course of the decade. Nonoil developing countries increased their borrowings (total bonds and credits) from $8.8 billion in 1973 to $18.9 billion in 1976. International earnings of the top thirteen U.S. banks grew at an annual compound rate of 36.4 percent between 1970 and 1975, while their domestic earnings only grew by .7 percent (Subcommittee on Foreign Economic Policy 1977).

The boom in lending altered the structure of the sovereign loan market. What had been an oligopolistic market, controlled by a handful of large banks, was now much more competitive. Banks that had little or no previous experience in the market quickly developed large portfolios of sovereign loans. They found the market much easier to enter. We are taught in introductory economics that a market becomes more competitive when lower barriers to entry allow small and novice firms to cut away at the market share of larger, established firms. This is not quite what occurred in the sovereign loan market. Barriers to entry did fall, but in a manner controlled entirely by the large banks.

What were the barriers to entry? Small banks stayed out of the sovereign loan market for two reasons. First, when countries requested credit, they asked for sums far larger than what small banks could provide. Second, putting together such a loan taxed even the most sophisticated international banks and was beyond the capabilities of a small bank familiar only with domestic markets. The syndicated loan eliminated these thresholds. Small banks were able to take on a piece of a loan commensurate with their size and could rely on the large banks to arrange and manage the loan.

Competition in this market grew more fierce toward the end of the decade, which took a toll on the risk-pricing mechanism within the banks. The difference between the interest spreads charged to high-risk and low-risk countries thinned as banks vied for the business of arranging loans to LDCs. In 1973, the average contractual fees on medium-term loans were .25 percent to 1 percent for developed countries, compared to 2 percent to 2.5 percent for developing countries. By 1975, the spread for developed countries had risen to 1.5 percent, while for developing countries it had fallen from 1.5 percent to 2.5

percent (Subcommittee on Foreign Economic Policy 1977). Falling spreads on developing loans were clues that banks were underestimating the risk to which they were exposed.

In hindsight, it should come as no surprise that banks underestimated the risk they faced. When analysts and line officers calculated the risk premium of a loan, they were in effect trying to measure the probability of events that had not occurred in recent memory. In the previous two decades, there had been no large-scale defaults. Those bankers who remembered the debt crisis immediately following World War II had long since passed away. Bankers in the mid 1970s were afflicted with "disaster myopia." Furthermore, risk analysts at banks were under pressure to minimize pessimistic assessments, because this went against the sentiment of line officers whose primary purpose was to book loans. Within the banks, the politics of sovereign lending favored those who blessed what was quite a profitable business. There was still a third reason for underestimating risk and shaving basis points off interest rate spreads: large banks were earning revenue not only from interest payments but from fees paid for arranging and managing the loans, fees paid long before the loan's maturity. There was less incentive to calculate the interest rate accurately because management and commitment fees could make up the difference. Average commitment fees grew from .25 percent to .75 percent between 1973 and 1975, and management fees grew from nil to .5 percent over the same period (Subcommittee on Foreign Economic Policy 1977)

These were the rules of the first phase of the debt crisis, but they changed abruptly by August 1982. A second oil price hike in 1979 created further demand for credit, but stretched the ability of borrowing countries to service debt they had already contracted. The unprecedented rise in interest rates strained their liquidity. The crisis in Poland signaled to some banks that a debt crisis was not so farfetched. When Mexico announced it could no longer service its external debt without outside help, the petrodollar recycling process came to a crashing halt, and the second phase of the debt crisis commenced.

THE SECOND PHASE

The Mexican crisis of summer 1982 was a case study in financial market failure. President Lopez Portillo reminded the world that financial markets are sensitive to that very mercurial commodity known as confidence. One hint that this confidence might be misplaced, and a market can freeze. Once banks doubted that sovereign borrowers had sufficient liquidity, they stopped providing that liquidity, creating a self-fulfilling prophecy of enormous magnitude.

With the freeze came an abrupt change in the rules of the market. As soon as banks realized that they were locked into bad exposure, it became apparent that sovereign lending was far from an ideal competitive market. While there may have been something akin to free entry during the competitive entry phase, there was little genuine free exit. Once a bank made a five-year loan to a country, it had little choice but to hold on to this exposure for the full term because there was no secondary market in which the asset could be liquidated. In the first phase this made little difference; in the second phase this was critically important.

Trapped between illiquid LDC borrowers on one side and an illiquid secondary market on the other, banks had little choice but to cooperate with each other to maintain a modicum of stability. A period of unprecedented collusion began between large and small banks, U.S. and non-U.S. banks, banks and governments, and banks and multilateral organizations. Collusion took place despite important differences in regulation and accounting standards which placed banks in relatively different positions vis-à-vis debtor nations. Several factors motivated this collusion. One was the distinct perception on the part of banks that short-term sacrifices would revive the sovereign loan market and restore it to its original condition. There was also the newly found religion that said that macroeconomic discipline would put countries on the right track.

Banks unwilling to collude faced steep costs. Even though the free-rider issue was discussed avidly in the early years of the debt crisis, it was not a serious problem. Most banks genuinely believed that if their intransigency undermined a debt agreement, a country's inability to make interest payments could cause unparalleled damage to the bank's capital base. Banks not persuaded by this argument came under fire from their respective central banks and the large banks in their domicile. Most of the time this pressure sufficed to secure agreements.

For five years, banks and governments behaved according to the rules of the freeze phase. These rules were very effective in achieving their first goal, averting financial disaster, but they were less capable of securing their second objective, to bring the crisis to an end. A proposition on which these rules were based was faulty. These rules said, in effect, that through a high degree of collusion, governments and banks could reverse the tide of markets. Nowhere was this proposition more explicitly laid out than in the Baker Initiative of 1985, in which U.S. Treasury Secretary James A. Baker III asked banks to increase their exposure to the fifteen most indebted developing countries while governmental institutions would do the same. But the paltry results that followed the Initiative suggested that, in fact, governments and banks would not be able to reverse the market. This was the first indication that the rules of the game were changing, and that we were on the eve of a new phase in the debt crisis.

Various unrelated factors concurred to change the banks' perception of the debt crisis. One was the secular move by commercial banks, especially in the United States, away from term lending altogether. LDCs were not the only borrowers having trouble meeting their obligations: U.S. farmers, real estate moguls, and oil riggers also struggled. At the same time, the Euromarkets were throwing up a cornucopia of new financial instruments that allowed borrowers to bypass commercial banks and tap directly into the capital markets. If banks were going to keep up with the times, they would have to adopt merchant banking strategies and compete squarely against investment banks, at least to the extent that the Glass-Steagall regulations allowed.[1] These were the days when Bankers Trust publicly considered giving up its commercial banking charter and entering wholeheartedly into investment banking. Regulatory changes encouraged this. By forcing banks to improve their capital adequacy, bank regulators increased the cost of adding new assets to a bank's portfolio, because more capital would have to be allocated against these assets. Instead, banks sought ways to earn fee-income rather than interest income, much the same way an investment bank operates. Traditional commercial bank lending was no longer as attractive.

Powerful new constituencies emerged inside banks around the merchant banking operations. They were a new breed of commercial banker, typically younger and often hired from investment banks or law firms. For them, the LDC debt crisis was nothing more than a prison locking up precious bank capital that could be better allocated elsewhere. As these constituencies grew stronger, so did their arguments for freeing up capital whatever the cost. Only with increasing difficulty could the old guard stand up for a more moderated approach to the debt crisis. If merchant banking changed the relative strength of camps within commercial banks, the balance of power among banks was jolted by the fall in the value of the dollar. The second Baker "initiative," the managed depreciation of the dollar, left U.S. banks holding the bag as non-American institutions found their dollar-denominated assets shrinking in terms of both risk and return. Foreign banks became less concerned with dollar-denominated sovereign debt problems and more concerned with taking competitive advantage of weakened American banks. Dollar-based banks saw

---

1. The Glass-Steagall Act of the 1930s established a set of regulations limiting the activities in which commercial banks could engage.

with some alarm their competitive positions eroding as foreign banks began moving in from their enhanced financial positions.

These centrifugal forces—merchant banking and the fall in the dollar—guaranteed the failure of the Baker Initiative. They were the backdrop against which entreaties from the United States for increased bank lending fell on deaf ears. They dealt a decisive blow to the proposition that governments could reverse the movement of markets. It was another proposition of the Baker Initiative that survived. Secretary Baker argued that the best way forward was to keep lending. The banks agreed, but for a different reason. He was hoping that greater lending would revive the sovereign loan market, but the banks believed that their only chance of exiting the market was to keep countries afloat long enough to pull out. Baker asked for renewed loyalty to the sovereign loan market. Banks were trying to keep the exit door open long enough to get out.

The rules of the game had changed subtly by the beginning of 1987, capped by Brazil's declaration of a moratorium. By halting interest payments, Brazil ushered in what we refer to as the competitive exit phase, with a new set of rules that govern the market today. Any viable plan to relieve the pressures of the debt crisis must be tailored to the new rules.

RULES OF THE GAME IN THE
COMPETITIVE EXIT PHASE

The emergence of modest liquidity is the characteristic that distinguishes the exit phase from its two predecessors. The presence of a secondary market in LDC debt and a growing number of innovative transactions that make use of this market raise the possibility that banks might exit from the sovereign debt market. Debt-for-debt swaps allow banks to recompose their portfolios to their liking. Debt-for-equity conversions provide direct investors with a vehicle for cheap financing. Debtor countries can modestly reduce their debt obligations as well. Investment bankers have begun proposing methods to securitize debt—converting it into tradeable securities—which would inject additional liquidity into the market.

But this liquidity has caused as much worry as hope. While the press reports have nothing but good to say about the secondary market—the latest evidence that free markets can solve this debt situation—large banks, especially in the United States, have resisted participating in it. Liquidity means that it would be harder to keep the smaller banks in the game. A massive recomposition of portfolios is just another way of saying that those banks that can exit will do so, and those banks that cannot will be left holding more of the problem debt. Keeping the smaller and non-U.S. banks in the game has taken on new urgency in the private dialogue among U.S. money center banks.

In this increasingly complex environment, banks as well as debtor countries are given to unilateral actions. In May 1987, Citibank set aside $3 billion in loan loss reserves, presumably to cushion the bank against poor LDC loans. Bank of Boston publicly admitted to writing down Latin American exposure in December. These actions, coupled with the Brazilian and Ecuadorean interest payments moratoria, legitimized moves that previously were considered out of bounds. The critical mass needed to restructure debt the old-fashioned way was crumbling.

Underlying the exit phase is a new and more complicated matrix of motivations. All banks would like to rid themselves of problem loans, but they approach this goal from increasingly divergent directions. The ease with which they can exit the market depends on a variety of factors, the most important of which are capital strength, level of reserves, the relative size of their LDC portfolio, and the regulatory and accounting regimes in which they operate.

Capital strength is critical. At the onset of the debt crisis, U.S. bank regulators were shocked by the amount of capital jeopardized by the largest LDC borrowers. In mid 1982, credits to Mexico represented 50 percent of the capital of the nine largest U.S. banks. Credits to Mexico, Argentina, and Brazil combined totaled 115 percent of the capital of these banks (Morgan Guaranty 1983). Led by the Federal Reserve Bank, U.S. regulators began a campaign to raise the ratio of primary capital to assets. Between 1982 and 1986, U.S. money center banks increased their primary capital from 4.8 percent to 7.1 percent of total assets. The respective ratio for regional banks grew from 5.5 percent to 7 percent.

Perhaps more critical was the market's perception of this capital. At the end of 1982, the median share of a money center bank was trading at 70 percent of its book value. By the end of 1986, it had only improved to 90 percent. A median share of a regional bank traded at 72 percent of book value at the end of 1982, but by December 1986 the share had risen to 131 percent (Morgan Guaranty 1983). Regional banks have gained a more healthy reputation, which improves their prospects for raising new capital if they so choose. Exiting the sovereign loan market is a more plausible option because the loss can be absorbed more easily.

Greater reserves also enable banks to contemplate exit more readily. This is one of the important differences between U.S. banks and banks from other countries, in particular Germany and Japan. U.S. banks tend to hold relatively low levels of reserves because of the great costs to holding these funds idle. In

Germany and Japan, banks may also have modest levels of explicit reserves, but they hold so-called "hidden reserves," unrealized gains in their securities portfolios that can be used to absorb losses without causing serious distress to the balance sheet.

Another factor distinguishing banks from each other is the importance of LDC loans in their portfolio. Obviously, banks with a greater proportion of LDC loans cannot contemplate exit as readily as others because the off-ramp is simply not wide enough to let all these assets out of the market. Banks also have strategic questions to resolve. Even if the sovereign loan business is dead, larger international banks still see markets in countries like Brazil and Mexico. Citibank, for example, is intent on building a large branch system in Brazil. To remain in good standing with the Brazilians, Citibank must tread carefully in negotiations over sovereign debt.

Finally, banks operate in different regulatory and accounting regimes, some of which are more hostile to innovations that might relieve the debt problem. In the United States, it is costly for a bank to defer interest payments, so costly that U.S. banks would prefer to extend new loans to guarantee these payments. In Europe, regulators and auditors (and shareholders) are more willing to let a bank capitalize interest (converting the missed interest payment into principal). This is one of the key differences that made it harder for U.S. banks to experiment with innovative options. During the freeze phase, the rules of debt management were tailored, in the main, to the U.S. regime. Non-U.S. banks are requesting that these rules be changed so that they may take advantage of the benefits of what is permitted within their regulatory environment. Regulatory rules can represent barriers to exit for any given bank. Those that face the highest barriers are U.S. money center banks. In almost every category in which they are at a relative disadvantage, U.S. regional banks are somewhat better off. German and Japanese banks are in a much stronger position, because of the weaker dollar and more forgiving regulatory and accounting systems.

As banks diverge because of their different characteristics, so do their strategies. U.S. money center banks cannot totally exit the market and therefore seek to minimize the liquidity and discounts on the secondary market. Smaller discounts represent smaller losses when banks use the secondary market. Large discounts can "contaminate" portfolios, either because regulators and accountants force banks to value assets to market, or more subtly if shareholders discriminate against large portfolios of heavily discounted assets. Large discounts also make it more difficult to negotiate with debtors. It is hard to persuade shareholders that new commitments to a debtor country are worthy investments when, at the same time, the market treats the country as junk.

Banks facing lower exit barriers take a somewhat different view. They, too, would like to see small discounts, but they prefer a secondary market with maximum liquidity. This would enable them to take advantage of the secondary market, and, because they are willing to take losses that money center banks want to avoid, these banks hope that the secondary market could one day swallow their entire portfolios. Many U.S. regional banks do not merely want to reduce their exposures, they want to eliminate them.

But money center banks fear liquidity. They see in greater liquidity the threat that they may be left holding the bulk of the exposure. In this scenario, the task of meeting the foreign exchange needs of debtor countries would fall to a small number of banks, and the costs of providing this credit would grow. On some occasions, money center banks have had to contribute more than their pro rata share of new money packages to make up for truant regional banks. U.S. regional banks are less and less sensitive to the entreaties and threats made by the U.S. government and the money center banks, and money center banks fear the possibility that this trend might accelerate.

The motivations of debtor countries have changed somewhat as well. During the freeze phase, they knew that to secure new loans and concessions they had to showcase their economies in glowing terms. Presidents might bemoan the sorry economic state of their countries, but finance ministers were appending highly optimistic economic forecasts to the term sheets of restructuring agreements. The rise of a secondary market had changed their strategic calculus. Large discounts open the possibility of debt relief. A steeper discount encourages investors to redeem debt for conversion into equity. It might also allow debt to be swapped in a way that reduces total debt (as the recent Mexican bond issue did to a limited extent). In the extreme, a steep discount might bring the price of debt to levels at which the country could afford to repurchase it.

In short, from a certain perspective a debtor country's optimal strategy might be to convince the market that its debt is utterly worthless. But there are costs to this strategy. By issuing pessimistic economic forecasts, a country jeopardizes its access to credit. Banks would have more difficulty arranging new money packages. A discount could also grow so large that it would discourage relief. Once a bank has charged off the bulk of its exposure to a particular country, the costs of holding on to the debt are relatively minor, though the country still owes the debt in full. Rather than selling the asset or swapping for equity, the bank might calculate that it is better to gamble on future interest payments rather than liquidate the asset at a deep discount. The country would then find that its only real option was to go into default, incurring an onus that most countries would rather avoid. Thus, in the competitive exit phase, countries face contradictory motivations. It is virtually impossible to discern a strategy that would maximize the discount on the secondary market while avoiding the attendant costs.

This new motivation matrix places banks trapped by high exit barriers in choppy waters. Other banks are getting out of the market, or at least threatening to do so. Within their own institutions there are groups advocating exit at any cost. Countries are behaving according to ever more complicated motivations, and are therefore less predictable. If the history of nonbanking sectors has any pertinence, it informs us that firms trapped in declining industries engage in increasingly destructive competition. Banks may follow suit by competing more fiercely for a competitive edge. This might have been one of the motivations behind Citibank's addition to reserves. As the largest bank in the U.S., it could afford to set aside these reserves. Indeed, its stock prices increased afterwards, reversing the typical pattern. Other banks were forced to follow but were in a much weaker position to do so. Another such round of reserves accumulation could easily wipe out the net worth of one or two money center banks, making the Continental Illinois debacle pale by comparison. If such chaos broke out among banks, the political and financial stability of the large debtor countries would be threatened. Most of the major debtor countries still rely on commercial banks for credit from abroad, and to be deprived of it could mean a period of extreme austerity.

MANAGING AN ORDERLY EXIT

While the competitive exit phase is operating according to a distinct set of rules, it is poised to become chaotic. For this reason there is a strong need to develop strategies to manage the exit phase in an orderly manner. We submit that there is an important role to be played by public policymakers in the exit phase, though it is a moderated one. Policymakers can make a contribution only if they consider the nature of the exit phase. First, we offer two propositions about the exit market that policymakers must keep in mind. The first is that the U.S. government, and OECD governments more generally, are at risk of having to shoulder an even greater share of development assistance given the exodus by banks from the sovereign debt market. The public and private sectors have shared the burden of development financing to date, but as we look ahead to the 1990s, that burden could rest almost entirely on public shoulders. Given the enormous pressure on OECD governments to reduce the size of the public sector, this burden can be ill-afforded. In addition, capital flows from the United States to LDCs are vital to supporting U.S. long-term commercial interests in these countries. An exodus by banks leaves the U.S. government as lender of first and last resort. It is thus in the U.S. national interest to prevent a categorical and panicked exit by commercial banks from the sovereign lending market.

The second proposition is that policymakers can modify market behavior at the margin but cannot alter its direction. This is particularly the case when financial intermediaries are scattered and fragmented. Other than macro-economic tools such as fiscal and monetary policy, policymakers have two basic mechanisms: guarantees and regulation. Neither of these can alter the direction of markets, but they can exert an influence.

To date, the proposals from policymakers have not heeded the second proposition. The Baker Plan was an explicit request that banks move in the opposite direction from the one in which they were inclined. We have mentioned the reason why the Baker Initiative failed. But proposals for an International Debt Management Authority were equally flawed because they asked banks to act collectively long after the impetus to collude disappeared. These proposals may have succeeded at the high point of the second phase, but in the present phase they are inappropriate. Instead, policymakers should realize that their greatest allies in the exit phase are those banks that feel trapped, that is, the large U.S. banks. Both OECD governments and these banks have similar interests, and could form a very influential strategic alliance.

In fact, large U.S. banks have already heeded the changes that have taken place in the rules of the game. Even though they would prefer not to inject liquidity into the secondary market, they recognize reality. If it is impossible to stop regional and non-U.S. banks from exiting, then the next best strategy is to structure this exit in the least damaging way. Hence, money center banks have proposed a variety of ways that other banks might reduce their exposure, such as the exit bonds in the April 1987 Argentina rescheduling or the bond issue devised by Mexico and Morgan Guaranty in December 1987. Several other "alternative participation instruments" are being contemplated in private by the banks on the various steering committees. Policymakers should follow the lead of trapped banks.

The Mexican bond issue was, in many ways, a model of how public and private actors could work together constructively during the exit phase. The program provided a mechanism for orderly exit by commercial bank players through the use of a government guarantee, but at no marginal cost to the tax-payer. It also provided debt relief to our most important neighbor to the south, singling out Mexico for cushioning against a possible default. Also, the plan kept banks in the market because the collateral on the bonds can be captured only after twenty years. But there were also flaws in the Mexico plan. The government guarantees were insufficient and misplaced, because they should have applied to interest rather than principal. Another flaw was that the players with the largest stakes and highest barriers to exit were the ones who least participated. The costs of exiting via the Mexican plan were still too high.

The Mexico program was yet another example of the failure of policymakers to perceive clearly the broader consequences of the policy choices made in the context of the exit market. In particular, the SEC ruling providing that banks must adjust their portfolio to the bid value,[2] even if unsuccessful, was damaging and short-sighted. The U.S. government participated in a policy process that benefited our offshore neighbors more than our own institutions, much the same way the weaker dollar has.

How can policymakers shape the exit process in a way that will discourage the categorical abandonment of the developing world by commercial banks? They might do so by tying the strong exit current by banks to longer-range policy goals of the public sector. Rather than block the flow and cause disruption, the flow can be guided creatively and constructively. The initial step is to acknowledge that all players want to get out, and second, that recent rulings have made it harder for banks to exit and therefore have encouraged a disorderly exit process leading to mutually damaging behavior. Tax changes and regulation that discourage loan loss reserves and increase the cost of funds have a deleterious effect on the banks involved in the exit process. We recommend that policies be fashioned in light of the new market realities.

More appropriate regulation can provide safer passage out of the debt crisis to those banks that promise to maintain some presence in Latin America, such as giving banks a tax advantage if they increased their trade finance in a particular country. This would allow a bank to exit from the long-term debt problem more easily, but the country in question would not lose access to the short-term trade credits that are desperately needed. By granting a tax advantage here and a supportive ruling there, the U.S. government can avoid having to pump large sums of money into a debtor country when the banks have left for good. But this is not enough. The U.S. government should also revive and assist the virtually moribund secondary market in LDC debt. The Mexico bond issue is a useful step in the right direction, but government policy crippled the plan with regulatory myopia. Similar creative uses of the guarantee mechanism are steps in the right direction.

We are witnessing the twilight of bank lending to developing countries. This is just one part of the overall decline in commercial banking.

---

2. That is, value the loans at the price at which it offered them to the Mexican government for repurchase.

Everywhere, banks are devising end-game strategies that will get them out of dying businesses without too much cost. Government officials can do very little to reverse the trend, for the direction of the market is simply too strong. The next best strategy, therefore, is to encourage an orderly exit. Otherwise, a war could break out in the banking system that could cause widespread harm. The U.S. financial system would be weakened and the U.S. government would be left assuming the cost of financing developing country growth. Rather than holding banks at bay, it is imperative that the government offer safe passage from this crisis.

III STRUCTURAL ADJUSTMENT: SOLUTION OR PART OF THE PROBLEM?

Many things made this seminar exciting, and perhaps the most catalytic ingredient was the presence of both high officials from international agencies— willing to speak openly and unbureaucratically—and academicians specializing in debt and structural adjustment issues. The result of this interaction comes out clearly in the chapters in this part of the book.

In Chapter 6, Robert Liebenthal and Peter Nicholas lay out clearly and with cautious optimism the experience of the World Bank with structural adustment lending. The role and posture of the World Bank on structural adjustment is particularly important, for, unlike the IMF, the Bank has in its charter the obligation to foster long-term development, not just macroeconomic stabilization. While Liebenthal and Nicholas are guardedly optimistic about the policy packages embodied in structural adjustment lending, Robin A. King and Michael D. Robinson in Chapter 7 are considerably less so. In a paper that represents a benchmark econometric study of structural adjustment, they conclude that the programs lead to little improvement in macroeconomic conditions or in the ability to service debt. Also skeptical is José D. Epstein, who in Chapter 9 provides an invaluable service by tracing the history of "policy-based lending" from an institutional point of view. The doubts he raises as to the assumptions implicit in the successful implementation of such lending make concrete the pessimistic empirical results of King and Robinson.

Closely related to these three chapters is Chapter 8 by Richard D. Fletcher, which focuses upon one specific policy instrument, exchange rate adjustment. In an argument that is both refreshingly blunt and disturbingly pessimistic, he concludes that developing countries have little choice but to pursue a "beggar thy workers" export policy if economies are to adjust to an unfavorable world economy. Fletcher's closing reference to the famous lament by Joan Robinson makes one pause to consider the equity of the prevailing system of international trade and finance.

6 WORLD BANK-SUPPORTED ADJUSTMENT PROGRAMS

Robert Liebenthal and Peter Nicholas

ORIGINS OF ADJUSTMENT

An escalating economic crisis in the early 1980s led the World Bank to emphasize more strongly than before the introduction of economic policy reforms by developing countries and to support the reforms through adjustment lending. There are two aspects to this crisis, the first of which is recession. Over the past nine years, there has been a major adverse change in the environment for almost all developing countries, caused by several events: the second oil shock; record-high real interest rates; the commodity price collapse; lower OECD growth coupled with rising protectionism; and the reversal of net lending flows. Not since the era of growth and development for LDCs got underway after World War II, with that development for the first time consciously fostered by international effort, have the circumstances been so unfavorable for global poverty alleviation.

It is therefore remarkable that LDCs as a whole have maintained some growth, albeit inadequately, in the 1980s. Real GDP has grown by 3.4 percent in 1980 to 1985, two-thirds of the growth rate of 1973 to 1980 and only half as fast as in 1965 to 1973. But almost all this growth has been in Asia. In

The views and interpretations in this paper are those of the authors and should not be attributed to the World Bank, to its affiliated organizations, or to any individual acting in their behalf.

Sub-Saharan Africa, average per capita incomes have fallen to 1960s levels, and in Latin America, performance has been little better. Net investment, essential to increase productive capacity, has practically ceased in several countries.

If these are the broad economic dimensions of the present crisis, it is increasingly associated with a social crisis, which is less easy to observe because of inadequate data, but abundantly clear on an impressionistic basis, and borne out by partial data, for the documentation of which a large debt is due to UNICEF (Cornia et al. 1987). Examples include the 70 percent increase in open unemployment in Mexico in 1981 to 1984 (Pfeffermann 1986: 11); a 40 percent reduction in real wages in Costa Rica in 1979 to 1982 (Pfeffermann: 17); and rising malnutrition among infants and children in a broad range of countries (Cornia et al.: 31-33). Recent work conducted at the World Bank suggests that some 100 to 150 million people in Sub-Saharan Africa (40 percent of the population) are "food insecure."

The second aspect of the crisis is the extension and intensification of long-standing difficulties in several countries' development strategies. In Sub-Saharan Africa, governments struggling to meet expectations of steadily improving living standards have often promoted policies that, instead of providing the basis for sustainable growth and poverty alleviation, have eroded the existing productive base. Contributing to this erosion has been a familiar litany of policy problems: a bias against agriculture;[1] inefficient state enterprises; unproductive government investment expenditures; a declining tax base as distorted exchange rates drive trade underground; and, when faced with declining tax revenues, a tendency to maintain or expand public-sector employment levels at the cost of reduced rehabilitation and maintenance expenditures. These problems have combined with high population growth and other structural problems to actually reduce living standards in an unfortunately large number of cases. While most countries were able to ignore the need for changes in economic policy in the 1970s when real interest rates were low or negative, external capital plentiful, and real commodity prices favorable, the onslaught in the early 1980s of drought, higher oil prices, and reduced commodity prices made drastic change inescapable. A few countries had also borrowed heavily at commercial interest rates, and for them the sharp rise in real interest rates that began in 1979 only added to their problems.

Up until 1983, comparatively few countries took steps to deal with these problems. Many more countries have now started to take action, such that some thirty African countries are, with IMF and World Bank support, trying to

---

1. See Chapter 12 by Jamal, where rural-urban and agricultural-nonagricultural biases in Tanzania are investigated.

cope with this crisis by introducing wide-ranging and courageously implemented programs of economic restructuring. A few, like Ghana, have already shown some successful results. In much of the continent, however, attempts at reversing years of economic deterioration and loss of government control of the economy have been compromised by powerful opposition and some understandable hesitancy on the part of governments.

In Latin America, the crisis of the 1980s was more sudden and unexpected. After a long period of sustained increase in per capita incomes and expanded government services, in part financed by huge external borrowing, the jump in interest rates and the subsequent cut-off of money from commercial banks, compounded by reduced access to the markets of industrialized countries and sharply deteriorating terms of trade, led living standards in much of Latin America to decline precipitously. To restore growth, these countries have been moving away from inward-oriented growth behind high protective barriers toward a strategy that emphasizes expanding export volumes to finance more imports and negative net financial flows. This strategy has met with varying success as countries have also faced increased protectionism and stagnant world trade. Except in 1984, external balance has been achieved much more through compression of imports than through expansion of exports. This has not only hurt the Latin American countries themselves, but also has had serious repercussions for export industries in other countries, particularly the United States.

For development assistance agencies like the World Bank, these problems were manifested in deteriorating micro (project) performance, especially in Sub-Saharan Africa. Shortages of domestic budgetary resources, inappropriate pricing policies, overextended public agencies, and restraints on trade were among the factors that reduced the returns on investment, including donor-financed projects. Prior to the 1980s, development assistance had emphasized investment as the primary instrument to achieve growth, development, and poverty alleviation. While investment lending by the World Bank had never neglected the policy environment, it was clear that the problems of the early 1980s in Sub-Saharan Africa and Latin America demanded instruments that put policy and institutional change at the forefront.

ADJUSTMENT STRATEGY

Attempts at economic restructuring in the face of these problems have come to be characterized as "adjustment," and support for restructuring from the multilateral agencies as "adjustment lending." The aim of all adjustment programs is to achieve an equilibrium, or sustainable macroeconomic balance (externally and internally), in response to external shocks, while at the same time improving the prospects for growth and poverty alleviation.[2]

When there are major macroeconomic imbalances, especially financing shortfalls, the issue is not whether to adjust, but how. The choice for government is, at one extreme, a disorderly adjustment in which import compression, inflation, and depressed investment levels perpetuate or even exacerbate declines in living standards and, at the other, an organized adjustment in which a combination of policy reform, investment, and external support leads to eventual recovery. The experience suggests that postponing adjustment is costly, especially for the poor, in both the short and the long runs.

The main elements of World Bank-supported adjustment strategies are:

1. stabilization—the elimination or reduction of macroeconomic imbalances— generally, though not necessarily, in association with IMF programs;
2. "switching"—shifting resources toward the tradeable sectors and consumption away from exportables;
3. efficiency improvement, measured by, for example, the reduction of incremental capital output ratios (ICORs), through public expenditure and state-owned enterprise rationalization and reduction in control and regulation; and
4. the mobilization and coordination of internal and external resources to support these efforts.

There are a number of common themes in adjustment programs, which can be conveniently grouped under four headings: trade, pricing, resource mobilization, and resource use.

Trade

Reform of incentives for production of exports and import-competing goods has been a key feature of almost all adjustment programs. Except in those African countries whose currencies are tied to the French franc, a devaluation has generally been the starting point for trade reform. Even those countries that did not allow their currencies to appreciate in real terms during the 1970s now face less favorable terms of trade developments as well as low-productivity

---

2. See Chapter 9 by Epstein, which treats the history of policy-based lending and questions its effectiveness.

export- and import-competing sectors, which imply a need for exchange rate depreciation.[3] In addition, in many countries high rates of domestic inflation actually led the real rate of exchange to appreciate, benefiting those with privileged access to foreign exchange, but inhibiting export and competing import growth. Increasing shortages of foreign currency in turn led to payments of large rents for access to foreign currency and to a parallel market at a more market-based rate, thus depriving the government of tax revenue. For this reason, some countries have experimented with foreign exchange systems or floats, which not only depreciate the official exchange rate, but reduce the incentive and opportunity for parallel markets. Despite the costs to the economy as a whole of an overvalued exchange rate, devaluation imposes heavy economic costs on certain groups, like urban wage earners or those in both the public and private sectors, who may lose their rents from control of foreign exchange or will have to pay significantly higher prices for imports, and who can therefore be expected to resist strongly.

On the export side, emphasis has been placed on two types of promotion measures: (1) the provision of financial incentives through tax rebates, subsidies on imported inputs to offset import controls, and preferential access to imports and credit, and (2) the reform of administrative procedures and the establishment of better institutional support for exporters. On the import substitution side, protection has generally been reduced to encourage efficiency and better exploitation of comparative advantage. The emphasis of most Bank-supported programs has been on the removal of quantitative restrictions and the introduction of more uniform rates of protection. Contrary to some accounts, Bank-supported programs have not generally favored rapid import liberalization, but phased programs in which the removal of restrictions was coordinated with an active exchange rate policy aimed at preventing a surge of imports and the destruction of potentially efficient import-competing industries.

The impact of these reforms, however, has been frequently hampered by failure to maintain a realistic exchange rate. In about half of the countries where adjustment programs have been supported by the World Bank, the effect of large nominal devaluations was quickly eroded by domestic inflation (sometimes caused in part by the devaluation itself). In addition, for low-income countries and those highly dependent on commodity exports, the short-run impact of devaluation on exports has been limited, because capacity constraints in the exporting sectors were greater than anticipated. These conclusions, rather than reducing the need for exchange rate and trade reform,

---

3. See Chapter 8 by Fletcher, where devaluation is treated in detail.

underline the importance of complementary policies to contain domestic inflation and to develop export infrastructures.

Pricing

Changes in economically strategic prices—particularly those in agriculture and energy—have been a feature of most adjustment programs supported by the World Bank. Pricing reforms have almost invariably focused on raising producer prices closer to international market price equivalents, and on cutting input and consumer subsidies. Most of these reforms, especially those related to the energy sector, seem to have had significant and visible benefits. There is evidence of increased agricultural production and improved rural incomes, and of increased conservation and efficient import substitution of energy resources. The main obstacle to raising agricultural prices is often the opposition of urban consumers who will face higher food or energy prices. In Zambia, for example, attempts to raise food prices in late 1986 had to be withdrawn in the face of urban riots. Furthermore, rationalizing prices is not generally enough on its own, and complementary improvements in infrastructure and services are also needed to produce a supply response. It is often convenient and necessary to address both price and nonprice factors in a single, comprehensive program.

Resource Mobilization

While the patterns of response to external shocks have varied considerably, the need to reduce resource imbalances implies some combination of reduced domestic investment or higher domestic savings. As the debt crisis has intensified, large shares of domestic savings have been externalized by the heavily indebted countries and have not been available to finance much-needed domestic investment. In addition, there were many situations in which it was important to channel resources to the private sector, especially in agriculture or export manufacturing.

Better resource mobilization has thus been an important objective of adjustment programs. To this end, the Bank has supported efforts to reduce public-sector dissaving. Many developing countries had already achieved quite high tax ratios to GDP; in these cases, Bank-supported programs have emphasized expenditure control and tax reforms aimed at better resource allocation. In other cases, programs have emphasized better revenue collection and sometimes the introduction of new taxes, like VAT. Expenditure reduction has emphasized direct cuts in low-priority government expenditure and control of the deficits of state and parastatal enterprises.

Financial-sector reform has also become an increasingly important feature of adjustment programs. Initially, adjustment programs emphasized raising interest rates to levels that were positive in real terms. More recently, adjustment programs have sought to reduce excessively high real interest rates by reducing public-sector recourse to domestic financing and by reducing financial intermediation costs. The most difficult aspect of financial market and banking-sector reforms has been ensuring an orderly transition for banking systems saddled with many nonperforming loans, sometimes of public enterprises, and liberalizing previously controlled lending and deposit rates. Financial reforms have been especially complicated in cases where the government has been using the financial system to promote exports and offset the bias of continued domestic protection. Here, close coordination of financial and trade reform is called for.

Resource Use

Bank-supported programs have not only sought to improve resource mobilization and reduce financial imbalances, but have also attempted to improve the efficiency with which resources are used, especially in the public sector. Public investment and expenditure reviews have been carried out in many countries, as a result of which governments have been able to identify low-priority investments and limit the allocation of resources to them while emphasizing maintenance and recurrent costs. These reviews have also helped governments in aid coordination by providing a framework for external support and a means of identifying priorities. The role of government as an operator of public enterprises has also been carefully studied. In a number of countries these studies have proposed the divestiture of public enterprises. Over twenty-five countries have announced plans to divest public enterprises, but actual implementation has been slow, not only because of political constraints, but because of technical complexity.

IMPLEMENTATION

The Bank has supported adjustment programs in 55 countries with 150 loans totaling $20 billion. These loans have disbursed rapidly—normally in one to three years—as countries have implemented reforms agreed between the Bank and the government concerned. Unlike the Bank's investment lending, which disburses for the imports needed for a particular investment project, adjustment lending typically disburses against general imports. The Bank has had two objectives in committing such large resources to adjustment lending: (1) to use the Bank's economic expertise and its relatively independent point of view to help countries develop their adjustment programs, and (2) to provide immediate financial support to help countries cover their balance of payments gaps as adjustment policies work to provide a longer-term solution through increased exports and greater domestic efficiency.

The Bank links its lending and disbursements to the implementation of an agreed program of specific actions. About three-quarters of all adjustment loans are experiencing delays in the release of funds as a result of tardiness in completing the action envisaged. The majority of such delays concerns reforms of public and parastatal institutions and enterprises, typically the most politically difficult and complex reforms being attempted under adjustment programs. It seems clear that governments and the Bank frequently have been overly optimistic about the speed with which these reforms can be carried out. More attention is now being paid to institutional factors, such as fiscal management, the management of key sectors, public enterprises, and overall public-sector management.

IMPACT

There are a number of obstacles in the way of reaching a reliable judgment on the impact of adjustment programs. First, the benefits of adjustment programs are not evident for several years, which makes it hard to judge their impact on the basis of short-term economic performance. Second, exogenous shocks, both favorable and unfavorable, occur and their effects are difficult to distinguish from those of adjustment. Third, the process of adjustment is almost never orderly or continuous. Changes in the timing of policy actions weaken the link between a planned reform program and short-term economic performance. And finally, differentiating between the effects of different policies which nevertheless form part of an integrated package is especially difficult. These obstacles could be overcome if comprehensive economic models, and the data needed to use them, were available. Since they are not, country experience is the only available guide to the results of adjustment programs.[4]

4. See Chapter 7 by King and Robinson, which uses a model to assess the impact of some major aspects of adjustment programs.

A recent paper reviewed macroeconomic indicators for sixteen countries that have undertaken adjustment programs (World Bank 1988). While no certain causal connections can be made between trends in the indicators and the adjustment programs, some conclusions do emerge. Indicators for GDP and exports show relatively strong growth for about two-thirds of countries following the introduction of adjustment programs. For each country, growth rates for GDP and merchandise exports in the period following the first Bank adjustment loan were compared with the equivalent figure for a group of similar countries. Of the sixteen countries surveyed, eleven had higher GDP growth than their comparator group, and ten higher export growth. Only two countries—Côte d'Ivoire and the Philippines—have suffered negative growth following their first adjustment loan, and eight countries—Costa Rica, Ghana, Korea, Mauritius, Morocco, Pakistan, Thailand, and Turkey—have so far achieved growth in per capita GDP. Trends in export volumes have varied widely. Jamaica has suffered a 2.5 percent per year export decline since initiating adjustment, while Korea and Turkey have 12 and 22 percent growth rates respectively. Twelve of the sixteen countries reduced their current account deficits, and nine their fiscal deficits, over their adjustment periods (although improvements in the current account may reflect shortages of foreign exchange rather than government policy). Half the countries had decreased both deficits, while only in Togo had both increased.

These assessments do not take into account variations in the degree to which planned actions were actually carried out, and the impact of world conditions. Such factors can only be incorporated by focusing on individual country cases. Even here macroeconomic models are not yet sufficiently advanced to allow rigorous analysis of the effects of reform packages on performance.

FUTURE DIRECTIONS

World Bank support for adjustment programs was initially viewed as an exceptional activity, both in terms of the volume of lending and the approach to design and implementation of Bank assistance programs. Adjustment lending now, however, accounts for about 25 percent of annual lending. More importantly, perhaps, the need for adjustment is influencing all Bank lending and giving rise to new directions in assistance program design.

Four broad hypotheses arise from the eight or so years of experience with Bank-supported adjustment programs. These relate to the global environment for adjustment and the need for adequate financial resources to resume investment and growth, the importance of addressing poverty concerns more directly in adjustment programs, the importance of institutional factors, and some evolution in adjustment program design.

Adjustment Program Financing

The financing of adjustment programs, broadly interpreted to include debt restructuring and possibly some debt reduction, has become *the* critical issue for the heavily indebted countries, as well as for low-income Africa. Without adequate financing, there is import strangulation, underinvestment, fiscal pressure, and a serious reduction in the incentive for countries to undertake adjustment programs. Not that the alternatives are at all attractive: Peru and Zambia are examples of countries undergoing serious economic difficulties as a result of not undertaking adjustment programs, despite unilateral reductions in debt servicing. Failure to mobilize adequate external resources of the right kind and on the right terms carries an increasingly heavy cost in terms of failed adjustment. The Bank is therefore giving increasing attention to the mobilization of finance, to debt restructuring and the "menu" of debt options, and to aid coordination in low-income countries.

Even if development finance becomes easier, however, the need for adjustment will remain. The basic parameters, like rapid population growth, weak commodity prices, and environmental and natural resource degradation, suggest continued emphasis on efficiency in the use of resources and the maximization of benefits from international trade and the world economy. Countries that have undertaken serious adjustment programs now need to extend the effort into specific sectors, to deal in depth with important development problems, like public-enterprise reform and restructuring, financial-sector reform, public-expenditure rationalization, and the creation of a supportive environment for private investment, enterprise development, and technology transfer. In low-income countries, especially Africa, the reform of food-sector policies, and the development of agricultural technology, infrastructure, and human resources feature strongly in development strategies. Some of these activities can perhaps proceed without a macroeconomic adjustment program, but the continuation of large macroeconomic imbalances typically confounds such efforts.

Adjustment and Poverty

The weak economic performance in developing countries in recent years has, as already noted, led to a serious deterioration in social conditions. This is in contrast to original expectations, which were not (as some have suggested) that the benefits of adjustment would trickle down to the poor, but that growth-oriented adjustment could succeed relatively quickly and set up an environment in which poverty programs could resume or expand. The longer-than-expected course of adjustment in most countries has led to growing concern about the impact of adjustment on the poor. Transitional costs of adjustment, resulting from the depression of output, employment, and consumption, almost inevitably affect poor groups adversely. In addition, changes in prices, subsidies, and exposure to market forces as part of adjustment programs lead some groups to gain and some to lose. And the process of shifting resources, especially in developing countries, is rarely smooth and frictionless. In many countries, adjustment involves the scaling-back or closure of facilities in poorer regions, where they were established precisely to create employment, but with weak economic justification.

Some of these costs are inevitably associated with adjustment. In these areas, there is a straightforward trade-off between adjustment and protection of the poor, as a result of which it may be necessary, if additional resources can be found, to slow down the adjustment process. In others, it is possible to protect the poor through the redesign of social programs (targeting), through the redirection of social expenditures, and through specific compensatory programs. These efforts are increasingly finding a place in World Bank-supported adjustment programs, as is the use of food aid to support poverty alleviation measures.

Institutional Aspects

The crisis conditions in which adjustment programs have been introduced have exposed several institutional and political weaknesses in many developing countries, especially in Sub-Saharan Africa. All too often, apparently well-designed adjustment programs have faltered because a limited number of key decisionmakers and technocrats must undertake a perpetual round of donor and creditor negotiations with negligible support from donor or domestic bureaucracies. More fundamentally, it is rare that an adjustment program can succeed on the basis of short-term "push-button" policies (devaluation, price changes) alone; sustained efforts to redesign policies, implement them, monitor performance, and feed back results for further analysis are needed and must become part of developing countries' economic management capacity. Adjustment programs have therefore increasingly emphasized improvements in the use of core economic policy instruments, especially public expenditure and investment, taxation, and external debt management; sectoral restructuring and policy reform; and public-sector management enhancement (pay, employment, and organization of public administration). These issues are often addressed through self-standing technical assistance loans or credits, in parallel with structural adjustment loans.

Adjustment Program Design

One of the effects of the adjustment era is to bring more closely together the various elements of economic and social policy in developing country governments, and in their external assistance. Thus, the need to assign priorities more rationally among competing sectors forces closer integration and discipline in public-expenditure management. Similarly, confronting generic problems in public-enterprise management demands a cross-sectoral approach. To produce the needed supply response in a sector requires broad-based and coordinated programs that address directly, or establish a framework for, both trade and pricing reforms, as well as the longer-term needs for enterprise restructuring, investment incentives, and technology development.

World Bank programs are increasingly acquiring these characteristics. Adjustment support is continuing, but is merging increasingly with a "new look" sector-investment approach, differentiated from project lending through its emphasis on a comprehensive sector-wide attack on a range of problems, and differentiated from adjustment lending by its attention to medium- to long-term problems (World Bank 1988).

7 ASSESSING STRUCTURAL ADJUSTMENT PROGRAMS: A SUMMARY OF COUNTRY EXPERIENCE

Robin A. King and Michael D. Robinson

This paper attempts to answer two important questions about the structural adjustment policies implemented as a part of debt rescheduling: What are the economic impacts of structural adjustment? And, do these policies improve a country's chances of meeting debt service obligations in the short term? Some studies have attempted to capture the economic effects,[1] but no study has addressed the implications of these effects on the future ability to pay of rescheduling countries.[2] Thus, there is a major gap in our knowledge about international debt rescheduling. This paper endeavors to fill this gap by determining the impact of rescheduling and adjustment on ability to pay.

We consider standard rescheduling policies and criticism of them and proceed to briefly outline the theory of the macroeconomic impacts of adjustment from the point of view of the IMF and its critics. A discussion of rescheduling and adjustment success and failure follows. Several steps are taken to empirically evaluate the economic impacts of adjustment on ability to pay: statistical estimates of the economic impacts of rescheduling are obtained from a comparison of rescheduling and nonrescheduling countries and from a vector

---

1. See Pastor (1987).
2. For previous work by the authors on this topic see King and Robinson (1988).

autoregression model. We continue the analysis by presenting evidence on the impacts of the policies on ability to pay. To determine the consequences of the economic impacts of rescheduling on ability to pay, the economic effects predicted as a result of adjustment are used in conjunction with our previous estimates of a logit model of debt service problems to predict default probabilities. By comparing the predicted probability of debt service problems in simulations with and without rescheduling episodes, the impact of the rescheduling on ability to pay can be estimated. These experiments indicate that rescheduling and adjustment policies improve balance of payments by decreasing debt service and imports, while concurrently reducing growth in GNP, exports, and commercial disbursements. These effects tend to offset one another, and we conclude that the net impact of the policies on ability to pay is negligible. By examining the results more closely, policy suggestions for improving debt management can be made, and we provide a brief discussion of these policy implications.

STANDARD RESCHEDULING POLICIES AND THEIR CRITICS

Three principles underlie standard adjustment practices: imminent default, conditionality, and burden-sharing. The situation must be quite serious for the restructuring process to begin. Default must be imminent—arrears must have accumulated. Conditionality rests on the principle that debt relief will not solve debt problems, good economic management will; care must be taken to ensure that a recipient debtor nation quickly regains its ability to service its debt. The premise of conditionality is that an outside agency, such as the IMF, can provide economic policy insight that might be lacking within a government. The typical IMF adjustment plan outlined in a letter of intent calls for limitation of money supply growth, decrease in the government budget deficit, control of credit, improved exchange rate policy (usually removal of an overvalued rate via a devaluation), lifting of price controls, and an improvement in the trade balance. Government intervention in the economy should be limited, and the market should be trusted to allocate resources according to price signals. For official debt rescheduled via the Paris Club, repayments of principal due over a two to three year period are consolidated, with 80 percent of the consolidated amount given new terms at market rates of interest for two and a half to ten years. The commercial bank long-term debt is typically rescheduled over five to ten years, with grace periods of one to four years. New money is often provided in a commercial bank rescheduling package. Burden-sharing attempts to place the costs of rescheduling on participants in a negotiation.

A number of critics of the standard rescheduling policies argue that the policies are doomed to fail because of the assumptions under which the Paris Club, the IMF, and commercial banks operate. Critics of the standard rescheduling process can be found in all economic and political camps.[3] Most criticism has focused on the deflationary adjustment programs of the IMF, which are characterized as concentrating too much on deflating demand while not paying sufficient attention to returning the debtor country to a positive growth path. An economy that is not growing will almost certainly have future debt problems. Some critics (Payer 1975; Pastor 1987) focus on the regressive nature of IMF adjustment, with labor's share of income bearing a large portion of the cost of adjustment. Others (Garcia 1985; Grinspun 1984; Ferrer 1984) argue that the burden of adjustment is shared unequally between creditors and debtor countries, with debtor countries expected to incur all of the costs of resolving the problem. To meet these costs, the populations in these debtor countries must lower their standards of living and growth in the economy will be reduced.

Despite the different focuses of the many critics, we find three main themes running throughout the critical literature: (1) the rescheduling and adjustment process does not encourage economic growth and development, (2) the costs of adjustment are borne largely by the debtor countries (more specifically by the less fortunate in such countries), and (3) the outcome of the process does not leave debtor nations better able to meet debt service payments after the rescheduling and adjustment. The remainder of this paper examines themes (1) and (3) in more detail. Empirical evidence is presented that suggests the criticisms may be justified.

MACROECONOMIC IMPACTS OF STRUCTURAL ADJUSTMENT

Before the onset of the debt crisis, IMF programs were referred to as "stabilization programs" and were explicitly expected to be short-term. With the advent of the debt crisis of the 1980s, "adjustment programs" have replaced the stabilization programs of the past, with lower expectations for the short run, and a longer timeframe allowed for success. The basic outline of the

3. On the IMF, see Bird (1984a), Killick (1984b), Feinberg and Kallab (1984); on the process in general, see Bradley (1986), Lever (1983), Kenen (1984), Rohatyn (1983), and Dornbusch (1986).

programs, however, has remained the same, with the IMF continuing to focus on stabilization, specifically on controlling aggregate demand. Long-term liberalization has been added to the basic short-run stabilization programs, resulting in structural adjustment programs. Typical adjustment policies recommended by the IMF include control of money supply, credit controls, control of budget deficits through limitations on government spending and increased government revenues, decreases in real wages, domestic currency devaluation, and liberalization of all markets. The last, liberalization, generally translates into the lifting of price, interest rate, foreign exchange, and foreign trade controls. Through attempting to control and limit aggregate demand, these policies are expected to return the economy to more appropriate levels of spending, investment, and growth. Government policy-induced "distortions" will be eliminated, allowing relative prices to reflect "true scarcities" of factor endowments. With "correct" relative prices, rational consumers and producers will make consumption and production decisions that are sustainable in the long run.

We can briefly sketch the expected effects of each of the policies recommended by the IMF in a typical stabilization program. Credit and money supply control will decrease inflationary pressures by discouraging further expansion of aggregate demand. Decreased government expenditures and increased taxes will also decrease inflationary pressures. Lower wages will lead to lower consumption on the demand side. On the supply side, they should encourage expansion of employment with movement toward the relatively more abundant factor endowment of labor. In the long run, this process is expected to lead to increased profits, which should encourage private-sector investment and economic growth. Devaluation of the domestic exchange rate will improve the trade balance. Overvalued exchange rates may encourage excessive use of imported inputs and intermediate goods, among them foreign capital. Liberalization of price controls is expected to lead to increased supplies of basic foodstuffs and to improve the government's deficit problem as public-sector prices increase. Liberalization in money markets will increase interest rates, reflecting the relative scarcity of capital. Higher interest rates can also lead to higher savings retained in the financial system and increased capital inflows. The lifting of foreign exchange controls, combined with devaluation and lifting of export taxes and import subsidies and licenses, should stimulate exports.

If the basic problem underlying the need for structural adjustment is not excessive aggregate demand, then the above policies may be inappropriate. A rescheduling country forced to undergo an adjustment program, by definition, is neither healthy nor does not necessarily have a highly integrated industrial and financial sector.   We should not be surprised to see effects that are not predicted by orthodox monetary approach to the balance of payments.   In a developing country, orthodox adjustment policies may have unexpected and negative results. Structuralist critiques of IMF-type adjustment policies argue that the resulting effects are most likely to be contractionary without solving the problem of inflation or establishing the necessary conditions for economic growth. More radical critiques focus on the advantages given to capital at the expense of the workers. What analysis lies beneath these criticisms?

Let us begin by briefly sketching the domestic and international situation during an adjustment episode. A country is unable to generate sufficient foreign exchange to meet its international financial obligations. It agrees to an IMF program as part of a rescheduling package, which should ease its foreign exchange burden, at least temporarily, by pushing current debt amortization payments into the future. The currency is devalued, markets are liberalized, and the government budget is slashed. One must take into consideration the effects of devaluation on debt service payments for the LDC government. The foreign debt service burden in domestic currency will increase with every devaluation, thus providing a stimulus to a burgeoning government deficit.[4] As a result, if the deficit is to be "under control," further cuts in domestic services and/or investment will be required. While tax increases are another possible way of controlling the government budget deficit, political reality makes it unlikely that progressive taxation will be implemented. Regressive sales taxes, the only politically feasible taxes, will inflict greater adjustment costs on those at the lower end of the income scale.

Devaluation is expected to generate increased foreign exchange through the expansion of exports and the reduction of imports. This effect, however, assumes that the Marshall-Lerner conditions hold, with the devaluation leading to a positive effect on the trade balance. This abstracts away from income elasticities and timing problems and focuses solely on price elasticities. In addition, it has not been proven conclusively that these conditions hold for all LDCs. For exports to increase, they must have markets. Therefore, one can say that adjustment programs require, as a necessary condition for success, a relatively free international trading system with access to all markets, particularly those of higher income countries with more free-spending consumers. Here the situation becomes more complicated: The observer needs to take into account the simultaneity of adjustment programs in many countries of the world. All debtor countries are encouraged to increase exports and cut imports.

---

4. The increased focus on this point has led to the increasing importance of "operational deficits," but much attention continues to be directed to the traditional budget deficits as well.

Logistical problems may result from this "maximize exports while minimizing imports" approach to adjustment (and, indeed, economic growth) if there is no country willing and able to purchase the net increase in exports from adjusting countries.

With the liberalization of financial and foreign exchange markets, the interest rate required to retain capital domestically (merely reflecting expected future devaluations) is likely to be high. While this will encourage capital inflows, it is likely to discourage productive investment while encouraging financial investment with its higher short-run returns. However, due to the easy mobility of capital and excessive speculation, the economy is rendered subject to more serious fluctuations.

Last, one must remember that the rescheduling process and IMF programs began with a short-run perspective. It was expected that significant capital inflows would soon return to productive uses in these countries. As it has worked out, adjustment policies have often been implemented within an environment of international financial austerity, with net transfers of resources flowing away from the LDCs, not toward them, as would be expected by traditional theory and the assumptions of adjustment programs. In short, one must take into account the possibility that IMF policies may not have the expected effects and may lead to further problems instead of making the process smoother and more efficient. It may be the case that it is not in a developing country's economic interest to follow these policies.

RESCHEDULING AND ADJUSTMENT SUCCESS AND FAILURE

To fully evaluate the macroeconomic effects of adjustment policies, some attention must be given to the impact of the policies and their economic outcomes on ability to pay. To facilitate this analysis, we have developed a definition of rescheduling episode success and failure:

> A rescheduling is successful if further reschedulings are not needed, that is, if a country's financial health has returned to a point where it can meet its financial obligations as previously contracted.[5]

5. This definition is not inconsistent with that given by Guitian (1982: 73-104), a senior analyst at the IMF: ". . . the Fund should adopt policies on the use of its resources that assist members in overcoming their balance of payment problems . . . and . . . to ensure that the use of the resources by members is temporary."

This rather pragmatic definition skirts the distributional issues raised above and should be thought of as a first test of adjustment. Adjustment should at a minimum improve the balance of payments and ability to pay of the rescheduling nation. If adjustment fails this test, then adjustment policies need to be reworked regardless of their distributional impacts. On the other hand, if adjustment policies do improve the short-term financial situation of a country, then consideration of the distributional impacts should be undertaken to determine if the costs of financial improvement are too high.

Under the rescheduling procedures and policies of the standard process, a hypothetical successful episode of debt crisis resolution can be outlined. A debtor nation with serious debt service arrears that appears to be in imminent default appeals to the Paris Club and its commercial bank creditors for help. After negotiating with the IMF on a set of economic policies designed to restore the debtor nation's economy to health, the terms of the rescheduling will be negotiated. During the grace period, the economic policies and other aspects of the rescheduling package should lead to improving financial and economic conditions, including decreased debt service obligations, decreased imports, increased exports, an improved reserve situation, renewed economic growth, and possibly renewed investor confidence in the ability to pay of the debtor nation as contracted financial commitments are met.

Several problems may arise that thwart the successful resolution of a debt crisis episode. As mentioned above, the economic policies agreed upon by the IMF and the country may fail to produce the economic revitalization necessary to resume debt service payments (or perhaps the policies are not implemented), the amount of debt consolidated may not be sufficient to allow the country to regain economic health, the length of time that the rescheduled debt has been postponed may be too short, or other unforeseen crises may occur (for example, natural disasters, unexpected export price fluctuations) that return the country to a position of requiring additional relief from debt service obligations.

Other definitions of rescheduling success are found in the literature and in the press, yielding the conclusion that rescheduling has been successful thus far in the debt crisis. That definition of success is held by the proponents of the "muddling through" strategy pursued to date, who argue that the international financial system has not yet fallen apart. Following this line of reasoning, the "success" of the process under tremendous strain has been resounding. Our definition, however, is more stringent. We are looking at the economic effects of rescheduling packages. Although difficult to find articulated publicly, the entire standard process is based on an implicit assumption that these debt service problems are merely transitory and we will return to "normal" conditions after a brief period of adjustment. The logical consequences of such an assumption imply a definition of success similar to ours, where a successful rescheduling lessens the need for further assistance.

MODELING THE MACROECONOMIC IMPACTS OF ADJUSTMENT

In this section the results of two statistical analyses of the macroeconomic impacts of adjustment are reported. Two approaches are taken. The first, similar to that used by Pastor (1987), Reichman and Stillson (1978), and Donovan (1982), compares the performance of countries recently involved in adjustment with countries not involved in adjustment programs. The second employs a "before" and "after" comparison for the same country. If Fund adjustment programs improve a country's balance of payments, decrease imports, increase exports, and improve economic growth, then comparisons of the economic performance under such a program before and after implementation should reveal program outcomes. In addition, comparisons can be made between the change in variables of interest between program and nonprogram countries.[6] The data for the entire analysis that follows were obtained from the *World Debt Tables* (1984), published by the World Bank, which cover the years 1974 to 1984 and include seventy-two debtor nations. Appendix B contains a complete country list, reschedulings used, and definitions of variables. We have assumed that each rescheduling episode is identified with an adjustment program and that the adjustment programs are equivalent. The economic variables included were those used in the Feder, Just, and Ross (1981) model of debt servicing difficulties, and include GNP, debt service, imports, exports, reserves, commercial inflows, and noncommercial inflows.

Tables 7-1, 7-2, and 7-3 report the results of tests of difference in means of growth in the economic variables. Table 7-1 compares all countries that have rescheduled in the last five years to other countries that rescheduled between 1974 and 1984; Table 7-2 compares these same countries to all other debtor nations; and Table 7-3 compares the economic variables the two years before rescheduling to the two years after rescheduling. Growth in imports was reduced by the program in each case, and in two cases the evidence indicates decreasing growth of debt service. These are the desired outcomes of adjustment and should improve balance of payments. However, growth in nominal GNP is reduced in each case, export growth is reduced in one case, and inflows of new money decreased. These results are not those predicted by the

---

6. See Appendix A for elaboration of the second model.

Table 7-1. Economic Variable Comparisons, 1974-1984[a, b]
(Mean Growth Rates by Rescheduling Status)

| | Growth Rate | | |
Variable	Countries Rescheduling in Last Five Years	Countries not Rescheduling in Last Five Years	T-Statistic[c]
GNP Growth	0.050	0.086	1.75[d]
Export Growth	0.075	0.088	0.47
Import Growth	0.062	0.109	1.77[d]
Debt Service Growth	0.177	0.277	1.65[d]
Reserves Growth	0.234	0.121	-1.53
Com. Inflows Growth	0.864	1.131	0.33
NonCom. Inflows Growth	0.117	0.323	2.45[d]

a. Sample size 338.
b. Countries rescheduling at least once during the period.
c. T-Tests are reported for either an equal variance or unequal variance test of means depending on the results of a test for equal variances.
d. Significant at the 90 percent level.

Table 7-2. Economic Variable Comparisons, 1974-1984[a, b]
(Mean Growth Rates by Rescheduling Status)

| | Growth Rate | | |
Variable	Countries Rescheduling in the Last Five Years	Countries not Rescheduling in the Last Five Years	T-Statistic[c]
GNP Growth	0.050	0.102	2.67[d]
Export Growth	0.075	0.142	1.99[d]
Import Growth	0.062	0.123	2.53[d]
Debt Service Growth	0.177	0.316	2.29[d]
Reserves Growth	0.234	0.121	-1.53
Com. Inflows Growth	0.864	1.689	1.23
NonCom. Inflows Growth	0.117	0.363	3.40[d]

a. Sample size 681.
b. All countries.
c. T-Tests are reported for either an equal variance or unequal variance test of means depending on the results of a test for equal variances.
d. Significant at the 95 percent level.

traditional monetarist model of adjustment and may be indicative of potential problems. The results on imports and debt service are broadly consistent with the research of Pastor (1987), Reichman and Stillson (1978), and Donovan (1982).

Analysis of this type can be subjected to a number of criticisms.[7] For example, such comparisons fail to distinguish between program effects and more general economic processes. Also, when comparing before and after rescheduling, external economic shocks may affect the results. To improve the analysis, a second econometric approach was undertaken that attempts to control for as many factors as possible. The details of this approach are presented in Appendix A. To obtain estimates of the impact of rescheduling on the economy of the debtor nation a simple vector autoregression (VAR) model of the economies of debtor nations was employed similar to the model used by McFadden et al. (1985). Included in the VAR process were dummy variables to measure the three-year impacts of the rescheduling and adjustment policies.

The net three-year rescheduling impacts estimated with the VAR model are shown in Table 7-4. The 10 percent decrease in debt service and the 6 percent decrease in imports are beneficial to balance of payments and reflect desired effects of the rescheduling procedure. Decreased growth in debt service payments should free resources to be employed within the domestic economy. Decreased growth in imports improves the current account and decreases outflow of foreign exchange. It also, however, could signify potential problems for firms that rely on imports in the production of goods for domestic consumption or export. Reserves are estimated to improve over 20 percent. The remaining effects are more troubling. A rescheduling episode reduces growth in GNP, exports, and inflows of foreign funds. The decreased growth in GNP indicates the general recessionary effects of the standard approach and does not augur well for future repayment problems. An economy that is not growing is likely to have future debt service problems, especially once principal amortization commences.[8] The lack of growth in exports is probably the most distressing sign for the creditors, as the orthodox strategy relies on generation of a trade surplus. The devaluations that often accompany implementation of the standard approach do not appear to have the desired effects of stimulating exports. The decrease in the growth of foreign exchange inflows

---

7. This criticism applies to the cited empirical work as well as to our own research.

8. This has not been lost on policymakers within the international financial organizations and the U.S. government. The growth-oriented Baker Plan announced by U.S. Treasury Secretary Baker at the IMF meeting in Seoul in September 1985 is one example. Another is seen in recent World Bank announcements about the need for renewed growth—"growing out of debt."

Table 7-3. Economic Variable Comparisons[a]
(Countries Rescheduling between 1976 and 1981)

| Variable | Growth Rate | | T-Statistic[b] |
	Before Rescheduling	After Rescheduling	
GNP Growth	0.050	-0.031	4.00[c]
Export Growth	0.059	-0.056	2.50[c]
Import Growth	0.104	-0.056	4.57[c]
Debt Service Growth	0.031	0.073	0.49
Reserves Growth	-0.434	-0.169	0.94
Com. Inflows Growth[d]	51.83	-0.690	2.04[c]
NonCom. Inflows Growth[d]	-77.60	-59.66	0.21

a. Sample size 18.
b. T-Tests are reported for an equal variance test of means.
c. Significant at the 95 percent level.
d. Measured as annual change, not as a percent.

Table 7-4. Three-Year Percent Changes in Economic Variables
Following a Rescheduling Episode
(Estimates from the VAR Model)[a]

Variable	Percent Change	$F(1,511)$[b]
Debt Service	-10.84	1.068
Imports	-6.62	3.382[c]
Exports	-2.38	0.221
Reserves	26.08	4.644[c]
GNP	-5.55	3.673[c]
Commercial Inflows	-48.47	5.146[d]
Noncommercial Inflows	-10.37	0.646

a. Derived from the parameter estimates of the VAR model shown in Appendix A.
b. $F(1,511)$ tests whether the entire estimated effect is significantly different from 0.
c. Significant at the 90 percent level.
d. Significant at the 95 percent level.

reflects the increased riskiness of the situation and consequent creditor hesitancy, particularly among commercial lenders, to commit new funds.[9]

A stylized picture of the economy of a rescheduling country in the years immediately after the agreement can be constructed from these results. The agreement lowers the debt service obligations of the country, and IMF-imposed economic policies reduce the growth in imports to the economy. This is consistent with the results reported by Pastor (1987), Reichman and Stillson (1978), and Donovan (1982). However, exports are not stimulated (in fact, they are reduced as part of the general economic slump), GNP growth slows, and banks in industrial nations are not forthcoming with new loans. The net impact on reserves is positive despite the mixed effects. Clearly, this analysis, while supported by the estimates in Tables 7-1, 7-2, 7-3, and 7-4, can be made only as a hypothesis. However, the results of the estimation clearly support the arguments of some of the critics of standard rescheduling practices who maintain that a scenario of this sort is the most likely outcome of a rescheduling episode.

SIMULATIONS AND ABILITY TO PAY ANALYSIS

The macroeconomic effects outlined above are only part of the story. In our definition of rescheduling success and failure, we stated that of particular interest is the net impact of the rescheduling and adjustment on ability to pay. To provide an estimate of the impact of a rescheduling episode on a county's economy that takes all possible interactions into effect and to estimate the impact of these effects on ability to pay, simulations were made for several Latin American countries using the vector autoregression model.[10] Two forecasts of the period 1984 to 1989 were completed for both countries. The first forecast assumed no rescheduling, while the second assumed a 1984 rescheduling episode. This experiment is designed for comparative purposes rather than as an actual forecast for the countries. The results of these simulations, which are quite similar to the static predictions, are shown in Table 7-5. Debt service and imports decline substantially by the fourth year after the rescheduling from the nonrescheduling forecast. GNP falls, as do commercial and noncommercial foreign exchange inflows.

---

9. See Chapter 4 by Lissakers and Chapter 5 by Sacks and Canavan for discussions of the impact of changes in bank regulation on the commitment of new funds in the 1980s.

10. These countries were chosen because of the authors' particular interest in Latin America. Other simulations could be produced on request.

Table 7-5. Simulations of the Impact of a Rescheduling Episode[a]
Simulated Results for 1989/Rescheduling in 1985
(Millions of U.S. Dollars)

Variable	With Rescheduling	No Rescheduling	Percent Difference
Debt Service			
Brazil	7718	8283	-6.82
Peru	677	727	-6.87
GNP			
Brazil	221172	232716	-4.96
Peru	16609	17475	-4.95
Exports			
Brazil	49175	50293	-2.22
Peru	6022	6159	-2.22
Imports			
Brazil	38258	43614	-12.28
Peru	4684	5339	-12.26
Reserves			
Brazil	10782	8319	29.60
Peru	2136	1648	29.61
Commercial Inflows			
Brazil	2566	4046	-36.57
Peru	296	467	-36.61
Noncommercial Inflows			
Brazil	218	244	-10.65
Peru	35	39	-10.25

a. From simulations using the model described in Appendix A.

Tables 7-1 through 7-5 indicate the impact of the economic policies associated with rescheduling on the economies of the debtor nations. The impacts are mixed with regard to increasing the creditworthiness of the rescheduling nations. Debt service and imports are reduced. This should increase reserves and the ability to pay of the country. However, GNP growth is reduced, which could negatively affect ability to pay. Exports are not increased; rather, they seem to fall with the decline in economic activity. Finally, the inflow of new reserves from external sources is severely curtailed after a rescheduling episode.

The net effect on ability to pay of the country is therefore not clear. A model of debt service difficulty can be used to determine the net impact of a rescheduling on the financial health of the debtor country. Several authors (King and Robinson forthcoming; McFadden et al. 1985: 179-201; Feder, Just, and Ross 1981) have used quantitative models to forecast debt servicing difficulty. These models predict the ability of a country to meet debt service obligations based on the economic and financial state of the country. Feder, Just, and Ross (1981) found that the following ratios were significant in predicting debt problems: debt service to exports, real per capita GNP to U.S. per capita GNP, reserves to imports, exports to GNP, and (non)commercial foreign exchange inflows to debt service. By modeling the ability to pay of Brazil and Peru from the simulations described above, some measure of the net impact of the rescheduling can be reached. If the rescheduling is a net success, the ability to pay of the country should improve as the impacts of the rescheduling and associated economic policies spread throughout the economy. If, on the other hand, the effects of the rescheduling decrease ability to pay or increase the probability of debt service difficulties in the future, the policies have failed. Using the King and Robinson estimates[11] of the Feder, Just, and Ross model of debt servicing difficulties, the probabilities of debt service problems were estimated for Brazil and Peru under both the 1984 rescheduling scenario and the no rescheduling scenario. These results, contained in Table 7-6, can be used to determine the net impact of the 1984 intervention.

The results from Table 7-6 show that the net impact of the various economic consequences that have been discussed throughout this paper is only marginally favorable for improving the ability to pay of the debtor nation. In both simulations the probability for debt service problems of the countries was reduced less than 6 percent in 1989.[12] These results would seem to indicate that the standard rescheduling practices have not been successful in solving the debt crisis or in improving the ability to pay of countries facing debt problems.

---

11. The estimated coefficients for the Feder, Just, and Ross model as they appear in King and Robinson (forthcoming) are as follows:

Variable	Estimate	Std. Error
Debt Service/Exports	5.51	1.32
Exports/GNP	0.73	0.51
Commercial Inflows/Debt Service	-0.39	0.20
Noncommercial Inflows/Debt Service	-0.16	0.10
Reserves/Imports	-1.08	0.74
GNP Per Capita/U.S. GNP Per Capita	-9.94	2.80
Intercept	-1.67	0.53

The probability of rescheduling is computed with the above coefficients in a logit probability form. Probability $= e^{b'X} / (1 + e^{b'X})$.

12. In simulations not reported with Chile, the rescheduling simulation actually increased the probability of repayment difficulty.

Table 7-6. Probability of Debt Service Difficulty[a, b]
Brazil and Peru, 1985-1989
(Probability of Repayment Difficulties)

	1984	1985	1986	1987	1988	1989
Brazil						
Rescheduling in 1985	0.141	0.146	0.125	0.124	0.143	0.146
No Rescheduling	0.141	0.152	0.130	0.129	0.143	0.150
Percent Difference	0.000	-3.940	-3.840	-3.870	0.000	-2.660
Peru						
Rescheduling in 1985	0.098	0.104	0.105	0.111	0.123	0.129
No Rescheduling	0.098	0.107	0.109	0.122	0.130	0.137
Percent Difference	0.000	-2.800	-3.660	-9.010	-5.380	-5.830

a. Computed from the Robinson-King estimates of the Feder, Just, and Ross model of debt service capacity.
b. From simulations using the model described in Appendix A.

In light of these results, it is interesting to consider why countries continue to participate in standard rescheduling practices, rather then seek other remedies. As members of the international economic and trading community, they are reliant on other countries as markets for their exports, sources of imports, and sources of trade and balance of payments finance. These important connections might lead to a reluctance to challenge the standard approach for fear of being further cut off from access to international markets and credit. Still, given these results, deciding to break with the standard approach, as Peru did publicly in July 1985, does not seem such an irrational decision. Indeed, the more relevant question may be why more countries have not adopted a similar attitude.

CONCLUSIONS AND RECOMMENDATIONS

Considerable debate has been engaged as to whether the standard rescheduling practices of the IMF and conditionality are a viable means of solving the debt crisis facing the world economy. This paper evaluated these policies in an econometric fashion. The economic impacts of rescheduling episodes from 1974 to 1984 are modeled by treating them as innovations to a vector autoregressive process. These estimates indicate that substantial economic impacts do result from rescheduling and the adjustment policies enacted as part of the rescheduling process. In the three years after a rescheduling occurs, debt service and imports are reduced to levels below what they would have been in the absence of the rescheduling. At the same time, reserves increase. These are desired outcomes of the economic policies of standard rescheduling practice. However, less positive changes occur as well: GNP, exports, and foreign exchange inflows are reduced to levels below those which they would have attained without the rescheduling. These changes would be detrimental to the ability to pay of the rescheduling nation.

The net magnitudes of these effects were examined in simulations of the economies of Brazil and Peru with and without rescheduling innovations. These simulations provide conclusions similar to those obtained from the estimates of the vector autoregression model. It appears as though rescheduling practices achieve only partial success in improving the health of debtor nation economies. To determine the net impact of the offsetting effects of declining debt service and imports and declining GNP and export growth, a logit model of repayment problems first used by Feder, Just, and Ross (1981) and reestimated by King and Robinson (forthcoming) was used to predict the probability of debt service problems for Brazil and Peru under the two simulation scenarios. In this experiment, neither Brazil nor Peru would develop substantially lower probabilities of repayment problems if they had rescheduled in 1985 than if they had not.

Despite the insights this analysis offers, one must be aware of its limitations. The vector autoregression model used here does not force structural consistency on the economies. In addition, any analysis done under the assumption all countries respond in the same manner should be viewed with caution. As more and better data become available, research with more complex models would be useful. Any updated model should attempt to capture policy changes that may be in progress. The actors involved in the rescheduling process have learned a great deal in recent years and have begun to modify their actions. Attempting to model these policy changes would provide useful insights into the ongoing debt rescheduling process. Having issued these words of warning, we repeat that our results suggest that standard rescheduling practices as implemented between 1974 and 1984 did not improve the prospects for debtor nations. The policies were successful in lowering debt service obligations and reducing imports. However, these gains were offset by the general slowdown in economic activity that follows a rescheduling and by a reluctance of creditors to provide new money to troubled countries. A rescheduling episode for a debtor nation, through its economic impacts, does not significantly decrease the probability that further debt service problems will emerge.

In light of the lack of success of the standard rescheduling approach, and given our results, two perspectives on policy become apparent. We have shown that exports are not increased by standard adjustment policies. The roles of exports and foreign exchange earnings clearly are critical in allowing a country to service its foreign currency debt. Export earnings, however, are subject to bilateral and multilateral regulations limiting access to markets. If a country is expected to service significant amounts of debt—in dollars, for example—it will be able to do this most easily if it has access to markets where it can directly earn dollars. Tying debt repayment to export earnings, as Peru's Garcia has attempted to do, is not an impractical strategy if it is accompanied by continuing negotiations. In fact, it might be possible to specifically tie debt repayment to one country's banks to that country's import purchases from the concerned debtor country. This would consist of U.S. banks, for example, receiving some portion of U.S. import purchases of a specific debtor's exports. This would serve to move at least part of the burden of stimulating exports from the debtor country to the commercial banks, which might be quite useful given the lack of export growth that our results indicate. A Garcia-type proposal has several advantages. It makes the connection between financial debt payments and trade earnings explicit. It would force the creditor banks—those with a direct stake in the repayment process—to assist their customers, the debtor nations, in gaining access to markets. Some of the political costs of adjustment are thus transferred to the creditor banks. While the mechanics may be difficult, one must remember that the entire rescheduling process as it stands absorbs significant amounts of time and resources, and thus has substantial costs of its own.

A second policy consideration is the apparent deterioration in the capital account implied by the reduction in foreign exchange inflows following adjustment. This result in part goes against current wisdom that an IMF agreement represents a seal of approval that should lead to increased bank lending. Our results suggest that rescheduling and adjustment would be more successful if continued inflows of new credit were maintained.

APPENDIX A: MODEL SPECIFICATIONS

To obtain estimates of the impact of rescheduling on the debtor nation, a simple vector autoregression model of the economies of debtor nations was employed similar to that used by McFadden et al. (1985). This represents a straightforward first approach. A more completely developed macroeconomic model capturing structural relationships should be possible sometime in the future as more data become available. In spite of the simplicity of the VAR technique, it has been used as a successful short-term forecasting tool by Webb (1984). Also, it has certain advantages over techniques employed by Pastor (1987) and used in other empirical work that do not control for the simultaneity of economic relationships. The state vector of the economy consists of the natural log of seven important economic variables. First, differences were employed to make the vector stationary. The equation that was estimated is shown below.

$$\log(X)_t - \log(X)_{t-1} = a + B_1'(\log(X)_{t-1} - \log(X)_{t-2}) + B_2'(\log(X)_{t-2} - \log(X)_{t-3})$$

$$+ C_1(R)_{t-1} + C_2(R)_{t-2} + C_3(R)_{t-3} + e_t$$

Where X_t is the economy state vector at time t, R_t is a dummy variable representing a rescheduling agreement in time t, and e_t is the error term in time t.

The model was estimated using data from seventy-two developing countries over the years 1974 to 1984. Appendix B contains a complete country list, a list of reschedulings, and further variable definitions. The economic variables included were those variables used in the Feder, Just, and Ross model of debt servicing difficulties. They include: GNP, debt service, imports, exports, reserves, commercial inflows, and noncommercial inflows. The source of the data was the World Bank's *World Debt Tables* (1983-1984, 1984-1985).

The use of pooled cross-section time series data poses some problems that must be acknowledged. We estimate a fixed-effects model, using the standard pooled cross-section time series treatment. Dummy variables are included to allow different intercepts across both time and region. The regions used are Latin America, East Asia and the Pacific, Sub-Saharan Africa, North Africa and Middle East, South Asia, and Europe and Mediterranean. The countries are placed in regions as defined by the World Bank. The error structure is assumed to be independent of both time and country, though the use of first differences minimizes potential problems.

A three-year first-degree distributed lag of each countries' rescheduling history was added to the economy vector of the autoregression to model the impact of rescheduling episodes. The three-year lag seems most appropriate because the typical grace period allows three years for the economic reforms of the rescheduling package to be enacted. Other lag structures were employed with similar results and are available from the authors. The results of the estimations are shown in Table 7-A1.

Table 7-A1. Vector Autoregression of Macroeconomic Variables[a]
(Including Rescheduling Innovations)

Dependent Variables

Lagged Variables	Debt Service	Imports	Exports	Reserves	GNP	Com. Inflows	NonCom. Inflows
Debt Service(-1)	-0.271	0.002	0.014	-0.112	0.007	0.071	0.047
	$(-6.05)^b$	(0.15)	(0.67)	$(-2.43)^b$	(0.61)	(0.62)	(0.87)
Debt Service(-2)	-0.009	0.022	0.018	-0.087	0.011	-0.164	0.011
	(-0.20)	(1.51)	(0.85)	$(-1.88)^c$	(0.95)	(-1.43)	(0.20)
Imports(-1)	0.026	-0.003	0.275	-0.080	0.073	0.882	0.209
	(0.18)	(-0.07)	$(4.05)^b$	(-0.54)	$(1.93)^c$	$(2.41)^b$	(1.18)
Imports(-2)	-0.093	-0.071	0.033	-0.393	0.004	0.345	0.070
	(-0.68)	(-1.54)	(0.52)	$(-2.79)^b$	(0.13)	(1.00)	(0.42)
Exports(-1)	-0.040	0.060	-0.424	0.297	0.043	-0.422	-0.018
	(-0.43)	$(1.76)^c$	$(-8.82)^b$	$(2.82)^b$	(1.61)	(-1.63)	(-0.15)
Exports(2)	-0.080	0.098	0.112	0.172	0.037	-0.458	-0.119
	(-0.91)	$(3.02)^b$	$(2.48)^b$	$(1.73)^c$	$(1.44)^c$	$(-1.87)^c$	(-1.01)
Reserves(-1)	0.024	0.089	0.075	-0.172	0.038	-0.046	0.004
	(0.05)	$(6.04)^b$	$(3.67)^c$	$(-3.84)^b$	$(3.36)^b$	(-0.42)	(0.08)
Reserves(-2)	0.024	0.094	-0.000	0.006	0.013	0.177	-0.053
	(0.55)	(3.28)b	(-0.01)	(0.14)	(1.17)	(1.58)	(-0.99)
GNP(-1)	-0.048	0.102	0.120	-0.032	0.159	0.453	-0.245
	(-0.26)	$(1.65)^c$	(1.40)	(-0.17)	$(3.29)^b$	(0.98)	(-1.10)
GNP(-2)	-0.143	-0.187	-0.265	-0.082	-0.231	-0.590	-0.033
	(-0.80)	$(-3.09)^b$	$(-3.15)^b$	(-0.44)	$(-4.89)^b$	(-1.31)	(-0.15)
Commercial Inflows(-1)	0.043	-0.003	-0.005	-0.009	0.002	-0.359	-0.011
	$(2.43)^b$	(0.56)	(-0.67)	(-0.51)	(0.55)	$(-7.98)^b$	(-0.52)
Commercial Inflows(-2)	0.029	-0.000	0.001	0.026	0.001	-0.208	0.035
	$(1.65)^c$	(-0.12)	(0.20)	(1.45)	(0.32)	$(-4.63)^b$	(1.62)

Table 7A-1 *(continued)*

Noncommercial Inflows(-1)	0.092 $(2.63)^b$	0.003 (0.33)	-0.009 (-0.56)	0.024 (0.68)	0.002 (0.32)	0.076 (0.85)	-0.285 $(-6.66)^b$
Noncommercial Inflows(-2)	0.044 (1.23)	0.007 (0.60)	-0.015 (-0.95)	0.013 (0.36)	0.005 (0.59)	-0.002 (-0.032)	-0.066 $(-1.52)^c$
Africa	0.002 (0.05)	-0.020 (-1.35)	-0.030 (-1.44)	-0.103 $(-2.26)^b$	0.003 0.293	0.008 (0.07)	0.023 (0.435)
East Asia	0.084 (1.38)	0.031 (1.53)	0.044 (1.55)	0.011 (0.18)	0.028 $(1.78)^c$	0.238 (1.54)	0.013 (0.18)
North Africa	0.095 (1.56)	0.017 (0.85)	0.027 (0.96)	0.001 (0.02)	0.046 $(2.87)^b$	0.066 (0.42)	0.005 0.07)
South Asia	-0.058 (-0.73)	0.040 (1.53)	0.016 (0.45)	0.063 (0.77)	0.017 (0.84)	0.130 (0.65)	-0.016 (-0.16)
Europe	0.028 (0.39)	0.011 (-0.56)	0.041 (1.23)	-0.027 (-0.37)	-0.018 (-0.95)	0.320 $(1.76)^c$	0.018 (0.21)
1978	0.107 (1.44)	-0.092 $(-3.67)^b$	-0.206 $(-5.86)^b$	-0.110 (-1.43)	-0.039 $(-1.99)^b$	-0.008 (-0.04)	0.080 (0.88)
1979	0.032 (0.44)	-0.005 (-0.22)	-0.074 $(-2.18)^b$	0.124 $(1.66)^c$	0.000 (0.02)	-0.396 $(2.16)^b$	0.087 (0.99)
1980	-0.046 (-0.63)	0.011 (0.45)	-0.010 (-0.31)	-0.186 $(-2.45)^b$	-0.153 (-0.78)	-0.304 (-1.63)	0.065 (0.72)
1981	0.010 (0.13)	-0.163 $(-6.36)^b$	-0.242 $(-6.78)^b$	-0.419 $(-5.37)^b$	-0.125 $(-6.22)^b$	-0.656 $(-3.42)^b$	-0.079 (-0.85)
1982	-0.117 (-1.59)	-0.215 $(-8.64)^b$	-0.329 $(-9.53)^b$	-0.412 $(-5.45)^b$	-0.120 $(-6.17)^b$	-0.517 $(-2.78)^b$	-0.205 $(-2.29)^b$
1983	-0.112 (-1.48)	-0.238 $(-9.25)^b$	-0.328 $(-9.19)^b$	-0.294 $(-3.76)^b$	-0.133 $(-6.60)^b$	-0.697 $(-3.62)^b$	-0.202 $(-2.18)^b$
1984	-0.143 $(-1.73)^c$	-0.160 $(-5.71)^b$	-0.173 $(-4.48)^b$	-0.399 $(-4.69)^b$	-0.117 $(-5.37)^b$	-0.547 $(-2.61)^b$	-0.066 (-0.65)
Rescheduling Effects	-0.112 (1.06)	-0.067 $(3.38)^c$	-0.024 (0.22)	0.240 $(4.64)^b$	-0.551 $(3.67)^c$	-0.622 $(5.14)^b$	-0.106 (0.64)
R-Squared	0.135	0.307	0.464	0.205	0.428	0.195	0.130
M.S.E.	0.164	0.025	0.036	0.173	0.011	1.048	0.244

a. T-Statistics in parentheses. For the rescheduling effects, coefficients represent the sum of the three-year lagged effects. F-Statistics testing the null hypothesis that the sum is zero are reported in parentheses.

b. Indicates significance at the 95 percent level.

c. Indicates significance at the 90 percent level.

APPENDIX B: DATA

Table 7-B1. Countries in Data Base and Reschedulings

Country	Rescheduling Years	Country	Rescheduling Years
Algeria	None	Malawi	None
Argentina	84	Malaysia	None
Bolivia	80,81,83	Mali	None
Brazil	83,84	Mauritania	None
Burma	None	Mauritius	None
Cameroon	None	Mexico	83,84
Central African Republic	81,83	Morocco	83,84
Chile	83,84	Nicaragua	80,81,82
Colombia	None	Nigeria	83
Congo	None	Oman	None
Costa Rica	83,84	Pakistan	74
Cyprus	None	Panama	84
Dominican Republic	83	Paraguay	None
Ecuador	83,84	Peru	78,80,83,84
Egypt	None	Philippines	84
El Salvador	None	Rwanda	None
Ethiopia	None	Sierra Leone	77,80
Fiji	None	Singapore	None
Gabon	78	Somalia	None
Ghana	74	Sri Lanka	None
Greece	None	Sudan	79,81,82,83
Guatemala	None	Swaziland	None
Guyana	82,83	Syrian Arab Republic	None
Haiti	None	Thailand	None
Honduras	82	Togo	80,81,83,84
India	None	Trinidad and Tobago	None
Indonesia	None	Tunisia	None
Israel	None	Turkey	78,79,81,82
Ivory Coast	84	Uganda	None
Jamaica	78,79,81,84	Uruguay	83,84
Jordan	None	Venezuela	84
Kenya	None	Yemen	None
Korea	None	Yugoslavia	83,84
Liberia	80,81,82,83,84	Zaire	76,77,79,80,81
Madagascar	None	Zambia	83,84

Sources: Economic Variables: GNP, Debt Service, Exports, Imports, Commercial Disbursements, Non-Commercial Disbursements and Reserves from the 1984-1985 *World Debt Tables.* Population from *International Financial Statistics Annual,* 1986. Rescheduling Episodes from Dillon et al. (1985).

8 UNDERVALUATION, ADJUSTMENT, AND GROWTH

Richard D. Fletcher

Devaluation—or "exchange rate action," as it is euphemistically called—has become a standard feature of IMF conditionality in the 1980s. In 1981-1983, for example, 80 percent of IMF-supported programs (excluding those involving members of currency unions) included devaluation as part of the package (Johnson 1985). The IMF's preference for devaluation is not generally shared by politicians in the LDCs. As the Finance Minister of Guyana recently remarked, "The IMF uses devaluation like a man with a hammer who believes that everything is a nail."[1] The skepticism of politicians about the usefulness of devaluation is understandable. After all, they can see from the unpleasant experiences of erstwhile colleagues that being associated with currency devaluation often cuts short an otherwise promising political career. Moreover, political fears are reinforced by doubts about whether devaluation will actually be effective in correcting balance of payments disequilibria. This aversion to devaluation is unfortunate because in economics, as in the practice of medicine, it is preferable that the patient as well as the physician have confidence that the prescription will work.

The views and interpretations in this paper are those of the author and should not be attributed to the Inter-American Development Bank.

1. Carl Greenidge, Guyanese Finance Minister, at the Caribbean Symposium on Exchange Rate Management, Trinidad and Tobago, January 1988.

HOW EFFECTIVE IS DEVALUATION?

In theory, devaluation is a very effective instrument: it will raise prices (in local currency) of exports and imports, leading to an expansion of exports and import substitutes, a decline in imports, and an improvement in the trade balance (Bird 1984b). In practice, however, there is a considerable delay before the improvement occurs. This can be seen, for example, in the recent case of U.S. devaluation, where it has taken nearly two years for the trade deficit to improve following a steep devaluation of the U.S. dollar. In LDCs, where infrastructure is lacking and the productive structure is less flexible than in the U.S., the response time is even greater—probably three years or more (Morawetz 1981).

Thus, devaluation should not be considered as an instrument for dealing with short-term balance of payments problems, but rather as an instrument for correcting longer-term imbalance between exports and imports. In this context, the relevant issue is not the effectiveness of a single isolated devaluation, but the effectiveness of a sustained strategy of keeping the exchange rate undervalued for a long period of time. The experiences of the LDCs in the 1970s and 1980s are very instructive in this regard. After the oil shock of 1973, it appeared that the most privileged LDCs were those fortunate enough to capture "rents" from the export of scarce primary commodities, such as oil and bauxite. Fifteen years later, it is sobering to note that virtually all the "rent earning" LDCs fell victim to "Dutch Disease." Their exchange rates became overvalued, and they lost the ability to compete in the export of products other than their rent commodity (Corden 1984). In contrast, the countries that performed best during the last fifteen years were those that did not have the option of exporting natural resources and were forced to develop a comparative advantage in the export of labor-intensive manufactures. These countries (for example, Singapore, the People's Republic of China, Hong Kong, and Korea) have maintained faster rates of growth of output and employment and enjoy better income distributions than the more privileged LDCs that export primary commodities (United Nations 1987b; Fields 1984). The lesson is clear: LDCs that developed a wide range of manufactured exports achieved success in the 1970s and 1980s. In those LDCs, export competitiveness was achieved and maintained in part by a deliberate long-term strategy of undervaluation of the exchange rate.

WHICH STRATEGY WILL WORK IN THE 1990s?

Evidence shows countries following a sustained policy of undervaluation had better results in the 1970s and 1980s than those that were overvalued. Will similar strategies work in the 1990s? Will it be counterproductive for all LDCs to attempt to become exporters of light manufactures? Will this result in excessive competition, a loss in the gains from trade, and even provoke protectionism in OECD markets? (Cline 1982; Ranis and Cline 1985). There is no categorical answer to these questions, but dangers appear to be small for two reasons. First, manufactured imports from LDCs are still a very small percentage of total consumption in OECD markets. Only in the case of clothing do LDCs supply more than 15 percent of the OECD market. Second, there are vast possibilities in South-South trade, which has grown from 20 percent of LDC exports in 1920 to 32 percent in 1986. It thus appears there should be adequate markets for LDC-manufactured exports in the 1990s (Balassa et al. 1986). Another issue is whether LDC manufactures will be able to compete in view of technological advances in the industrialized world. Again, there is no definitive answer, but it is likely new technologies will impact primary commodities most adversely (Overseas Development Council 1988), so that diversification into manufactures makes sense if only as a defensive strategy. There are also strong indications that LDCs that develop a broad capacity in manufactured exports have the flexibility to roll with the punches and will be better able to adapt to new technology than exporters specializing in raw materials (Ranis 1984).

POLITICAL OBSTACLES TO UNDERVALUATION

The economic rationale of the undervaluation strategy is very powerful, and has been around for a long time. As early as 1950, W. A. Lewis argued that the only viable strategy for industrialization of the (then) British West Indies was to achieve competitiveness in labor-intensive manufactured products (Lewis 1950). Yet few LDCs have chosen to follow this approach—evident from the small number that has become successful exporters of manufactured products— because political difficulties of an undervaluation strategy are immense. In most LDCs, the political forces that benefit from undervaluation are weak, at least in the short run (Nelson 1986). Groups that favor overvaluation comprise a broad range of powerful interests: wage earners, consumers, importers, trade unions, civil servants, academics, and members of the security forces, all of whom would be adversely affected by increases in import prices following a devaluation. Groups that would benefit from undervaluation are exporters (often foreign firms), peasants, and those who eventually will be employed in the expanded export sector. In countries that do not have a tradition of exporting manufactures, these groups are poorly organized and wield little political influence.

The pressure from powerful groups is usually sufficient to persuade a government to delay devaluation. But unless the country is fortunate enough to benefit from a windfall (for example, an unexpected rise in the price of its commodity exports), a disequilibrium caused by lack of export competitiveness will not be cured by procrastination. On the contrary, the disequilibrium will worsen, the country will lose foreign exchange reserves, and the government eventually will be forced to implement a drastic devaluation combined with recessionary demand management. In this situation, the political costs will be even greater than those that would have been incurred by an early devaluation, and the economic benefits will take even longer to materialize.

The lesson from the above is that attempts to avoid the short-term political costs of devaluation inevitably lead to even greater political costs in the longer run. And yet, in most competitive democratic systems the short-term concerns predominate. The result is that virtually no open, competitive, democratic regimes have been able to follow a sustained policy of export-promoting undervaluation in the 1970s and 1980s.

HOW TO DEVALUE SUCCESSFULLY

The political problems caused by devaluation are so serious that no LDC government will take this step with enthusiasm. Yet it is clear that LDCs that get into balance of payments problems are obliged to take this step sooner or later. The question of how to devalue successfully is therefore more relevant than the question of whether to devalue at all.

The key to success is timing. Early decisive action will permit a less drastic devaluation. Moreover, it is better to correct overvaluation while there are still sufficient foreign exchange reserves to allow output and incomes to expand while the productive structure is adjusting.[2] In other words, early action will both reduce the immediate political costs and allow the economic benefits to be realized before the electoral day of reckoning. To take early action, policymakers need to have fair warning that the exchange rate is overvalued. The danger signal most frequently used is the level of reserves, but this is a flawed indicator because reserves may actually increase during the early stages of "Dutch Disease." A much better indicator is the rate of growth of labor-

2. Conclusions of the Caribbean Symposium on Exchange Rate Management, Trinidad and Tobago, January 1988.

intensive exports. If these are growing rapidly, more than 15 percent per year, then this suggests that exports are competitive and the exchange rate is satisfactory. If labor-intensive exports are stagnant or declining, then one has a sign of loss of competitiveness and overvaluation.

A second issue is the choice of the "correct level" of the exchange rate. Economic theory prescribes that the rate be calculated using the price elasticities of imports and exports. However, this is of little practical value, because data on elasticities are usually unavailable. In any event, the important issue is the country's ability to develop new exports rather than the expansion of traditional exports. Another approach is to restore the real effective exchange rate to the value it had during a period in which the economy was in equilibrium. But this is too general and does not specifically address the issue of competitiveness in the rate of labor-intensive exports. The most useful approach is to determine the exchange rate that will ensure profitability of those products the country plans to develop in the relevant markets (Nashashibi 1980).

The third issue, as indicated earlier, is the importance of sustaining a situation of undervaluation long enough for production to respond. This is not easy because there will be pressures to revalue the effective rate through increases in money wages. These pressures must be fought with an appropriate combination of incomes policy and prudent monetary and fiscal policy. If, despite these measures, money wages continue to rise, then it will be necessary to have further devaluations. In this regard, it is probably better to have small frequent adjustments of the rate rather than large infrequent changes, because the latter will produce large variations in profitability and undermine the confidence of exporters.

The fourth issue is how to reduce the lag in realizing the economic benefits from devaluation. The most important consideration is to give exporters confidence that there is a long-term commitment to ensure the profitability of labor-intensive exports. This means that in addition to keeping the exchange rate competitive, the government should support the export effort with a broad array of measures, including fiscal policies that favor exports, the provision of finance, the ready availability of imported inputs, institutional support, and close collaboration between the public and private sectors in solving the myriad day to day problems of exporting (Rhee et al. 1984).

FINAL COMMENT—THE MORAL ISSUE

There is convincing evidence in the last fifteen years that those LDCs following a sustained strategy of undervaluation reaped substantial economic rewards in terms of rapid growth of exports, output, and employment. Those LDCs that overvalued their currencies had much less favorable results. The political difficulties of implementing a strategy of undervaluation are considerable, especially in democratic systems with a competitive electoral process. These difficulties can be minimized, however, if action is taken early and is supported by other policy measures. Apart from political problems, the strategy of undervaluation raises an important moral issue. For LDCs, undervaluation essentially involves exploitation of labor. To develop export competitiveness, the exchange rate must be devalued until costs of production are comparable to prices available in international markets. In the case of labor-intensive manufactured products, the major item is the wage cost, so it is this which must be reduced. Moreover, for most LDCs other cost items such as profits, cost of capital, and even managerial costs are now pegged at international levels and consequently are not subject to control by domestic policies. Unfortunately, given productivity levels in most LDCs, the wage rates that result from the need to establish export competitiveness are a fraction of the minimum wage in the developed economies. This is unpalatable from a moral standpoint. It is unjust that economic success in the LDCs should depend on their workers being obliged to work cheaply to produce goods that are enjoyed by relatively well-off consumers in the industrial countries. And yet, the experience of the last fifteen years suggests that other alternatives are no better, for even at low wages, employment and growth are preferable to unemployment and economic stagnation. Which leads to the sad conclusion arrived at some twenty-five years ago by Joan Robinson: "The misery of being exploited by capitalists is nothing compared with that of not being exploited at all" (Robinson 1964).

9 OLD WINE IN NEW BOTTLES: POLICY-BASED LENDING IN THE 1980s

José D. Epstein

NEW BOTTLES

On March 30, 1988, Secretary of the Treasury James A. Baker III testified before the Appropriations Committee of the Senate Subcommittee on Foreign Operations in support of the FY1989 budget proposals for multilateral development banks, in particular the World Bank. He made several references, in several contexts, to policy-based lending and its impact on the private sector:

> . . . policy-based lending is an important element of Bank private-sector development efforts. Such lending has become an important component of World Bank activity. The impact of such lending is broader than project loans, affecting the borrower's macroeconomic policies rather than a specific activity. There is normally a requirement to meet preconditions before the loan will be submitted for board approval. The loans are tranched, and require additional action by the borrower before a second or third tranche will be disbursed.

With regard to the success of such programs, he added quite candidly:

> Currently about three-fourths of all policy-based loans are experiencing implementation delays . . . which are fairly unavoidable given the uncertainties in implementing politically difficult and complex reforms in such areas as public and parastatal enterprises, which account for the bulk of the delays . . . .

131

The policy reforms are only abandoned less than 10 percent of the time. Loans have been cancelled altogether due to lack of agreement between the Bank and the country over economic policy.

Baker concluded this part of his testimony by speaking about the difficulties found with policy-based lending, despite the "quite good" label he accords the World Bank for the quality of its PBL, and by stating specifically: ". . . while we have been impressed with such lending we still have some concerns, including the impact of PBL on the poor. Therefore . . . we have asked the Bank to review policy-based loans." Throughout this important testimony there are two further mentions of PBL in other connections. First, when Baker gave a progress report on debt strategy, he referred to the debtor nations' need for financial resources and for ". . . sustained, market-oriented reform of their economic structure . . . to make these nations more attractive for future investment." The other reference came when he drew attention to the showpiece countries in debt management, specifically Colombia, Mexico, Uruguay, and the Philippines. He stated specifically: "The World Bank has provided strong support . . . through both fast-disbursing, policy-based loans to support structural reforms, and project loans to enhance production and development."

The concentration on PBL, one of the more important messages conveyed by the U.S. administration to Congress in support of budget proposals for International Financial Institutions (IFIs), is all the more surprising when one takes into account that 75 percent of World Bank lending is devoted to its more traditional form of finance, namely project loans. Perhaps even more surprising is to rediscover that virtually all U.S. administrations have frowned on IFIs' deviation from their project-based lending approach, which is embodied in their charters. Indeed, it was the borrowing LDCs that in the past insisted that structural adjustment (program loans) was more important than project loans for development. This was particularly true for the newly industrialized countries (NICs), whose capacity for producing capital goods had been on the rise but was unmatched by their ability to provide credit to their domestic capital goods industry. What happened to provoke this turnaround by the U.S. government is the subject of this chapter.

OLD WINE

I begin with a working definition of policy-based loans, or structural adjust-ment lending (SAL) in the new jargon: a quick-disbursing response to the balance of payments . . . intended not only to provide more immediate funding than is usually the case with lending for specific projects, but also to influence a country's decisionmakers to adopt policies which the [lender] deems to be in the best interests of the recipient country" (Stevenson 1988). PBLs are associated with policy reform proposals, which in turn are related to the appearance of conditionalities that are attached to the particular loan contracts by the lenders and accepted by the borrowers. The central question is, as put bluntly in a recent study by the World Bank, "Does PBL work?" At the risk of stealing my own thunder, I would have to reply with typical economists' answers: either "it depends," or "more research is needed." What does seem certain is that PBL often accomplishes policy reforms, or part thereof, that were stipulated at contract signature. Yet a considerable amount of backsliding occurs, and it is by no means certain that all the adjustments contemplated in the loan contract are necessary, desirable, or feasible for the recipient country.

Policy-based lending is not new, although the World Bank gave it a status of major policy innovation when it began the process in 1980. It used to be called program financing when USAID made it part of its lending policy in the early 1960s. The utilization of the loan had relatively little to do with the target sector, as is the case now with the World Bank. Indeed, AID program lending was routinely available to cover all types of imports. The only restriction was that the domestic currency resulting from the sale of financed imports be made available for the purposes stipulated in the loan contract, usually budget and/or balance of payments support. I am uncertain when or for what reason AID gave up the practice of program lending, but I suspect abandonment of PBL had to do with lower availability of aid funds and also with the disappointment with policy adjustments as targets of lending. In any case, PBL by AID involved the rare coincidence of the desires of the lender and borrower, particularly the Ministries of Finance in developing countries, which have been clamoring for nonproject financing for a long time. In fact, recipients seem to prefer the program-financing instrument to discrete projects, for reasons I will try to explain later.

PROGRAM-LENDING BY COMMERCIAL BANKS

With the exception of strict trade-financing, most lending by commercial banks has been program-financing (that is, nonproject in character). Unrestricted-use commercial bank lending boomed with the accumulation of huge offshore deposits on the Eurodollar market after the oil shock of 1973-1974. Large resources on deposit with the offshore banks, owned by oil exporters with insufficient domestic investment requirements because of low population pressure, were transferred by commercial banks serving as intermediaries, with a surcharge ("spread") over the London interbank rate (LIBOR, the base rate the banks agreed upon with depositors). This arrangement between depositors (oil-exporting governments) and banks resulted in variable (floating) rates of interest to borrowers. The borrowers, principally governments of developing countries, were of course at that time under great pressure to finance balance of payments deficits that resulted from higher oil prices. Balance of payments pressure threatened to interrupt or slow domestic investment programs, especially in social infrastructure. Commercial lenders signaled their flexibility to rescheduling the short maturities, and borrowing countries became habituated to "roll-overs" of their loans. By 1980, the debt crisis emerged in full force as the second oil shock occurred and LDCs found themselves suffering the consequences of industrial countries' recessions.

Until the heady days of the early 1970s, commercial banks had been accustomed to performing a country-risk analysis, which emphasized political and economic stability, "know-thy-borrower" being a lending tool with careful dispensing of new loans and cultivation of traditional clients. The incentive to "recycle" the petrodollars seemed to obviate the need for careful behavior, and banks followed a herd instinct by running after each other's clients, as well as trying to discover new ones. This lending took place without any reference to projects, even token. Banks had done this type of lending much earlier, but the amounts involved were minuscule when compared to the billion-dollar loans of the 1970s. Over the years of the boom, commercial bank lending served to finance budget deficits, counterpart requirements of project loans by IFIs, cofinance operations with the World Bank and regional banks, and postpone adjustment measures, particularly those related to unpopular items such as tax increases, fiscal discipline, exchange rate devaluation, and control of capital flight.

Why did Ministries of Finance resort to commercial bank borrowing at variable interest rates and short maturities? Several reasons come to mind. First, the resources of IFIs for project finance are always in short supply, because they are granted at fixed rates, long maturities, and important grace periods. Second, commercial borrowing involves no long negotiation, no counterpart requirements, no lengthy project preparation, and no complex loan analysis. Disbursements are very fast; indeed, speed is desired by the lender, who does not begin earning interest until disbursements take place. Moreover, a psychological element is also important: The length of a typical Minister of Finance's tenure is relatively short, and his term might be over before the loan matures. While it is true that commercial bank lending has contributed heavily to the emergence of the debt crisis, the banks alone cannot be faulted.

Before granting a loan to a foreign borrower, commercial banks traditionally would consider the degree of ability of a country to ". . . allow its residents to repay external obligations on a timely basis . . ." (Trifari and Villamil 1983: 102). Country-risk analysis would include exchange rate risk, sectoral risks,[1] and other risk components. At present, a country-risk table (such as that produced periodically by the *Institutional Investor*) refers to repayment experience rather than individual component elements of risk analysis. These tables include indices of what bankers might consider good economic management, such as incentives rewarding risk-takers for productive endeavors; a legal structure stimulating the private sector; corrections to market distortions, including appropriate fiscal policies; and simplicity and predictability of policies. All such requirements should be supported by highly competent officials at central banks and Ministries of Finance; a cadre of mid-level officials with knowledge of economic management; an independent central bank; a minimum of red tape; and an economic team that communicates well with politicians.

Moreover, country-risk analysis by commercial banks, when resulting in a favorable appraisal of lending recommendations, has included strategy considerations that took into account factor endowments of the borrowing country, an open economy approach to realize the country's comparative advantage, and reasonable investment expenditures commensurate with domestic savings, with a low incremental capital-output ratio. Finally, the analysts look to short-term policies that result in a fiscal policy that seeks to reduce the share of public-sector expenditure as a proportion of total GNP and emphasize a non-inflationary approach to monetary policy.

PBL IN THE 1980s

Do these country-risk prescriptions look familiar? The list is strikingly similar to the criteria and conditionalities of IMF and World Bank PBLs; the difference, of course, is that IFIs can impose the criteria and conditionalities while the banks cannot. Component elements of adjustment policies affect a wide variety

---

1. For example, Argentina lowered tariff barriers from 1976 to 1980, which caused many bankruptcies. Brazil in the mid 1960s decided to import newsprint rather than allow domestic production to supply demand at higher prices, but impeded borrowers from paying their foreign creditors.

of policies, principally trade, fiscal, monetary, price and wage, and foreign exchange. Other conditionalities include public-sector investment priorities and institutional organization. The overall purposes are to promote export-oriented development. Present-day emphasis on structural adjustment exhibits a strong bias toward outward-oriented development, in favor of export-led growth and private markets as principal vehicles of economic activity. Not so long ago, in the dark days of $30-per-barrel oil, adjustment normally meant upward revision of domestic oil and food prices. This is in contrast to an earlier period when "structuralist" analysis, especially in Latin America, called for land reform and warned against over-dependence on the export sector and excessive emphasis on imported technology. It seems we have come a long way from that earlier epoch.

We have been dwelling on adjustment options because PBLs and SALs have incorporated them, particularly in World Bank nonproject loans since 1980. PBLs are conceived to provide foreign exchange for a number of purposes, including rehabilitation of industry and infrastructure, maintenance and counterpart requirements of ongoing projects, and, above all, covering import requirements supposedly designed to expand export performance. So Stevenson correctly states, ". . . . SAL programs focus on opening up the country to the world market through the restructuring of incentives—prices, tariffs, taxes, subsidies, interest rates—with special emphasis on liberalizing the trade sector in order to improve the competitiveness of exports, review of public-sector investment priorities . . . and high-priority sectoral adjustments" (Stevenson 1988).

The introduction of SALs in the World Bank in 1980 (and shortly afterwards the equivalent experiment by the IDB with sectoral adjustment lending) was by no means without controversy. The legal base in IFIs for performing nonproject lending has been thought by some of their attorneys to be questionable, if not downright in violation of the Bank's charter. Yet the pressure to do nonproject lending came from both "donor" nations and borrowers, and the World Bank approved an experiment of structural adjustment lending for a limited period and a limited amount (not more than 10 percent of total annual lending). By mid 1987, the World Bank had granted forty-three SALs to thirty-one countries for a total of $6.5 billion; in 1986, almost one-half of all lending to Latin America consisted of nonproject loans, and the trend seems here to stay.

SALs were to be limited to no more than five operations in as many years for any country, but only one country, Turkey, received all five. Most remaining countries received one or two SALs, and four programs—in Senegal, Bolivia, Guyana, and Pakistan—had been discontinued by the end of 1986 because of noncompliance with conditionality stipulations. While SALs as such have been deemphasized and substituted by sectoral adjustment loans, the issue of adjustment requirements and conditionalities is virtually the same. The IDB had made two somewhat hesitant experiments with sectoral adjustment loans—in Guyana (rice production stimulation) and Peru (agricultural sector)— but the operations were not deemed successful. Sectoral adjustment loans have now taken over where structural adjustment loans left off. The World Bank made over $10 billion worth of the former loans from 1979 to 1987.

It is quite possible that policy-based lending by IFIs was greatly influenced by the growing reluctance of borrowing LDCs to continue contracting large-scale infrastructure loans. Their heavy counterpart requirements increasingly impinge on domestic investment budgets because of larger import demands and the slowing down of commercial bank lending offers. Besides, a trend among NIC members of the IFI community had been for a long time that program lending was preferable to strict project financing, with its overtones of paternalism and "the lender knows best" philosophy. A subtle underlying factor for the acceptance of PBLs by LDCs has also been the long, drawn-out discussion about financing of local (borrowing country incurred) costs with foreign exchange proceeds of the loan, a tedious and complex issue with overtones of economic development theory, which occupied the boards of IFIs during much of the 1960s and the early 1970s. PBL certainly obviated the need to demonstrate import component of inputs, calculate foreign exchange multipliers and marginal propensities to import, and justify the transfer of dollars for payment of domestic costs.

Structural adjustment loans are designed to be fast-disbursing, ideally within two years, broken down into several tranches, each subject to the measurable fulfillment of a number of conditionalities, of which there may be as many as seventy in a loan agreement. In most cases, SALs are to be used for import financing, with a small list of excluded imports (weapons, conspicuous consumption items). Conditionalities focus around sectors of the economy closely connected to balance of payments problems, and often include conditions such as the passing of specific legislation or the abolition of custom tariffs conceived as too high, so as to oblige domestic industry to become more competitive. The last chapter of PBLs has not yet been written. It is neither the solution to all debt and development problems, nor the villain of capitalist intervention in LDC economies as detractors have labeled it.

It does seem certain, as the analogy of old wine in new bottles suggests, that we do not know whether SALs (and their cousins, the sectoral adjustment versions) accomplish the goal of promoting structural adjustments in the sectors and to the degree foreseen in the loan documentation. Many of the conditions contained in the contracts are either impossible to monitor or cannot be fulfilled within the very short disbursement period. Even assuming that the adjustment needs were jointly arrived at during the period preceding the loan between lender and borrower, SAL installments already have been disbursed, and the leverage, if any, of the lender has disappeared. Policy-based lending is based on faith in the free market model of neoclassical theory, with its efficiency conditions of perfect knowledge, flexible prices, no market entry barriers, and all costs internalized into the price mechanism, all of which are rarely present in the real world. It is ironic indeed that structural adjustment lending could be seen as responsive to the concerns of the early structuralists, who would bristle at being identified with neoclassicism. They would, however, find solace in discovering that the conditionalities now surrounding SALs are not only impossible to enforce but are difficult even to monitor. Turkey's first SAL in 1980 had eleven conditions in five areas; its fifth SAL in 1984 had seventy-five conditions at the sectoral and national policy levels. Formally, these should have been met within the normal two-and-a-half year disbursement period.

Policy-based lending, while by no means new or innovative given the long AID (and now seven years of World Bank) experience, does seem an eminently suitable, albeit partial, mechanism to support debt management and to assuage the crushing cash-flow problems produced by debt service requirements. This is also one of the criticisms leveled on PBL in the sense that it is sometimes labeled an instrument to bail out commercial banks by providing the debtor countries with foreign exchange liquidity not specifically tied to development investment. The other criticism is closely linked: One of the more serious consequences of the debt crisis has been the postponement and even abandonment of infrastructure. PBL will certainly not help to reactivate development projects, except insofar as it might create conditions for development by forcing recipient countries to implement policies more attractive to investors both domestic and foreign.

LATIN AMERICAN EXPERIENCE WITH PBL

It is instructive at this point to look briefly at the experience of Latin American countries with PBL. Under policy regimes associated with World Bank and IMF programs, Brazil, Argentina, and Mexico strongly compressed their imports and increased their exports (by over 6 percent per annum between 1981 and 1984). A similar shift occurred throughout Latin America. The increase in exports partly accounted for a renascent protectionism trend in the industrialized countries, particularly in the United States. The overall swing in the Latin

American balance of trade with the rest of the world moved from a $10 billion deficit in 1981 to a $35 billion surplus in 1984, almost enough to cover the interest on the external debt. As can be seen, efforts toward adjustment on the external front, while not easy by any means, were successful in a relatively short span.

As for domestic adjustment, the performance has been disappointing due to a poor reaction in national savings. The results were severe recessions and accompanying inflation.[2] As a result, public-sector savings were dramatically affected. Aggregate investment ratios fell from 24 percent of GNP to 18 percent in the two-year span from 1983 to 1984, and in more recent years did not show great improvements. Further, the social cost of adjustment usually has been high. Improvements in current account of the balance of payments were achieved by sacrificing living standards, with the main burden falling on wage earners. Moreover, the continuity of investments in social infrastructure was interrupted. Nonetheless, the cost of adjustment policies can often be lowered if good exchange rate policies prevail, maintaining a parity between domestic and international prices. This is facilitated by a freely floating exchange rate, and it is worth noting that the IMF has completely reversed its earlier (pre-1970s) resistance to deviations from fixed rates.

Adjustment measures are normally constructed after the external debt-burden indicators are analyzed by the IFI. These ratios include long-term debt burden (total debt/GNP); short-term debt burden or annual service payments; average maturity of debt portfolio (total external debt/annual amortization payments); and the ability to meet interest payments (interest payments/international reserves). These ratios have changed consistently over recent years. The World Bank used to consider a short-term debt burden of 10 to 12 percent reasonable, but presently a 25 percent ratio is considered tolerable. Nonetheless, this ratio exceeds 50 percent in many countries.

The traditional opposition of the United States and other developed countries to policy-based loans evaporated in the wake of the Latin American debt crisis. In 1985 in Seoul, Korea, Secretary Baker stated:

> For the World Bank and the IDB capital increases . . . we will assess how these institutions strengthen their lending policies. Well-defined economic and country strategies to enhance economic reforms which encourage growth [will be taken into account]. Given a firm commitment by the IDB . . . it should be permitted to introduce a major program of well-targeted nonproject lending.

---

2. See the discussion of inflation and debt service in Chapter 14 by Dornbusch.

The most volatile aspects of adjustment policies find expression in price and wage policies. The cost of adjustment in Latin America between 1982 and 1984, for example, resulted in accelerated inflation (even though most countries closely adhered to IMF-prescribed measures), reduction in real wages, loss in real output, and a rise in unemployment. Thus, while success can be claimed for the balance of payments effect of PBL in Latin America, the domestic costs appear to have been quite high. With this in mind, I return to the discussion of PBL to raise certain nagging questions.

A number of things are not at all clear. I indicate these in a series of leading questions. First, if structural reforms, including policies and institutions, are so vital, why do not the affected LDCs proceed with such reforms on their own, without the incentive of policy-based loans? Does this not once again smack of paternalism, or "the lender knows best"? Second, what is a critical mass for a recipient country to proceed with policy reforms based on loans from abroad? Is it possible to quantify minimum amounts below which a country would not find it worthwhile to implement policy reforms? Third, given the quick-disbursing feature of the loans (even in tranches), what happens to policy reforms not implemented after disbursements have ceased and the presumed leverage of lenders to press for restructuring has ended? Is there enough of a commitment from the borrower to continue the reforms even when no new disbursements are expected? Fourth, PBL, by its very nature, has not produced a direct stream of foreign exchange to generate repayments when they are due. What resources will the borrower rely on to make repayments if there are no resources directly or even indirectly attributable to the loans? Or, conversely, one of the most important features of project lending has been their self-liquidating character, that is, their ability to generate resources to service the loan. What does a country have to show as a consequence of PBL, beyond policy reforms that may or may not have been successfully implemented?

I would submit that these questions have not as yet received adequate responses. Therefore, countries would do well to examine closely the commitments they undertake when assuming PBLs. In any event, a judicious mixture of PBLs with project loans seems the better course to follow. PBLs are by no means the ultimate, much less the ideal, instrument to provide development financing in these troubled times for international lending.

IV STRUCTURAL ADJUSTMENT: IMPACT IN THE THIRD WORLD

In the first part of the book, Rolph van der Hoeven provided a survey of the impact of external economic shocks on Third World countries. In Part IV, three authors take that analysis to a less aggregative level, with the emphasis on the two areas most affected by structural adjustment programs, Latin America and Africa.

In Chapter 10, William L. Canak and Danilo Levi provide an interpretation of the role of the multilateral agencies in the management of the debt crisis, then apply this analysis to Latin America. While data are somewhat limited (partly due to the relative newness of the application of structural adjustment), they provide strong circumstantial evidence of high social and economic costs of World Bank and IMF policy packages. This is a particularly useful paper, for it is a view of the multilaterals that is strongly held by nationalists in the Third World. With social and economic costs have come political ones, and these are treated in Chapter 11 by Peter Hakim and Louellen Stedman.

The book would not be complete without at least one in-depth study of a specific country, and this is admirably provided by Vali Jamal in Chapter 12. While one must be hesitant about generalizing from a single case, Jamal's analysis of Tanzania brings to light a number of trends and tendencies that seem common to much of Sub-Saharan Africa. Particularly important is his argument that the structural adjustment program implemented in Tanzania was largely redundant—he demonstrates that many of the changes it sought to bring about had occurred prior to the institution of the new policy regime. This chapter is especially valuable because it focuses on an African country, while most of the discussion of the debt problem places undue emphasis on Latin America.

10 SOCIAL COSTS OF ADJUSTMENT IN LATIN AMERICA

William L. Canak and Danilo Levi

The objective of this paper is two-fold: first, to develop a theoretical framework for understanding the relationship between constraints on international economic growth and the development of an interorganizational rationale for regime policies; and second, to consider the effects of structural adjustment policies in Latin America. In the following sections we will discuss the issues, the institutions, the policies, and the consequences of structural adjustment policies.

THE ISSUES

The neoclassical model for economic growth, which has been the foundation for most economic studies of development, is a world without transaction costs and institutions (Coase 1960; North 1981). Historically, national wealth has been regarded as closely tied to trade, and the international division of labor has been viewed as the basis for productivity growth. Development studies have treated exchange processes as neutral or unimportant determinants of economic performance. However, transaction costs have always defined the key constraints on gains from trade. The capacity of political and economic institutions to define and enforce the legitimate normative order in a given territory, not transportation costs, has been the key to defining transaction costs (North and Thomas 1987; see also Weber 1968).

Economic growth based on impersonal exchanges requires development of institutions that enable actors to engage in interdependent activities with other actors about whom they have little information and no personal capacity to control or directly penalize for violation of an agreement. Governments and a normative order have allowed estimation of exchange costs and enforcement of property rights and contracts (North and Thomas 1987). States, however, are not neutral third parties and tend to use their monopoly over legitimate coercion to the advantage of specific groups and at the expense of others. Moreover, while political institutions may function to enable market exchanges, their organizational interest in ensuring access to and controlling their resource base tends to lead them to create policies that undermine economic efficiency and guarantee support from powerful groups (North 1981 and 1984).

The most dramatic change in the world economy since the 1960s is that exchange rates for national currencies are now driven by capital flows instead of trade in goods.[1] International financial markets have rapidly integrated. As a consequence, a relatively minor impact of national economic policy on interest rates may result in large-scale international shifts of capital. Technological advances have reduced the costs and increased the speed of such transactions. Their effect on exchange rates can overwhelm the role of trade revenues, and without policy coordination currency volatility can only increase. Indeed, Dornbusch's theory of exchange rates predicts just this.[2]

Over the course of several centuries, the developed western industrial societies have created institutional mechanisms for controlling exchanges and enforcing the normative order of property rights. These institutional structures developed to control participants and reduce transaction costs that may arise from cheating or foot-dragging (Becker 1965; Lancaster 1966; North 1981; Barzel 1982). Although this elaborate set of institutions increases transaction costs for society, the gain from stable predictable trade and the low cost to participants in any one transaction have led to high rates of growth for these nations.

1. "Get Ready for the Phoenix," *Economist,* January 9, 1988.
2. Goodhart (1988) notes a number of events in which exchange rates have either seemed unaffected by national policies or where changes have not been tied to new information. He also cites the "random walk" movement of exchange rates and failure of exchange rates to tend toward equilibrium as evidence of failings in the Dornbusch model. He does not, however, investigate the role of institutions affecting transaction costs as a factor underlying long-term trends in exchange rates, particularly greater stability than would be predicted otherwise.

The complex, specialized and interdependent structure of international capital markets makes the potential cost of transacting very high, because the capacity to measure the future value of a currency may be difficult, and enforcing the terms of an exchange may be problematic, particularly with national governments. Rapid growth of international trade and capital flows in the postwar era has necessitated the development of an institutional structure that seeks to decrease uncertainty and turbulence associated with such exchanges. The stability of an institutional structure governing capital and product markets increases participants' confidence in their ability to predict the consequences of their activities. These institutions, however, are governed by an imperative that compels them to establish policies that contradict efficiency. Concern for survival leads these institutions to formulate and enact policies that enhance their ability to monitor and control their resource base and to bend to the interests of dominant international interest groups.

International transaction costs can be measured to the extent that they occur in a market economy, but in Latin America and much of the periphery of the world system, unmeasured transaction costs—including corruption and delays—are so important that they may undermine the market completely. Economic and political institutions that facilitate markets and guarantee the normative order should develop to reduce transaction costs, but such institutions will not necessarily produce policies that are efficient or neutral toward all parties in the marketplace.

THE INSTITUTIONS

Throughout the postwar era, the complex institutions overseeing official capital transfers aimed at fostering development and introducing orderly market processes in the international economy have functioned, in Europe and Third World nations, to limit nationalist and socialist groups' capacity to influence state policy (Block 1977; Payer 1982; Pastor 1987; Wood 1986).[3] First the Marshall Plan and later IMF-sanctioned lending served to transform national class relations and political power and reinforce processes of internationalization. Aid, grants, loans, and subsidized investment were in general linked to the liberalization of national economic policies and evidence of a domestic capacity to "control" populist demands. National regimes were presented with a limited repertoire of acceptable development policies (Sanderson 1985: 20-21). Thus, the debt crisis of the 1980s is not a crisis that threatens the

3. This section draws on material from Canak (1988).

monetary and fiscal stability of the developed countries. Rather, it is a structural feature of a new stage in core-periphery dependency in which the integration of Latin American nations in the world market is conditioned by the disciplinary authority of supranational agencies over national regimes.

Theorists attempting to conceptualize the structure and developmental processes of this New International Division of Labor (NIDL) have drawn distinct themes. The Postimperialism theorists (Becker et al. 1987) have focused on development of multinational corporations and processes of class formation in the Third World. They view "indebted industrialization" in countries like Brazil and Mexico as the expression of an alliance between domestic elites and international financiers that is transforming the political and economic structures of both OECD and Third World nations. They assert that internationalization of dominant class interests from OECD nations and the development of a dominant national bourgeoisie in Third World nations renders the framework of dependency and imperialism obsolete.

Fröbel et al. (1985) also identify the new patterns of trade and the relocation of production from OECD countries to the Third World as evidence for an NIDL. Based on cheap labor, fragmented production processes, and new technologies of transportation and communication, a truly world market is now possible. They argue that in the 1960s these conditions first became operative and set in place tendencies that are transforming the historical division between industrialized and developing countries on the one hand, and encouraging the increased geographic and operational division of manufacturing processes on the other (1980: 45).

One set of theorists has focused on the developmental logic of capital accumulation in the world system (Sanderson 1985; Marcussen and Torp 1982; Nyilas 1982). These analyses depict world economic processes as ". . . a function of the expansion of capital and its valorization and reproduction at a global level . . ." (Sanderson 1985: 9). While this perspective recognizes the importance of multinational corporations and national states, their importance is secondary to fundamental processes of capital accumulation that are both national and international. Capital accumulation—the expanded reproduction of capitalist social relations through the transformation of surplus value to new constant and variable capital—is the driving force that incorporates and integrates specific institutions and locations into a capitalist world economy. As capitalist social relations (proletarianization) become a global reality, and the transnational coordination of capital (bank and production) occurs, the significance of trade has been reduced by the capacity to internationalize production (1985: 15). Finally, international production and global coordination of capital increasingly require the structural adjustment of national economic policies. In contrast to the predictions of Postindustrialization theorists, this perspective asserts that transnational production undermines the autonomous political capacity of national regimes. Protectionism is not an option for countries whose critical "resource dependency" is tied to foreign debt refinancing and structural adjustment programs presented as a condition for access to world credit markets.[4]

Global coordination of capital and the direct sanctioning of national regimes has been focused on a set of institutions founded in the 1940s. We will briefly review these multilateral institutions and their developing role in the NIDL. The system governing international monetary and trade relations from 1945 until the early 1970s was negotiated at Bretton Woods in 1944. Representatives of forty-four nations attended, but the proceedings were dominated by the two principal industrial powers, Britain and the United States. At Bretton Woods, U.S. officials were concerned that the postwar monetary system should avoid the uncertainties and instability created by floating exchange rates and uncontrolled devaluations of the 1920s and 1930s (Damm 1982: 88). It was hoped this monetary system would sustain free trade and avoid the protectionist policies of the interwar period, which was to be achieved through the creation of multilateral institutions: the International Monetary Fund, an International Bank for Reconstruction and Development (World Bank), and an International Trade Organization (ITO). The latter was short-lived, but the first two became fundamental components of the postwar internationalization process. These institutions were a preliminary effort of global coordination of capital accumulation within a system of sovereign states. The more complete fulfillment of that intention necessitated the global integration of trade, finance, production, and labor markets. The transformation of international financial markets in the 1970s and the subsequent debt crisis/credit crisis of the 1980s transformed the role of those institutions and their relationship with national states and private financial institutions. That process continues with the need for solutions to problems created by uncoordinated national economic policies (Bell 1988: 24). The IMF's original functions were quite specific: to establish fixed exchange rates and currency convertibility and to help governments through short-term liquidity crises

4. "Whether in cases embracing the low state neoliberal authoritarianism of Chile or the high state mobilization of Brazil, the political capacity, or power, to guide industrial and agricultural internationalization shrinks before the transnational locus of production changes. The imperatives of export promotion, debt refinancing, import constraint, regressive wage policies, competitive devaluation (realistic exchange rates), and fiscal austerity dictate that the states of Latin America have less real capacity to negotiate their entry into the new international division of labor" (Sanderson 1985: 21).

resulting from a negative balance of payments. The aim was to eliminate the impact on international trade of seasonal and short-term fluctuations. Loans were tied, at least in theory, to each government's contributions (Moffitt 1983; Brett 1985; Pastor 1987). Although conceived as an international organization, governance was to be weighted to reflect each nation's quota, thus guaranteeing the United States and Great Britain a dominant role in defining policy. At base, the goal was to replace the gold standard with a set of fixed exchange rates and reserve currencies that would be amenable to "regulation." Exchange rates were to be regulated by multilateral organizations controlling a fund comprising members' contributions. The system was based on the ability of nations to maintain stable exchange rates, the convertibility of currencies, and national policies supporting free trade and balance of payments equilibrium (Brett 1985: 111-112).

The World Bank, also created at the Bretton Woods conference, was to make long-term loans at commercial rates to finance infrastructure development projects in economically weaker nations. Had it been endowed with sufficient resources, the World Bank may have functioned to increase development investments and promote more balanced international trade (Brett 1985). The Americans at Bretton Woods worked to constrain government contributions to the Bank. Forced onto private credit markets, it reinforced commercial rates and credit policies while absorbing the risk of loans to countries otherwise unable to obtain credit. In addition, project loans were guided by performance criteria. In 1956 and 1960, additional components were created to form the World Bank Group: the International Finance Corporation (IFC) to provide loans to private corporations (without government guarantee) and the International Development Association (IDA) to provide very long-term loans (fifty years) to governments. Since IDA money was targeted for countries with weaker economies, little went to Latin America. Indeed, the original purpose of these organizations was to reestablish trade in the industrialized world. The foundation of this system was a stable U.S. currency, backed by gold reserves. When that system collapsed in the early 1970s, the World Bank, like the IMF, was compelled to find its way in a newly uncertain international division of labor.

In the 1960s, the World Bank's priority was agriculture, but bank project loans focused more on poverty after 1973.[5] Bank statements consistently assert that economic criteria are the sole basis for its lending decisions, but the distribution of World Bank loans has been toward regimes favoring foreign

5. Payer (1982: 43) notes that this shift closely tracked changes in U.S. aid marked by the U.S. Foreign Assistance Act.

investment, free trade policies, and unrestricted capital flows, even when such policies have exacerbated inequality and poverty and reinforced the use of violence by national regimes in defense of international interests (Bornschier and Chase-Dunn 1985: 44-45). In essence, the World Bank's policies subsidized development of a national capitalist class allied with international business and antagonistic to autonomous national economic policies (Payer 1982: 117).

The third multilateral institutional pillar of the postwar international economy was GATT (General Agreement on Tariffs and Trade). It is not an organization per se, but a treaty first signed in 1947 by industrial and developing countries—currently 105 countries participate—formally ratifying their commitment to end the protectionism that they viewed as one cause for the intractable nature of the Great Depression. It was originally conceived as a part of the International Trade Organization that would complement the IMF and World Bank's governance of the postwar international system.

Ironically, the ITO, established by the Havana Charter in 1948 and signed by fifty-three nations, provided extensive regulatory powers but failed to secure U.S. support when American business and Congress protested external controls on trade policy.

Financed by members according to their share of world trade, GATT promotes trade equity by providing that any restrictions on trade be in the form of tariffs and not discriminate against any member. While members automatically have "most-favored nation" status with each other, negotiating membership may require that applicant countries restructure their economic policies.[6] GATT influence promotes policies that reduce constraints on trade and capital transfers. Since the adoption of the agreement forty years ago, average tariffs of industrialized nations have dropped from roughly 40 percent to 5 percent. Nevertheless, growing protectionism in the 1970s—particularly in the United States and Common Market countries—and glaring gaps in GATT controls (for example, agriculture, services, and information) have undermined its credibility.

Parallel to trends in relations among the World Bank and the IMF and individual governments, GATT as an institution has emphasized development of standardized negotiation procedures for disputes and institutionalized performance criteria. The principal industrial and dominant trading powers (the European Economic Community, the United States, and Japan) have dominated past policies, but developing countries have often violated the principles of GATT. Nevertheless, they have been unable to establish a coordinated set of

6. When Mexico joined GATT in 1986, the cost involved an end to existing policies on import licenses, reduced tariffs, and lowered subsidies.

proposals. Indeed, as with the functioning of the World Bank and the IMF, GATT negotiations have reinforced the disunity of Third World interests.

The functioning of these multilateral institutions in the immediate postwar years was somewhat dampened by the Marshall Plan's massive transfer of resources to Europe. U.S. intentions at Bretton Woods and in the Marshall Plan were directed at establishing an international economic order in which national capitalism—state interventions limiting free trade and investment— would be controlled (Wood 1986; Dietz 1987). European recovery and the defense of capitalism against the alleged Soviet threat, however, also would be based on the development of Third World markets for industrial products and raw materials exports to the United States (Wood 1986: 40-41). Indeed, developing countries as a whole experienced considerable growth between 1950 and 1980 (Srinivasan 1982: 92). Significantly, the Bretton Woods system did not distinguish between advanced industrial nations and the Third World. No specific mechanisms were developed to direct external finance from countries with a surplus to developing countries. Nevertheless, a succession of actors did play this role in the postwar decades. Foreign direct investment burgeoned in the 1950s; in the 1960s—after the Cuban revolution—official aid programs expanded; and in the 1970s—seeking to recycle petrodollars—international banks provided funds. The debt crisis of the 1980s stems in part from the lack of new external financing for Latin American development (Griffith-Jones 1984: 5), as these commercial banks restricted new loans to debtor nations.[7]

By the 1960s, however, contradictions inherent in the Bretton Woods agreement began to compel changes. First, the incapacity of the U.S. economy to eliminate deficits meant that foreign liabilities were outstripping its capacity to fulfill gold exchange commitments. Although the dollar functioned as the reserve currency for the international monetary system, U.S. balance of payments deficits tied to its military obligations and the Vietnam War meant that those nations with a surplus were paying for U.S. policies if they did not convert their dollars into gold. However, if the United States had ended its balance of payments deficits, gold production at the fixed value of $35 per ounce was insufficient to meet the needs of an expanding world economy (Triffin 1978). The leading industrial nations worked within the structure of the IMF to create new forms of credit that would counterbalance U.S. deficits. In 1967, the leading industrial nations and the IMF created an additional reserve asset called Special Drawing Rights (SDR), which was available to all IMF members. But this did not halt the flow of dollars from the United States, and

---

7. See Chapter 4 by Lissakers and Chapter 5 by Sacks and Canavan for discussions on commercial bank lending (or nonlending) to developing countries in the 1980s.

fixed exchange rates and dollar convertibility for gold were increasingly anachronistic commitments that eventually fell in 1971.

THE POLICIES

The IMF's function as fiscal disciplinarian was initiated in the 1950s via a set of rules that addressed new problems relating to Third World members' currency requests. Within a defined proportion—"tranche"—of each country's contribution quota, approvals were virtually automatic. Beyond this threshold, approval was to be conditioned on evidence that the funds would be used to support "an effective program for establishing or keeping the stability of the currency of the member country at a realistic exchange rate" (IMF 1959: 404). IMF standby agreements increased in importance in later years, and a formal bureaucratic protocol for applications and supervision came to dominate IMF activities. Thus, the IMF's relationship with less-developed nations became that of an auditor and fiscal disciplinarian (Frenkel and O'Donnell 1979: 174-175). The rationale for its actions rested on self-defined technical and objective criteria regarding the general welfare of the national and international economy.

The specific set of measures imposed on borrower countries characteristically includes: (1) devaluation; (2) reduced public spending; (3) elimination of public subsidies; (4) wage restraint; (5) increased interest rates; (6) taxes to curb demand; (7) elimination of state-owned or -supported enterprises and greater access for foreign investment; (8) reform of protection for local industries; and (9) export promotion and application of new foreign exchange to the debt service. The general thrust is to promote market-oriented open economies geared to agricultural and industrial export production (Loxley 1984: 29). By late 1983, seventeen adjustment agreements were operating in Latin America and the Caribbean (ECLAC 1986: 102).

In 1979, the World Bank initiated a new lending instrument, the Structural Adjustment Loan (SAL), similar in most respects to IMF conditional loans and reflecting the developing functional convergence of these two institutions (Wood 1986: 185; Loxley 1986b: 138-139).[8] These loans are aimed at restoring balance of payments strength sufficient to allow developing nations to finance imports. The loans are to sustain imports while debtors implement institutional and policy changes. Like IMF conditional loans, SALs' main intent is to promote exports and reduce import substitution industrialization (Loxley 1986b: 131). SALs rapidly became the World Bank's predominant

8. See Chapter 9 by Epstein for a discussion of policy-based lending.

form of program lending, but, excepting Bolivia and Panama, Latin America did not participate in the first few years (Wood 1986: 185).

Bank monitoring of economic performance has focused on specific policy compliance and not on quantitative development performance. The criteria of compliance suggest that information and control are the basic objectives. These goals may be compatible with incentives that contradict national development policies. Indeed, the World Bank's review of its SALs concludes they have lowered incomes and have an anti-consumption bias (Balassa 1981). Increased unemployment, higher prices, and reduced social programs may adversely affect the poor, but basic human needs have not been criteria for judging policy performance. Similarly, questions of equity have been deemphasized and "growth" criteria given more weight. SALs, therefore, represent a commitment to supply-side, "trickle down" assumptions about social welfare.

According to Robert Wood, "Outward-oriented policies with low protection are the basic aim of structural adjustment lending. Although the range of policy areas has varied among different SAL recipients, all have agreed to institute changes in trade policy designed to orient the economy more toward international market forces and exports" (Wood 1986: 187).

Prior to the 1970s, IMF "conditions" had only minor importance for Latin America. In the 1960s, 75 percent of net capital flow was composed of direct investment and official credits (Ffrench-Davis et al. 1985). In the rush to recycle petrodollars, international commercial banks engaged in aggressive loan policies that often were unaccompanied by analysis or judgment of client solvency. Throughout the 1970s, easy access to private loans and high inflation combined to encourage many governments' acquisition of debt. Third World public debt increased from $75.1 billion in 1970 to $634.4 billion in 1983 (Wood 1986: 130). The rapid growth of private bank lending in the 1970s appeared to offer developing countries an opportunity for greater autonomy (from the IMF) and a chance for debt-led growth (Griffith-Jones 1984: 69-70). By 1980, however, private banks' lending proportion of net capital flow had reached 70 percent. When Federal Reserve Board policies initiated an era of high interest rates and tight money to break inflation, bank lending terms reversed. Higher interest rates and short-term amortization and refinancing created a credit crisis that annually produced large increases in total indebtedness.

In this new environment, balance of payments deficits and bank debt compelled a rise in requests for standby loans from the IMF. As the central institution defining the terms for access to credit, the IMF's role was magnified. Coordination of creditor policies (IMF, World Bank, private banks, bilateral aid) effectively prevented debtors from playing one credit source against another;[9] differences in specific debt conditions, trade structure, and national resources combined with variations in the actual implementation of conditionality (Korner et al. 1986: 61; Walton 1987) to undermine the possibility of debtor cartels.[10] Debtor governments seeking to travel their own course by placing national development priorities ahead of debt payment and IMF-mandated structural adjustments faced domestic turmoil and had nowhere to turn. Without IMF approval, foreign investment and credit flows declined precipitously.[11]

NEGOTIATIONS AND RENEGOTIATIONS: THE ROLE OF INSTITUTIONAL LOGIC

The harsh IMF and World Bank conditionality and structural adjustment terms for debtor government access to new credits and renegotiation of old loans are commonly noted to have a creditor bias. The impact of these policies on the population and economic structure of debtor countries is viewed as a necessary price to pay for maintaining orderly markets and the financial stability of international institutions. Calls for a more equitable distribution of the costs of the debt crisis receive little sympathy from these agencies and/or international banks.[12] In the first years of debt accumulation, the $52 billion (ECLAC 1986) in net capital transferred to Latin America (between 1976 and 1979), was more than matched by a net outflow of $113 billion in 1983-1986 (Feinberg 1987: 205). In short, 5 percent of Latin American GNP has been

9. "Governments in industrial countries, led by the United States, are working to increase the collaboration among these three (IMF, World Bank, IDB) multilateral institutions in order to ensure that they offer consistent advice backed by the maximum degree of leverage" (Feinberg 1987: 206).

10. Indeed, coordinated actions by private bank advisory committees and the IMF have ensured that negotiations with major debtors are staggered, thus undermining one structural basis for debtor leverage in negotiations (Riding 1988a: 1).

11. In early 1987, a decline in currency reserves led Brazil to suspend virtually all payments on its $113 billion foreign debt. The immediate goal was to step outside the rules of formal negotiation to compel improved terms from creditors. Other debtors were hopeful, but passive. The international financial community and OECD governments acted. Foreign investment declined, credit flows were reduced, and trade sanctions were applied.

12. ECLAC (1986: 30) summarizes IMF and World Bank rationale as follows: "They assume that . . . the problem is one of short-term liquidity, that is, a temporary conjunctural crisis caused by factors beyond the control of the agents involved . . ." It is claimed that this crisis will automatically be resolved when the world economy recovers, since financial equilibrium will then be restored within a few years and normal international credit operations resumed. In other words, it is assumed that, on recovering their capacity to service external debts, the developing countries will regain their image of creditworthiness and their former access to the international credit markets.

exported to meet the conditions imposed by the commercial banks and the IMF. The mandate of the IMF and the World Bank is to stabilize and regulate the international financial order and sustain open international trade. Private banks' objectives are to lower their potential losses, increase payments, and provide the minimum necessary credit to guarantee that debtor countries continue to pay (Foxley 1987: 101). However, the capacity of debtor countries to implement the structural adjustment policies upon which new loans and credit are contingent is limited by the processes of internationalization, which characterize the New International Division of Labor.

Internationalized production processes, labor markets, and financial markets, when coordinated through the organization of multilateral institutions and corporations, effectively undermined national regimes' capacity to use traditional monetary, trade, and fiscal policies to control the economy (Furtado 1987: 40). On the other hand, heterodox stabilization policies and austerity policies are fraught with contradictions that threaten the political legitimacy of national governments. Caught within these compelling cross-currents, debtor governments have found themselves forced to accept a routinized process for rescheduling loan payments. They must present a plan for economic stabilization that conforms to the conditionality and structural adjustment criteria demanded by the IMF and the World Bank as the certification of credit-worthiness. Negotiation with agencies of industrial nations' "aid regime" follows to obtain official loans on below-market terms and secure trade agreements within GATT. Finally, negotiations with commercial banks determine access to new private credit (Garten 1982: 280).

In practice, these routine negotiations with one set of institutional actors present contradictory demands that, ironically, are contingent upon satisfactory negotiation with another set of creditors. These separate negotiations create an environment of institutionally determined performance criteria, which are unrelated to the welfare and security of the debtor country population or traditional development goals, but which redistribute organizational power within debtor states. The IMF annual review procedures create an imperative for debtor governments to establish economic monitoring procedures and state institutions that allow continued supervision and standardized reporting procedures. In addition, the World Bank's shift from project-specific to broad structural adjustment policies and more short- to medium-term lending reduces the role of special purpose institutions and increases the importance of central banks and finance ministries within national regimes (Carvounis 1984: 62-84). The convergence of IMF and World Bank loan policies has increased the leverage of multilateral institutions by centralizing information and negotiation strategies for creditors. The effectiveness of IMF conditionality and the negotiated rescheduling process in controlling the overall policy mix in debtor countries is based on the ability to monitor borrowers' economic performance (Williamson 1982: 25).

Indeed, the negotiating procedure brings the IMF into the process of fashioning the economic policies for the debtor nation, including decisions that have powerful effects on domestic conditions. At the same time, the IMF insists that adjustment take place without recourse to heightened trade and exchange controls, and this also disposes the IMF to go beyond policy approval and into policymaking (Carvounis 1984: 68; see also Neu 1979: 239).

In the 1980s, Latin America's principal debtor nations have produced a strong net outflow of capital based on reduced wages, reduced imports, and dismantling of state sector programs and institutions, especially public-sector capital investments. Conditionality has required that surpluses generated by balance of trade surpluses be used to satisfy multilateral and international creditors. National regimes are constrained from shifting resource dependence to the local economy by raising domestic revenues. Thus, the functions of all state institutions are increasingly buffered by those state agencies that negotiate access to new credit. And, as a result, IMF conditionality and World Bank structural adjustment can be viewed as a set of institutional criteria incompatible with development goals, a set which delegitimates the sovereignty of national governments.

In addition, satisfaction of IMF "conditions" has become the routine first step required for debtor country loan negotiations with OECD nations through the Paris Club.[13] This structure has produced a maximum amount of uncertainty for debtor nations and a maximum amount of flexibility and control for creditors. Debtors seeking bilateral loans and debt rescheduling face ad hoc procedures, short-term loans requiring constant negotiating, domestic policies aimed at rapid measurable results, and official indifference to the domestic consequences of required policies (Carvounis 1984: 73).

Finally, commercial creditors' loans are conditional upon Paris Club agreements, and the negotiation process for rescheduling loans follows no established routine. Again, this increases debtor uncertainty. The information search by debtor countries attempting to reschedule loans incorporates them into a perpetual round of prenegotiations, negotiations, and renegotiations wherein they must respond to new demands for information on policies and

---

13. The Paris Club was created in 1956 as a multilateral organization to coordinate the policies of OECD creditor nations that have bilateral loans with Third World nations. Creditor nations have thus been able to centralize negotiations and routinize procedures. Debtor nations therefore must confront creditors in a negotiating framework where bilateral loans and rescheduling of loans are uniform across sources of credit.

policy performance. To "play the game," debtor country negotiators thus find themselves compelled to conduct three separate sets of parallel negotiations with creditors who place mutually contingent but independent performance demands upon the debtor government's economic and social policies.

To conclude, Latin American debtor nations find themselves operating in a New International Division of Labor wherein internationalization has produced profound shifts in trade, production processes, finance, and investment. More important for the processes of policy formation and implementation, however, the coordination of multilateral, official, and commercial finance capital has created an environment of organizational priorities that are divorced from the functioning of the domestic economic and political marketplace in debtor nations. "Aid has been structured to promote a certain type of industrialization, which is characterized by private ownership, openness to foreign capital, and reliance on market forces, and which is, increasingly, export oriented" (Wood 1986: 188). The fundamental rationale of structural adjustment is, first, to compel peripheral nations to accept the logic of comparative advantage in exchange relations by concentrating on export-led growth, and, second, to dismantle the state capitalist institutional structures, which increase transaction costs for international capital. These policies are, of course, asymmetric in that they may raise transaction costs for some social groups in peripheral nations. Wage laborers, local businesses, and consumers are faced with increased uncertainty and volatility, not greater certainty and predictability, in their market relations as a result of the actions of these multilateral agencies.

SOCIAL CONSEQUENCES OF STRUCTURAL ADJUSTMENT

Demography

Data on Latin American population processes must be interpreted cautiously due to the unreliability of statistics in the region (Hakkert and Goza 1988). The presumption that structural adjustment policies implemented in Latin American nations during the 1980s had a negative social impact is intuitively appealing. Unfortunately, efficient civil registration systems are uncommon in Latin America, and fertility and mortality data must be interpreted cautiously. Moreover, decreased government spending also affects collection of data on health, migration, and labor force characteristics (Martine et al. 1984). Demographic social indicators, however, may provide a more accurate assessment of structural adjustment policies' impact on the well-being and life chances than simple income distribution measures.

Roett (1987) asserts that structural adjustment policies have a direct impact on health, and UNICEF (1987) concludes that child mortality in Brazil has increased, but these findings are somewhat controversial given the nature of the data. Nevertheless, IMF- and World Bank-influenced orthodox policies produced recessions throughout the region, resulting in increasing unemployment, and declining levels of consumption and real wages. Government investment spending dropped precipitously, particularly expenditures on health and education. However, time lags, countercyclical trends, and separating the impact of austerity from long-term trends all complicate the question of determining the social costs of structural adjustment in Latin America.

From 1979 to 1983, per capita real expenditures on health in Latin America declined by nearly 60 percent and educational spending by 59 percent (UNICEF 1987). As a consequence, one might expect the following demographic consequences: increased malnutrition, especially among children; larger proportions of deaths due to malnutrition and infectious diseases; increased labor force participation of women and children; reduced marriage rates; lower birth rates; increased marital instability and divorce rates; increased crime rates, including child abuse; changes in the prevailing patterns of internal migration; and increased emigration where possible.

In Chile, a decade of monetarist economic policies and overall cuts in health care, including privatization of many services (Scarpaci 1988), has been accompanied by continuing declines in infant mortality rates (Haignere 1983; Foxley and Raczynski 1984; Raczynski and Oyarzo 1981). However, increased rates of malnutrition among preschoolers and increased infant mortality rates for mothers with no education may be linked to reduced government nutritional aid programs (Foxley and Raczynski 1984). In 1984, when unemployment declined and nutrition programs were improved, malnutrition declined.

In Costa Rica, Rosero's analysis covering 1910 to 1981 demonstrates a systematic increase in infant mortality during recessions, a pattern which holds in the 1980s. However, child malnutrition continued to decline between 1979 and 1982 in spite of reduced child nutrition programs (Costa Rican Ministry of Health). Suicides increased from 0.98 percent of deaths in 1982 to 1.4 percent in 1983 (Ministry of Justice). The economic recession appears to have led to increased urban migration as the differential between urban and rural wages increased (MTSS 1986).

From 1975 to 1985, slower economic growth in Brazil was accompanied by government intervention with expanded urban services, especially sanitation, which led to a decline in infant mortality rates (Vetter 1983). The infant death/birth ratio, however, is up from 56 per 1,000 in 1982 to 60.9 in 1984 (FIBGE 1987). Brazil's homicide rate doubled in the past decade, and suicides attributable to financial problems rose from 187 in 1982 to 332 in 1983, when the financial crisis compelled Brazil to petition the IMF for assistance. Shifts in the marriage rate have tracked the economy, increasing with improved economic conditions and declining with recession. As of 1986-1987, both the birth and marriage rates were at their lowest levels in this century. The impact of austerity on fertility rates, however, is difficult to judge conclusively in the short term. The observed shifts may simply be intensifying trends already present, or they may represent a change in timing of births and presage increased birth rates in the future.

The recessionary impact of structural adjustment policies has led many observers to expect increased emigration from South and Central America. Internally, one may anticipate an increase in migration, but perhaps a decline in migration to cities where the recession and reduced government spending have hit labor markets hard. In Colombia, Bogota's growth has remained below the predictions of the United Nations. Costa Rica, however, where agricultural wages dropped below the official minimum wage and the differential with urban wages remained high, experienced growing urban migration. Mexican migration to the United States continues at a high rate. Venezuela, historically a target of international labor migration, has experienced a net outmigration of foreigners (Van Roy 1984). Finally, in Brazil, return migration to the Northeast (Martine et al. 1984) and outmigration from the new frontier states has accompanied a decline in job opportunities (SEPLAN). In the United States, the Immigration and Naturalization Service estimates that annual illegal migration rose from 1 to 1.8 million between 1980 and 1986.

Income, Employment, and the Economic Costs of Structural Adjustment

The negative impact of low wages, oligopoly, and insufficient consumer demand on economic growth is asserted by those researchers who conclude that "inequality" is an important cause of stagnation in peripheral nations (Lustig 1980; Dutt 1984; Marshall 1988). In the 1980s, Latin American nations operating under structural adjustment policies have experienced declining wages. The consumption capacity of the low-income population, often an important market even for consumer durables, has been reduced by a series of economic and political shocks. Lower consumption levels have been paced by slow export growth, reduced industrial production, capital flight, and increased foreign debt. Short-term recoveries and brief periods of economic "stability" tied to heterodox policies have been followed by rapid inflation, rampant speculation in place of investment, and an elevated sense of insecurity, uncertainty, and turbulence. In this context, declining physical and institutional infrastructures, and a reduced state control of contractual laws, has greatly increased transaction costs in the local economy. In response, informal economic relations have grown and may be limiting economic growth.

An important component of structural adjustment policies is an attack on wages. Such policies assume that wage increases have an adverse effect on prices and imports, contradicting the goal of servicing the foreign debt. Given slow export growth and small export surpluses, "excessive" consumption is targeted as the source of trade deficits. The benefits of labor's increased consumption capacity are unexamined. However, Cline (1972), Cortes and Marshall (1986), and Garcia (1987: 3-47) provide evidence from Latin America that a more equitable income distribution has no impact on imports.

The economic cost has been severe in high-debt countries implementing structural adjustment policies. Brazil's minimum monthly salary of US$50 will not support a family's basic needs. Indeed, Estado de Minas (1987) estimates that an increase in the minimum wage of 600 percent would be required to achieve that level. At the start of the debt crisis in Mexico, over 30 percent of the economically active population received the official minimum wage while 54 percent earned below that level (Carr 1986). During the early 1980s, 60 percent of Chilean urban families earned less than the minimum income needed to purchase the basic "food basket" (UNICEF 1987). Costa Rican household heads earning the minimum wage or less increased from 24.4 percent in 1979 to 30.8 percent in 1982, an increase that was accompanied by a drop in meat and dairy consumption.

Between 1980 and 1985, Latin American per capita income in a group of twenty-three Latin American nations dropped 9 percent (UNICEF 1987). From 1979 to 1984, Costa Rican real wages fell 40 percent (Pollack and Uthoff 1984). In Mexico, real wages declined 30 percent between 1981 and 1984 (UNICEF 1987). In Brazil, SEADE (1987) records a 38 percent drop in urban wages in the 1986-1987 period. From 1981 to 1984, real wages in Chile declined 16 percent. It appears that the poorest sectors of the population were most severely affected in these cases. In 1981-1982, real income declined 10 percent for the poorest 40 percent of Chilean wage carriers (Altimir 1984: 91-112). Argentina's stabilization programs of the mid 1980s have dropped real wages below their level of the early 1970s. In addition, by 1985 labor's share of national income was only 70 percent of its 1970 level (PREALC 1986: 63; Marshall 1988). In Mexico, real wages fell 9.6 percent in 1982, 18 percent in

1983, and 1.3 percent in 1984 (IDB 1985). Mexico's minimum agricultural wage declined 31 percent in real terms from 1981 to 1983 (World Bank 1986).

Structural adjustment policies have also been related to increased unemployment and poverty throughout Latin America. Klein and Wurgaft (1985) report that from 1980 to 1984 the weighted average of urban unemployment for twelve Latin American countries increased from 5.8 to 7.9 percent. Some evidence indicates that unemployment among young workers has been particularly strong. In Brazil between 1979 and 1985, youths aged ten to fourteen had their proportion of the labor force drop from 6.7 percent to 5 percent, and the fifteen to nineteen age stratum declined from 15.4 to 14 percent (FIBGE/PNAD). In Mexico, unemployment rates rose to 12.3 percent in 1986, with "underemployment" affecting 45 percent of the workforce (*LAM* 1987). The impact in Bolivia, however, has been expressed in an increased dropout rate for primary school youth, rising from 2.2 percent in 1980 to 8.5 percent in 1983 (UNICEF 1987). There is also evidence of increased labor force participation of females and the elderly, as formerly dependent members have increasingly entered the labor force to counteract lower wages for heads of households.

There is much evidence that structural adjustment has produced an increase of informal employment activities (Garcia and Tokman 1985; Saboia 1986; United Nations 1986c; Portes and Johns 1988). Employment growth in the informal sector now surpasses formal sector job creation in Latin America (World Bank 1986; Portes and Johns 1988). In Brazil, Argentina, Peru, and Costa Rica, informal sector growth has been associated with declining real wages of between 23.5 percent and 39.3 percent (Hakkert and Goza 1988). In Argentina from 1970 to 1980, skilled labor dropped from 40 percent of the workforce to just 25 percent. Self-employment increased by 5 percent in the same period. Tertiary sector workers increased to 50 percent of the labor force (Rofman 1988).

Social Responses to Austerity

Debtor nations following IMF- and World Bank-mandated structural adjustment policies are increasingly confronted by popular responses. Since 1976, some seventy-seven strikes, riots, and demonstrations against the austerity policies typical of structural adjustment have marked the experience of twenty-six debtor nations, thirteen in Latin America (Walton and Ragin 1988). It is not surprising that as the costs of structural adjustment policies have fallen principally on the poor and wage earners, popular resentment in Latin America is increasingly taking the form of spontaneous riots, community-based militance, and various forms of "disengagement," which observers link directly to these policies (Portes and Johns 1988; Grindle 1988).

In Mexico, peasants have engaged in popular protests against government structural adjustment policies (Carr 1986; Prieto 1986; Fox 1987; Grindle 1988). Nevertheless, mobilizations and protest have not been the characteristic responses in rural areas. Rather, disengagement strategies paralleling those described by Portes and Johns in urban areas typify household adaptation to ensure economic survival (Grindle 1988). Survival strategies are used by households that combine sources of income from agriculture, commerce, industry, and migratory activities.[14]

In the 1980s, structural adjustment-related riots have contributed to the downfall of Latin American and Caribbean governments in Peru (1980 and 1984), Brazil (1983), Panama (1985), and Haiti (1986) (Walton and Ragin 1988). Popular protests have risen parallel with the debt burden and the rate with which austerity measures are imposed. Loxley (1984: 30) links urban riots directly to the impact of structural adjustment on the working class. Petras and Brill (1986), however, argue that state control and legitimacy relations between the state and civil institutions determine popular responses to austerity programs. Robert Kaufman (1986) finds that measures of "economic concentration" and "populist tradition" determine the emergence of destabilizing coalitions, such as those which developed in Brazil, Argentina, and Mexico.

CONCLUSION

After World War II, rationalization of international markets was facilitated in part by the creation of multilateral agencies such as the IMF and the World Bank, and treaties like GATT, that sought to establish a normative order within which transaction costs among diverse actors could be regulated. The functions of the IMF and the World Bank have evolved from regulation of short-term balance of payments crises and project-oriented development loans to coerced structural adjustment of debtor nations to guarantee repayment. These multilateral lending institutions' and GATT's influence over debtor nations' access to credit and export markets have allowed them to dictate national economic and social policies that reduce constraints on capital and goods markets and dismantle state institutions.

14. See Chapter 12 by Jamal for a similar phenomenon in Tanzania.

The policy rationale for IMF and World Bank structural adjustment loan policies tends to be subordinated to these same institutions' organizational interests and to those of dominant international actors. The effects of SALs often contradict the stated goals of international economic development and democracy and are necessarily affected by power relations within each country and internationally. Their social and economic costs are unequally distributed; these costs are shifted by the more powerful actors (governments in developed nations, commercial banks, multilateral lending institutions) onto the less powerful (wage earners, local small-scale business). Moreover, the specific measures imposed on debtor countries not only may be ultimately incompatible with the promotion of development, but may also exacerbate already glaring inequality, delegitimizing and destabilizing democratic governments.

The response to SALs in Latin America is likewise mediated by national and international power structures. Within each country, the particular constellation of social class alliances, the military, and the state will determine not only the form of popular responses to austerity measures, but also the state's own posture in reference to those responses. Brazil, Argentina, Mexico, Peru, and Venezuela are limited in their capacity to fully implement structural adjustment. Organized constituencies of state-sector employees, labor unions, industry associations, and other interest groups confront the regime with cross-cutting demands and resistance to SALs. A pattern of intermittent austerity policies, popular mobilization, state resistance to conditionality in the name of national interest, and renegotiation with creditors will continue. Where nondemocratic regimes have effectively demobilized such interest groups and maintained a strong coalition of the military, export businesses, and foreign capital, the social costs of austerity will not produce similar contradictions. Thus, Chile implemented the broadest and most sustained structural adjustment policies in Latin America. As a result, rapid improvement in conventional economic indicators has been accompanied by severely deteriorating physical and economic conditions for much of the population.

Export-related business groups benefit from their nation's favorable trade status with developed economies. Aside from some complaints, their response to structural adjustment loans seems to be acquiescence. The reaction of working classes is more problematic and contingent on their economic and political strength vis à vis other national political actors. Where working-class organization and political involvement is high, the ability to compel national regimes and multilateral lending institutions to moderate SALs increases. Where working class organization is relatively weak, renewed emphasis on subsistence agriculture and urban informal sector activities is likely.

As SALs produce declines in relative and absolute living standards for wage earners and local business, political unrest and destabilization may be expected. In this situation, the response of the military becomes a crucial factor. In a region with long traditions of military intervention in political affairs, the strengthening or reemergence of authoritarian regimes seems a likely outcome. The perception of austerity policies as a shifting of dominant groups' obligations to the poor, typified by the slogan "Let the ones who stole the money pay back the money," can only sharpen political polarization in Latin American nations. The middle classes and other hegemonic groups, in turn, will tend to become more rigid in protecting their interests (that is, the status quo) and less flexible toward protests from below. The threat of instability also increases the probability of military intervention and repression.

The situation may be construed as a zero sum game in which power determines who bears the costs involved. Thus, developed countries, through mediation of multilateral lending institutions regulating flows of capital and trade, can shift the cost of maintaining the international regime onto developing economies whose critical dependence on foreign debt refinancing and access to world credit markets makes resistance to structural adjustment policies, which are conditions for further credits, virtually impossible. In the national setting, the cost of adjustment is passed down the path of least resistance to the less powerful classes, those not under protection of the international regime or unable to establish coalitions to gain some protection.

11 POLITICAL CHANGE AND ECONOMIC POLICY IN LATIN AMERICA AND THE CARIBBEAN IN 1988

Louellen Stedman and Peter Hakim

The debt crisis has deeply affected the lives of Latin Americans. After three decades of uninterrupted growth, the economy of nearly every Latin American and Caribbean country went into a tailspin in 1982 and 1983. Now after four straight years of slow growth (1984 to 1987), the region's per capita income is still some six percent below its 1980 level. Throughout Latin America and the Caribbean, wages have fallen; jobs have disappeared; housing, schools, hospitals, and other public services have deteriorated; and Latin Americans have endured food shortages and mounting street crime. Poverty and already skewed distributions of income have worsened in most countries, bringing to a halt promising improvements in nutrition standards and infant mortality rates.

Yet these developments have not brought the outright social and economic turmoil that many predicted would result from the debt crisis of the 1980s.[1] At times, austerity measures have provoked outcries from people in debtor nations, as workers have gone on strike to protest declining real wages, and riots have greeted increases in food and transportation costs. But these reactions have by and large been of short duration and have not had major political consequences. Most Latin Americans have quietly tolerated austerity, hardship,

1. See, for example, Roett (1984).

165

and sacrifice, moderating their demands and expectations in light of the severity of the economic crisis facing their countries. For example, after five years of profound economic crisis and more than ten years of lessening government popularity, no political breakdown or metamorphosis has occurred in Mexico (Aguilar 1987-1988: 53). And, in fact, Latin America's turn toward democratic rule has persisted throughout the crisis; economic setbacks have not interrupted elections in any country.

The economic difficulties brought about by the debt crisis have, however, had political consequences in virtually every country of the region. Since the crisis began six years ago, most governments in power in Latin America and the Caribbean have suffered sharp losses of credibility and popular support that are directly attributable to economic problems. In country after country, as governments have been unable to restore economic growth and meet even the minimal demands of their citizens, their support has eroded, and opposition forces have gained ground.

Since 1982, presidential elections have been held in eight Latin American and Caribbean countries in which civilian rule was already in place. In all but one of these countries (Costa Rica), the opposition candidate won. Personalities and other political issues certainly played an important role in these elections, but the dominant issue in every one was economics.

1. The Revolutionary Nationalist Movement's Victor Paz Estenssoro was elected in Bolivia in August 1985 as the successor to President Hernan Siles Zuazo. At the time, Bolivia's economy had virtually collapsed, with inflation raging at an annual rate of nearly 30,000 percent. The incumbent party received less than 10 percent of the vote.

2. In Colombia, Conservative President Belisario Betancur was defeated in 1986 by Liberal Virgilio Barco Vargas in an election emphasizing economic distress and political violence in the country.

3. In the Dominican Republic, the aging and nearly blind Joaquin Balaguer returned to the presidency, defeating the governing Dominican Revolutionary Party's candidate.

4. In Ecuador in 1984, businessman and Conservative Party candidate Leon Febres Cordero was elected president, defeating the candidate of the incumbent Christian Democratic Party.

5. In Honduras, the governing Liberal Party split in two, with the dissident party candidate winning 26 percent of the vote. Although the candidate of the opposition National Party took 43 percent of the vote, the combined vote of the two liberal candidates was higher, and the Liberals held on to the presidency.

6. In 1985, young and charismatic APRA Party Leader Alan Garcia was elected in Peru to lead the country out of the economic disarray left by his predecessor Terry Belaunde. Belaunde's Popular Action Party received only 6 percent of the vote, and an APRAista became president for the first time in the party's history.
7. And in Venezuela, 1983 brought the election of Jaime Lusinchi, leader of the Democratic Action Party, and the defeat of former President Rafael Caldera of the governing Social Christian Party.

Notably absent in these elections was any consistent ideological trend. In four of the elections, the winning candidate favored more open, free-market approaches; in three others, the reverse was true.

Since this early round of elections in the 1980s, governments in power have continued to lose prestige and support. There are few Latin American presidents who are stronger today than they were two years ago. Opposition groups are winning legislative and local elections, and polls reflect the declining popularity of sitting presidents.

But in the subsequent round of elections in the late 1980s, there appeared to be an ideological trend. Populist and nationalist groups seemed to gain ground. These groups called for less conciliatory postures toward international creditors and demanded relief from intolerable debt burdens. This trend reflected the growing resentment toward continued austerity and orthodox economic programs imposed to maintain debt payments and good relations with creditors. People appeared to lose faith that such standard approaches would bring an improvement in their nations' financial and economic circumstances, turning away from leaders who promised more of the same.

POLITICAL TRANSITIONS AND THEIR IMPLICATIONS

At the time this chapter was written, presidential elections were due in the next two years for eleven countries in the region, including the four largest debtors: Brazil, Mexico, Argentina, and Venezuela. The indications were that at least some of these elections will bring significant political transitions.

It has not been easy for governments to promote economic reform. Shortages of foreign capital and cramped domestic budgets have constrained efforts at structural change. Public and private enterprises, for example, lack the resources to exploit new export opportunities. Many countries initiated tough measures to control fiscal deficits and inflation, but they could not sustain them because of political opposition. The stop-and-go performance of most Latin American economies has eroded the confidence of business and financial communities throughout the region, reducing incentives to invest in future production. In sum, there is little willingness in any sector to accept further sacrifices because few Latin Americans still believe that such sacrifices will produce significant and lasting results.

In many places, opposition is increasing to market-oriented policies that people often associate with austerity, unemployment, and reduced social expenditures. Organized labor actively resists reforms that threaten to eliminate jobs and lower wages. Other resistance comes from owners of businesses anxious to preserve protected markets and state subsidies, and from public employees concerned about their jobs and influence. For most Latin Americans, the standard approach to debt management—austerity at home and massive interest payments abroad—has come to a dead end because it has failed to bring growth. Although elections in all countries are not necessarily fully representative of the attitudes and interests of all population groups, the broad public frustration with economic management is certainly likely to be reflected in upcoming election results. These results will in turn significantly influence the course of economic policy and the management of foreign debt in the hemisphere.

Mexico

Mexico will be the first major debtor to face presidential elections in 1988. In an upcoming election, the PRI will almost certainly assert its continuing dominance of Mexican politics through the victory of the party's Carlos Salinas de Gortari, one of the main architects of current President de la Madrid's economic policies. Salinas is more likely to bring continuity than marked change to the Mexican economy. Nonetheless, there have been significant shifts in Mexican politics in the past six years. The upcoming election has brought more debate about economic policy, and is more contested, than any in Mexico in the recent past.

Assuming office in December 1982, President Miguel de la Madrid adopted a policy of accommodation with the international financial community, which he has maintained throughout his term of office. Mexico was rewarded with larger amounts of new external financing than any other Latin American country. With the help of these funds and a shift toward exports, the country was able to produce a sizable trade surplus, build up large foreign reserves, and strengthen its economy overall. Yet the Mexican people have suffered great hardship. Real economic growth, manufacturing output, and investment have declined (Bailey and Watkins 1987).[2] Real wages remain extremely low and by mid 1987 were 50 percent of their 1976 level and 9 percent lower than in the previous year (1987). Government efforts to maintain reserves and the trade balance through devaluations have produced considerable discontent among the Mexican people.

Consequently, the PRI in this election year is more vulnerable than in the past. Salinas does not have the enthusiastic backing of the PRI rank and file that previous candidates had. Criticism of the party's undemocratic internal governance is loud, led by former PRI member Cuauhtemoc Cardenas, the son of Mexico's most popular president, who is running for the presidency under the auspices of three small, left-oriented parties. Both Cardenas and the candidate of the business-based National Action Party are highly critical of the PRI's economic management. These opposition candidates are likely to do better at the polls (presuming reasonably fair elections) than they ever have.[3]

PRI candidate Salinas will withstand these challenges and win the election. But another battle will begin once he enters office. His own campaign reveals concern with the changing dynamics of Mexican politics and the design of acceptable economic policies. Salinas himself now maintains that repaying the country's $105 billion foreign debt must be linked to the achievement of sustainable economic growth.[4] He also acknowledges that the severe economic crisis has made more imperative the need for change in the Mexican political system. But Mexico is not likely to alter in any fundamental way its economic course or its close economic relationship with the United States.

Venezuela

The likely return of Carlos Andres Perez to the presidency in Venezuela would produce changes in domestic economic management and relations with foreign creditors. The nomination of Perez, who held the presidency from 1974 to 1979, followed a struggle within the Democratic Action Party that pitted Perez against current President Jaime Lusinchi. Perez advances a more populist

2. See the discussion of Mexico's experience with structural adjustment in Chapter 14 by Dombusch.
3. Various sources record this trend, including "The Peons Turn on Mexico's Ever-Ruling Party," *Economist*, March 5, 1988, pp. 43-44.
4. "Salinas Begins to Define Positions," *Latin American Weekly Report*, Oct. 22, 1987, p. 4.

alternative to the governance of Venezuela than did either of the previous two presidents.

During his earlier term, Perez nationalized the oil industry and promoted a series of social reforms that made him popular with the poor and working classes. Industry and business sectors, on the other hand, have always been wary of him (Collet 1988). Perez's former priorities in domestic matters will probably not change significantly, although economic and financial constraints will limit his policy choices. In the international sphere, Perez has called for debt repayment to be conditioned to new loans and stronger export earnings (1988). Perez seems more willing than his predecessors to consider reducing growth-hindering foreign debt payments, but he has been cautious about calling for unilateral action to abandon Venezuela's foreign financial obligations.

In what could prove an important development, Perez has expressed his intention—if elected—to extend his leadership beyond the borders of Venezuela. He has pledged greater priority to Venezuela's external relations and is unlikely to maintain Lusinchi's conciliatory relationship with the United States. Perez does not advocate a debtors' cartel and cannot, therefore, be expected to lead an outright rebellion against the current international debt strategy. But as president, Perez might well convert Venezuela from a quiet and docile debtor to a regional leader in the search for an escape from the debt crisis.

Brazil

The decision of Brazil, Latin America's largest debtor, to suspend unilaterally its debt service payments to commercial banks in February 1987 was perhaps the most dramatic and destabilizing development in the five-year-old debt crisis. The suspension led directly to the decision by U.S. banks to establish large reserves against losses on Third World loans. Brazil acted to avoid depleting its foreign exchange reserves, which were dwindling rapidly as the country's overheated economy had caused imports to surge and exports to decline (as production shifted to satisfy domestic demand). Despite the recovery of exports and resumption of growth that occurred before the end of 1987, it was more than a year before Brazil reached agreement with its creditors to resume interest payments. This delay reflected the political dynamics in Brazil, which have grown more complex as the country prepares for its first presidential election since the transition to civilian rule in 1984.

Domestic politics has consistently played a major role in the management of the Brazilian economy and the country's external debt. The popular and innovative Cruzado Plan failed largely as a result of President Sarney's refusal, against the counsel of many advisers, to slow economic growth prior to key gubernatorial elections. The governing party won a clear victory in the elections, but inflationary pressures had been released, and foreign reserves were largely depleted by the boom. The moratorium on interest payments was almost an inevitable result.

With the subsequent contraction of the economy, the popularity and credibility of the Sarney government plummeted, and political divisiveness increased. Brazil is now politically and economically demoralized. The Brazilian Popular Democratic Movement Party (PMDB), ostensibly the governing party, is divided, making it difficult for Sarney to carry out a consistent economic policy (Truell 1987). A new strategy by Finance Minister Mailson Ferreira da Nobrega to stabilize the economy through real wage cuts and deficit reduction is not given much chance of success, due to popular opposition as well as the resistance of the military to the wage measures (Cohen 1988).

Presidential elections are due in 1989, and candidates still remain to be chosen. Many consider Leonel Brizola, a former governor of Rio de Janeiro, to be the leading candidate. Brizola offers a strongly populist approach to Brazil's economy and its debt problems. He favors nationalization of the banks, a harder line on external debt, and inward-looking solutions to the country's economic plight (Whitefield 1988). If elections were held today, many observers believe he would be the likely victor.

Despite his popularity, Brizola, or whoever gains the presidency in 1989, will be constrained by political and economic realities. Among these realities is the military, which continues to play a major role in Brazil's political affairs, and it is possible that the military would prevent Brizola from taking power at all. Army Minister General Leonidas Pires Goncalves sounded a warning when he declared in December 1987 that "military interventions are provoked not by 'the nature of regimes but rather by the incompetence of those in government'" (Riding 1988b). President Goulart's ties to Brizola contributed to the military takeover in 1984.

Brazil is in a political and economic quandary, with little popular support for economic austerity or continued cooperation with private and official creditors. Yet it is difficult to see any easy resolution of the country's economic problems without such measures. Populism and nationalism may propel Brizola or a similar candidate to the presidency in 1989, and the results may be greater confrontation with external creditors and further setbacks for Brazil's economy.

Argentina

Argentina faces the most difficult economic future of the major debtor countries. While its debt level ranks third in the region, its ratio of interest payments to exports, a crucial indicator of solvency, in 1987 reached 56 percent, compared to 35 percent for Brazil and 38 percent for Mexico (ECLAC 1987). And gross domestic product per capita has declined further than in other debtor countries (World Bank 1987c: xi). Today, observers describe the Argentine economy as "exhausted, chaotic, and out of control" (Christian 1988). Strikes for wage adjustments have become commonplace; a general strike debilitated the entire country in early 1988. The labor movement has been particularly vocal in rebelling against the government's "submission to the 'policies of hunger' of the IMF'" (1988).

In September 1987, voters dealt a stunning defeat to President Alfonsin's Radical Party in gubernatorial and legislative elections. The victorious Peronists based their campaign on a populist condemnation of the government's failure to take a stronger position on debt repayment and improve living standards. As 1989 presidential elections approach, the Peronists now seem to have the upper hand over President Alfonsin's Radical Party. Popular support for Peronist economic positions will clearly influence policy over the next few years as Alfonsin tries to regain lost ground. This is not the same Peronist party that lost the election to Alfonsin. It has moderated its positions on a number of fronts. The party no longer advocates deficit spending, development through import-substitution, protectionism, or fervent economic nationalism (Hewko and Chediek 1988). The new Peronist Party favors a tougher stance toward the IMF and external creditors, but it also calls for privatization and reduction of the immense budget deficit in Argentina (1988). And the party may become even more moderate if it gains national office.

But the Peronists must still satisfy their labor constituency, even as they have been able to broaden the party's base. They oppose tough austerity measures that keep wage increases below price rises and are not ready to dismantle state-owned enterprises or raise taxes. Many of their supporters will continue to press for a suspension or reduction of external debt payments.

Other Countries

Elections in other countries of the region are likely to follow patterns similar to those of the four largest debtors. Continued economic stress seems likely to lead to increased support for populist approaches to economic policy and external debt management. Political developments in Jamaica and Ecuador provide further evidence of this trend.

Current Prime Minister Seaga of Jamaica has sought for seven years to promote a market-oriented economy for his country. In this he has been strongly supported by the United States and international financial institutions. He can point to significant improvements in the economy, but the people are tired of the relentless austerity they have faced.

It now appears that Michael Manley, whom Seaga replaced in 1981, will return to power. Manley contends that the Seaga-orchestrated recovery of the past seven years has never reached the poor, condemning the serious decline in public education, health, and social welfare standards. Although he has moderated many of his stated positions and plans to retain many of the Seaga economic reforms, Manley still advocates a stronger role for the state in the economy and is likely to have a far less cordial relationship with Jamaica's creditors.

Ecuador provides another example of the hemispheric trend toward populism. President Febres Cordero pursued free market, export-oriented economic policies, again with strong support from the United States. Although these policies initially brought reductions in inflation and the budget deficit and promoted growth in exports and production, the sharp drop in oil prices and a devastating earthquake brought this progress to a halt (Hollihan 1988). In January 1988, Febres Cordero was soundly defeated in the first round of presidential elections, and two more populist candidates reached the run-off election. Both Democratic Left candidate Rodrigo Borja and Roldo-sista Party candidate Abdala Bucaram called for a greater role for the state and less cooperation with external creditors (Golden 1988). Borja, the more moderate of the two, won the election, but a clear turn away from market approaches to economic management and toward tougher negotiations with international organizations and banks can still be anticipated.

TRENDS AND OUTLOOKS

We have discussed thus far six upcoming elections in Latin America and the Caribbean. As in the earlier round of elections held in the 1980s, the parties in power in most countries face probable rejection at the polls in the next few years. Unlike the previous elections, however, the leading candidates at this stage tend to favor more populist policies and to reject market-oriented approaches. They will call for higher wages, price controls, and greater social spending. These prospective leaders are also less prone to promote exports at the expense of internal consumption and are likely to be less accommodating to their international creditors.

The determination and ability of political leaders to carry out election promises is always difficult to assess. Political rhetoric reflecting ideological positions can be particularly harsh and polarized in Latin America, and most successful presidential candidates are likely to moderate their policy objectives once they assume office and are faced with the task of governing. Nonetheless, preelection statements do distinguish candidates. And if they do not precisely predict the course a government—once in power—will follow, such statements do suggest likely policy directions.

Given the preelection debates emerging throughout the region, this round of elections may well bring important shifts in economic policy in Latin America and the Caribbean. The internal economic consequences of less orthodox and more populist approaches are uncertain. But countries following these approaches—Peru, for example, which after two years of expansion and growth is now out of reserves and on the brink of collapse—have not fared particularly well over the past several years.

12 THE DEMISE OF THE LABOR ARISTOCRACY IN AFRICA: STRUCTURAL ADJUSTMENT IN TANZANIA

Vali Jamal

Structural adjustment programs as currently applied in African countries exhibit many common features, including restraints on wages, suspension of subsidies on food products, liberalization of markets, and devaluation. The objective of these measures is to shift resources in favor of rural areas. The common justification for this shift is that past policies have created distortions that support inflated living standards in the urban areas. Pricing policies for agricultural crops and wages policies for urban workers are particularly singled out as culprits. As a result, urban wage earners allegedly gain through price twists and terms of trade transfers at the expense of farmers. The squeeze on agriculture destroys farmers' incentives to produce for the market, precipitating

This paper draws upon analysis of the Tanzanian economy done during several ILO missions, particularly the Basic Needs Mission in 1981 under the leadership of Paul Streeten. The author would like to thank, without implicating, Fred Bienefeld, John Harris, Ian Livingstone, Ajit Singh, Frances Stewart, and Paul Streeten for helpful suggestions and discussions during the writing of that report. Many of them have also commented on the author's subsequent papers on Tanzania, on which this paper also draws. The author would also like to thank Brian Van Arkadie, Reg Green, Rolph van der Hoeven, and John Loxley for discussions on recent trends in the Tanzanian economy. Opinions expressed are solely those of the author.

crises in African countries. What is allegedly needed to raise these countries out of the crisis are structural adjustment programs to correct the major imbalances in the economy.

Adjustment programs in Africa are thus based on some notion of "urban bias," which in Africa was almost invariably translated to imply a bias in favor of the urban wage earners. That such a bias exists in African countries has been a feature of African economic analysis ever since serious analysis got underway. Elliot Berg was certainly not the first to remark on it, but he did it most forcefully, deliberately seeking controversy on the grounds that "there had been too little of it [controversy] in the past" (Berg 1966: 185). Writing in 1964 on wages policy in Africa for a conference of the International Institute of Labour Studies, he observed: "African wage earners are in general a relatively privileged group. They enjoy more of the benefits of modernization and growth than any African social group" (1966: 189). His point of reference was the "nonwage sector," by which he meant the agricultural sector. He quoted figures from the Belgian Congo and Senegal to show a gap of up to 2.5 times between the incomes of wage earners and farmers (1966: 190). The notion of a wide and widening rural-urban gap in Africa became entrenched in the literature.

Tanzania became caught in this scheme of things quite early on. In the same year as Berg was writing, an ILO document (ILO 1964) identified Tanganyika as the African country in which money wages increased at the highest rate between 1959 and 1962 (62 percent). At the subsequent conference in 1967, Tanzania's position was more than confirmed, as it emerged first among all African countries surveyed in terms of wage increases. Money wages increased by 175 percent between 1956 and 1964, translating into a 153 percent increase in real wages (Smith 1969: table 1). Noting that per capita income rose by much less, it was remarked that "very high increases in real wages . . . have been accompanied by a relative—and sometimes absolute— deterioration in living standards in the subsistence sector. Since the living standards of wage earners were . . . above those of subsistence workers the large increases in real wages need special scrutiny" (1969: 32).

The farm-wage inequality gave rise to a school of "gap economics" by which almost all economic trends in African countries were to be understood. This school, as we might have gleaned from the passage with respect to Tanzania, sought to establish a causal link between the two poles of the gap— workers' wages and farmers' income. If wage earners were gaining, it was at the expense of farmers. Berg showed some of the axes of the transfer: farmers pay the most taxes in African countries and hence finance the wage-induced increases in the government wage bill; and farmers face higher prices for commodities they buy and receive lower prices for export crops to offset higher wages (Berg 1966: 204). In essence, this was the forerunner of the urban bias model unveiled by Lipton in 1977, a model said to be of universal validity (Lipton 1977).[1] By the time Lipton wrote his influential book, the urban bias model as described above had been standard fare in African economic analysis for at least a decade and a half. Its manifestations in Tanzania were the "Turner Reports" to government on wages policies (ILO 1967 and 1975), a chapter in the ILO/Jobs and Skills Programme for Africa (JASPA) Employment Mission report (ILO/JASPA 1978), and the invaluable terms of trade studies of Frank Ellis in the early 1980s (Ellis 1982, 1983, and 1984). In 1982, JASPA's Basic Needs Mission report was also published (ILO/JASPA 1982; also published in part in Jamal 1982), which pointed out for the first time the dire consequences of the Tanzanian crisis for the real income of wage earners. The World Bank's censorious report on Africa in 1981 (IBRD 1981), written by Elliot Berg, epitomized the urban bias model as an explanation of the malaise afflicting African countries, while Bates (1981), in another influential book, brought together all the various strands of urban bias in Africa.

One reason for the general acceptance of the urban bias model in Africa was its supposed link to rural-urban migration. Michael Todaro (1969) accorded center stage to the rural-urban gap as the cause of migration, given the probability of securing a town job: the higher the gap, the bigger the flow of migrants into towns; and because urban employment was not increasing fast enough, the higher the gap, the higher the level of urban unemployment. Thus, the complete "gap model" in Africa went something as follows: Government was squeezing the agricultural sector through various forms of taxes and terms of trade twists, the benefits of which went to wage earners; the consequent farm-wage gap encouraged migration and hence unemployment; and in the rural areas the squeeze on agriculture was the cause of stagnating output.

In short, everything one ever wanted to know about Africa could be found in the gap model. In particular, when the "African crisis" gripped world attention, the gap analysts knew the cause—economic mismanagement, which was really shorthand for all past misguided wages and pricing policies. These questions were never asked: To what extent was the assertion of the rural-urban gap true? What was its size at any given time? If the rural-urban gap existed in the 1960s and 1970s, does it still exist (as implied by the structural adjustment

---

1. As a curiosity, it should be mentioned that Lipton put Tanzania in the category of countries in which there was no urban bias (Lipton 1977: 74 and 264). Later, under some attack, he retracted, saying he was "too ready to accept claims that [socialist, less developing countries such as Tanzania] featured relatively little urban bias" (Lipton 1984b: 142). He was quite likely mistaken on both accounts—at the time of his book there was urban bias in Tanzania, notwithstanding the avowed socialism, and by 1984, most of the overt signs of urban bias had disappeared.

remedy)? I examine these questions, using the case of Tanzania as an example. (For other countries see Jamal and Weeks 1987, 1988, and forthcoming b).

WAGES AND PRICES POLICIES

The policies that are most relevant in analyzing the wage-farm gap are government policies affecting prices and wages. Farm prices have a direct bearing on agricultural incomes (though, as we shall see, not as much as might be thought) and an indirect bearing on wage earners' real incomes. Wages may congruently affect farmers' real incomes by their impact on the general price level. Indeed, as we saw earlier, many analysts made a direct connection between the two incomes, taking it as axiomatic that a gain in one implies a loss in the other through price impacts. Such a simple connection was made in Tanzania by Turner.

Wage Policy

As far as government policy for wage earners is concerned we can discern seven periods in Tanzania: 1959-1962, laissez faire; 1963-1966, laissez faire; 1967-1972, wage policy; 1973-1975, "catch up"; 1976-1979, wage restraint; 1980-1981, "catch up"; and 1982-present, market-oriented restraint.

The first two periods merge, with the operative theme being market-oriented wage policies. At the start of the first period, a minimum wage was laid down for the first time in Tanganyika (as it then was) at Sh. 82 per month in Dar-es-Salaam (Table 12-1). This minimum remained in force until January 1963, when it was almost doubled, to Sh. 150 per month. In the meantime, the non-agricultural sector wage increased by 62 percent between 1957 and 1962 (a year before the promulgation of the new minimum wage), attesting to the labor market conditions prevailing in the country at the time. It may be noted that this is the trend captured by the two ILO reports previously cited that did so much to project Tanzania as a "high-wage economy." If wage increases in Tanzania were higher than elsewhere it was because of underlying market forces.

At this time, as in the other East African countries, the Tanzanian government had embarked on a policy of "stabilization" of the labor force. The "target worker," the worker who sought a fixed money income for a set period, was at the center of this policy. It was believed that the target worker was

Table 12-1. Wages in Current and Real (1969) Terms, 1957-1983
(Shillings per month)

	Current Terms		Real Terms		
	Minimum Wage	Nonagricultural Sector Wage	Minimum Wage[a]	Nonagricultural Sector Wage	National Consumer Price Index[b]
1957	82 (Apr.)	100	103	125	80.0
1963	150 (Jan.)	210	186	261	80.5
1964	"	224	182	272	82.6
1965	"	302	170	343	88.0
1967	"	347	160	370	93.8
1968	"	359	153	366	98.1
1969	170 (July)	381	170	381	100.0
1972	240 (July)	416	206	356	116.7
1973	"	432	186	335	128.9
1974	340 (July)	686	221	445	154.1
1975	380 (May)	659	174	339	194.3
1976	"	672	183	324	207.6
1977	"	708	164	305	231.8
1978	"	710	146	273	260.0
1979	"	967	129	329	293.0
1980	480 (May)	1036	126	271	382.0
1981	600 (May)	1105	131	230	480.0
1982	"	1191	97	192	619.5
1983	"	1060	76	135	787.0
1984	810 (June)		65		1071.9
1985	810 (June)	[1400]	57		1428.8
1986	1035 (June)		47		1892.8
1987	1230 (July)				

a. Deflation is based on effective minimum wage for the whole year.

b. National Consumer Price Index is used rather than the Dar-es-Salaam wage earners' index for reasons explained in footnote 4.

Sources: Jamal (1982) and ILO (1988), supplemented by ILO (1967 and 1975).

harmful to both urban and rural sectors, as he would have no foothold in either sector and no incentive to improve his productivity. The transitory and migratory pattern of wage employment this engendered could only be broken by enabling the worker to earn a sufficient wage in the city to support his family. The wage increase granted between 1957 and 1964 was designed to curb circulatory migration. It pushed up the purchasing power of the minimum wage from an ability to buy the necessities for two adults to the ability to buy for a four-member family.[2]

During the second period, government's wage policy existed only in a negative sense, as government did very little to influence the wage structure, either by changing the minimum wage or by legislating the maximum permissible wage increases in the private sector. In the meantime—and no doubt because of the lack of policy—trade unions managed to get huge wage awards. The average wage increased perceptibly, with the nonagricultural average earnings rising from Sh. 163 per month in 1962 to Sh. 347 in 1967. These increases were necessarily confined to a small section of the population—those represented by powerful trade unions who were concentrated in larger firms. Thus, the notion of "labor aristocracy," comprising this small group of wage earners, arose. Professor Turner, who was asked at this time to advise government on its wages policy, made the strong case that wage earners were gaining at the expense of farmers by means of a trade squeeze. He compared this to the tendency for the primary producing countries' terms of trade to fall on the external market (ILO 1967).

Turner recommended a wage freeze. The government acquiesced and inaugurated a wage policy in 1967. Prior to this came the Arusha Declaration, which signaled a reordering of Tanzania's economic structures. The ensuing nationalizations and expansion in the number of parastatal bodies increased the government's power over wages. Thus, by 1968 the government controlled 53 percent of the wage employment and 57 percent of the wage bill in the country. This control increased continually throughout the early 1970s, reaching 65 percent and 70 percent respectively by 1976. The government used this power to implement its policy of wage restraint. The average wage increased altogether by only 8 percent between 1968 and 1971, the nonagricultural wage by 11.6 percent, and the minimum wage by a mere 20 shillings.

2. I should make it clear that in looking at African wages my prejudice is for a family wage. Berg, in his IILS article, argued strongly against it, viewing the migratory system "as the most efficient way to meet money needs in the village" (Berg 1966: 147). He also argued that the labor stabilization policy was costly, requiring large social overhead investments in housing and other facilities.

But the period of wage restraint could not survive the great increase in inflation that started around 1972. By this time the purchasing power of the minimum wage—fixed at Sh. 170 since 1969—had fallen to Sh. 145 in terms of 1969 prices. In the face of this, the government abandoned its wage-restraint policy and sought to compensate the wage earners by raising the minimum wage. Compared to the single adjustment in the minimum wage in the first nine years after its introduction, there were three increases between 1972 and 1975, raising the minimum wage successively from Sh. 170 to Sh. 380.

The government once again called in Professor Turner. Turner gave a clean bill of health to the incomes policy that had been in operation between 1967 and 1971, which of course he saw as "his" incomes policy; before the policy, 1960 to 1966, wages increased by around 20 percent per annum, whereas during the incomes policy, 1966 to 1971, they increased by only 5.5 percent per annum (ILO 1975: 210). Before the incomes policy, total employment declined at 3.4 percent per annum, whereas during the incomes policy, it increased by 3.1 percent per annum. As for inflation, Turner wrote, "The average annual rate of inflation in Tanzania, which had risen dangerously in the three years 1964 to 1967, was approximately halved in the four following years" (1975: 34).[3] However, everything was not rosy, as "the gap between employees' and peasants' living standards (and probably that between urban and rural living standards) continued to widen between 1967 and 1972, though at a very much slower rate than before the incomes policy" (1975: 39).

Turner, we should note, was writing his second report toward the end of 1974. By then the wages policy, with the raising of the minimum wage in 1972 and 1974, had been abandoned; Turner lamented this (1975: 41-42). The problem for the future, however, was what to do about wages given the "violent inflation" in the last few years (shown to be 53 percent in 1973 to 1974). The inflation that so disturbed Turner and that he tried to explain in terms of the "wage-price spiral" (1975: 48) was actually caused by a statistical error during the changeover to the metric system.[4]

3. The figures were as follows (percent per annum change in Dar-es-Salaam wage earners' retail price): up to and including 1963-1964, 1.3 percent; 1964-1965 to 1966-1967, 4.6 percent; 1967-1968 to 1970-1971, 2.9 percent (ILO 1967: 34).

4. The error exists in the Dar-es-Salaam wage earners' price index only. The full story can be found in ILO/JASPA (1982: Technical Paper 15). Around this time Tanzania changed to the metric system and prices started to be collected on the basis of kilogram. These prices were entered untreated in the Dar-es-Salaam wage earners' index along with the previous per pound prices. For example, the price of maizemeal was Sh. 0.40 per pound in December 1973 and Sh. 1.00 per kg in December 1974. These two prices were entered directly in the price index. Of such raw material are economic theories made and important policies recommended! Note that in Table 12-1 we have used the National Consumer Price Index as a deflator because of the problems with the Dar-es-Salaam wage earners' index.

Turner recommended that future wage policy aim to establish a "viable level of minimum wages" (1975: 62), which he took to mean the 1969 real wage plus 5 percent (1975: 50). Once such a wage was attained, "the broad aim should be to stabilize the real purchasing power of the legal minimum wage. This should be done by adding a cost of living allowance to the minimum wage periodically" (1975: 50). All this is rather curious, because the 1969 wage increase was Turner's main culprit in causing the widening rural-urban gap; now he was recommending a restoration of the real wage to the 1969 level. As for the rural-urban gap, in a rather confusing argument Turner suggested that "changes in the general level of food prices must be decided at the same time, and through the same central machinery as the average increase in wages for each forthcoming year" (1975: 56). He then said that "food prices and the prices of industrial goods and services should be kept in step" (1975: 56). One might wonder if this would not encourage the wage-price spiral that had so concerned him.

The minimum wage was raised soon after Turner's mission, and its value returned in real terms to the 1969 level. However, there then followed five years of remarkable wage restraint during which the minimum wage lost around one-third of its purchasing power. Between 1980 and 1981 there was another period of "catch up," followed by wage restraint, followed by some halfhearted attempts to raise the minimum wage. Tanzania by this time had indeed gone into the league of the hyperinflation countries, and the wage increases granted after the mid 1980s made hardly a dent in the erosion of purchasing power. Altogether the value of the minimum wage fell by almost *80 percent* between 1974 and 1986, while the value of the nonagricultural-sector wage fell by 70 percent within even a shorter period—1974 to 1983.

What is remarkable about Tanzanian wage trends is the turnaround in wage earners' fortunes around 1975. At precisely this time we see a reversal in agricultural prices, so that the wage-farm gap began to narrow sharply and finally went in favor of farmers.

Agricultural Prices

Farm prices of export crops have been controlled by the Tanzanian government for many years now. Over the years food crops also became subject to official control, with prices being set for most important crops, such as cereals, oilseeds, beans, and sugar. This left bananas, plantains, potatoes, sweet potatoes—fruits and vegetables—and eggs as about the only agricultural items traded without state intervention. However, it should be pointed out that even where prices were officially set, a large part of the produce was marketed outside official channels. In most cases a parallel market existed because marketing arrangements were lacking in particular localities, or because farmers could get a better price by supplying on the open markets.

As a criterion for setting prices, the government tried to ensure that farmers got a "fair" return for their crops. In the case of export crops, the department within the Ministry of Agriculture concerned with recommending agricultural prices, the Marketing Development Bureau (MDB), advocated that farmers should receive the highest possible proportion of the "export realization." In between export realization (or export parity, one might say) and what the farmers actually receive is the export tax, over which the MDB has no control. Its price recommendations are based on its forecast of export prices and accommodate themselves within the export tax structure.[5]

As far as food prices are concerned, the criterion of "fairness" to the farmer was tempered by the need for "fairness" to the consumer. The balance was struck by bringing in other considerations, such as trends in farmers' and wage earners' real incomes, the need to provide farmers an incentive to increase food production, and trends in farmers' input costs. Until 1973-1974, the desire to keep down urban food prices outweighed other considerations, and farm prices stagnated. But the food crisis in that year, combined with the poor performance of export volumes, led to a drastic change in policy. The prices of food crops were increased significantly in the 1974-1975 season, again in 1975-1976, and to a smaller extent in 1976-1977. In the next two seasons the prices remained steady, but they were again raised in 1979-1980. The full time series is shown in Table 12-2, where to carry the discussion forward we have also provided prices of maize and cotton as representative.

The series divides into two periods, with the break at mid 1970. Until then government policy could be said to have favored wage earners, with minimum wage being raised twice, altogether by 60 percent between 1963-1964 and 1974. In the meantime, food prices stagnated, increasing by just 16 percent. In 1974, food crop prices were raised significantly, by 36 percent, for the first time.

The swing to the farmer, discernible in 1974-1975, became a well-established trend in the next five years as the minimum wage stagnated, while food crop prices increased by 51 percent (1975 to 1980). The freeze on

5. It should be noted that since 1980 no export taxes have been collected from export crops.

Table 12-2. Indices of Crop Prices and Minimum Wage
in Current Terms, 1963-1988
(Selected Years)[a]

	Food Crop Prices	Export Crop Prices	Maize Prices	Cotton Prices	Minimum Wage	Memo Item: NCPI[b]
1963	100	100	100	100	100	100.0
1969-70	100	105	100	106	113	126.4
1972-73	105	109	100	110	160	152.6
1973-74	116	113	118	110	160	175.9
1974-75	151	128	179	145	227	216.4
1975-76	228	217	278	190	253	249.7
1976-77	253	295	286	191	253	272.9
1977-78	309	225	304	217	253	305.6
1978-79	315	214	304	230	253	343.5
1979-80	345	246	357	283	253	419.3
1980-81	354	262	357	320	320	535.5
1981-82	464	327			400	683.1
1982-83	534	380	625		400	873.7
1983-84	713	518	789	600	400	1154.9
1984-85	1055	717	1429	630	540	1553.6
1985-86					540	2063.5
1986-87					690	
1987-88	[2100]				820	

   a. All figures are in current terms because our objective is to compare trends. Deflating by a common price index would give similar trends.
   b. National Consumer Price Index (NCPI) is averaged for corresponding years.

Source: For all crop prices (including maize and cotton) between 1969-1970 and 1979-1980, Ellis (1982); 1963 from ILO/JASPA (1978: table 4.3); food crop and export crop prices for latter years from Marketing Development Bureau data as quoted in Ndulu (n.d.), and ILO (1988). Minimum wages from Table 12-1.

minimum wage, as we saw, resulted in a great erosion in its purchasing power. Partly in compensation, at the start of the 1980s there was somewhat of a swing back to wage earners, which proved short-lived. Wages in nominal terms doubled in seven years after 1980, whereas food prices doubled within four years and doubled again by 1987-1988 compared to 1984-1985. Maize prices show similar trends to food prices in general.

These findings may come as somewhat of a surprise to those who know the justly renowned work of Frank Ellis, which highlighted the catastrophic declines in Tanzanian farmers' terms of trade in the 1970s. Altogether, Ellis's estimates show that between 1969-1970 and 1979-1980 farmers' terms of trade (for all crops) fell by 36 percent (Ellis 1982: 273). However, in line with our argument of a turnaround at mid 1970, Ellis's figures confirm that the decline happened before 1974-1975. Farmers' terms actually improved (by 7.2 percent) in the next five years, led by an increase of 15.8 percent in real food crop prices. During the same years, the purchasing power of the minimum wage fell by almost a quarter. Two points are worth underlining regarding Ellis's analysis: (1) pricing policy changed in favor of farmers after 1975, and (2) farmers fared much better than wage earners. It is also worth noting that food crop prices remained strong beyond the period analyzed by Ellis. Thus, between 1980-1981 and 1984-1985 the figures given in Table 12-2, along with the cost of living data in Table 12-1, suggest that terms of trade of food crops declined at the most by 9 percent, while real wages practically halved.

A point of wider applicability should also be noted vis-à-vis Ellis's terms of trade analysis. Ellis calculated farmers' income terms of trade and found a decline of 33 percent, from which he tended to conclude that farmers' real incomes fell by 33 percent. This is erroneous. Terms of trade figures merely show what happened to the purchasing power of agricultural crops sold. If all crops are sold, then we may translate changes in the terms of trade to corresponding changes in real income. But where crops are used for own consumption, terms of trade calculations have no direct bearing on real income.[6]   In Tanzania, retained crops comprise one-half to two-thirds of a farmer's income properly counted (income gained from cash crops plus the

6. For example, if in two successive periods price terms of trade fell by 36 percent but farmers produced (and consumed) the same amount of produce, then while the so-called "income terms of trade" would indicate a 36 percent decline, in real terms there would be no decline at all. The purchasing power of crops fell, but since farmers were not selling crops but consuming them themselves, their real income was unaffected by the market prices. These points were first made by the author in ILO/JASPA's Basic Needs Mission report (ILO/JASPA 1982: Technical Paper 16) regarding Ellis's terms of trade analysis. In a later study (1984), Ellis took full note of this as well as of the finding about the fall in wages. That subsistence-oriented farmers are immune from government price policies forms the core of Goran Hyden's study (1980).

valuation placed on own-consumption). Any terms of trade decline would translate into a decline of only one-third or one-half as much in total income.

The full story from terms of trade analysis is that farmers' income terms of trade or real cash incomes declined by up to two-thirds between 1969-1970 and 1983-1984, which translates into a drop of 25 to 33 percent in total income. Compared to this, minimum wage declined by over 60 percent. If we carried the story up to the present period, we would find that things got even worse for the wage earners compared to the farmers in the second half of the 1980s.

THE FARM-WAGE GAP

No doubt after the above analysis we could dispense with showing what happened to the farm-wage gap. Quite obviously it declined. But it is still worth showing that the gap now stands in favor of farmers, and even at its height was much smaller than all the talk of "labor aristocracy" would have one believe.

Clearly, the important thing in deriving the rural-urban gap is not its exact magnitude, but the order of magnitude: Do we believe that an urban family depending on the minimum wage is worse off now than a farm family, or is the urban family considerably better off? Answering this question requires a perception of the two types of families in terms of their consumption levels. Let us approach the matter heuristically by noting the nondiscretionary expenditures a Tanzanian town family would have to incur simply to survive. The total of these expenditures would then be compared to the urban wage. The nondiscretionary expenditures that have to be included are food, transportation, housing, clothing, fuel, lighting, and water. Such calculations are normally referred to as a poverty datum line. Table 12-3 shows an estimate of a poverty line for a town-based family at the end of 1985, and the total comes to Sh. 1865. Compared to this, the minimum wage was Sh. 810. Food expenditure alone would over-exhaust the minimum wage by 64 percent. Even the average nonagricultural-sector wage (estimated at Sh. 1400 per month) would not have sufficed to buy the minimum food basket. As opposed to this, one would find that an average rural family provided at least 80 percent of its food from its own farm, and provisioned itself with housing, fuel, and water. If we value the farm family's own production at town prices, then we put a figure of Sh. 1330 as its income in 1985 (Sh. 1060 worth of food and Sh. 270 worth of other items). On top of this, rural families had around Sh. 150 in cash income. Thus, a Tanzanian farm family in mid 1980 was much better off than an urban family seeking to subsist on the minimum wage.

Table 12-3. Poverty Line for an Urban Family, December 1985
(Shillings per month)

Food	**1325**
Maizemeal (75 percent)	950
Beans (15 percent)	176
Fats (5 percent)	133
Sugar (5 percent)	67
Nonfood	**540**
Clothing	150
Rent	150
Fuel and Water	120
Transport	120
Total	**1865**
Memo Items	
Minimum Wage (Sh. p.m.)	810
Nonagricultural-Sector Wage (Sh. p.m.)	1400
Maizemeal Price (Sh. /kg)	13.75

Source: Estimates to provide a minimum consumption basket for a five-member family based on prices prevailing in Dar-es-Salaam in December 1985. In the case of food, the basket is set to provide 2,200 calories per capita day, with the composition as indicated.

Picking up the story of "labor aristocracy," in 1974, when the minimum wage was at its highest level in real terms, and, as previously mentioned, government policies tended to favor the wage earner, an average food basket of the type described in Table 12-3 would have cost around Sh. 170 per month— that is, minimum wage at its maximum represented the ability to buy two basic food baskets. Adding other nondiscretionary expenditures would exhaust the minimum wage. Compared to this, a farm family produced its own food (Sh. 170 per month) and had Sh. 40 worth of cash income. Obviously, one should not push such figures too far, but at the order-of-magnitude levels, they illustrate that even at the height of the rural-urban gap there was not all that much to choose between farmers and wage earners in Tanzania.

IMPLICATIONS FOR STRUCTURAL ADJUSTMENT

If by structural adjustment is meant restoring the price structure in favor of the rural areas, then that sort of adjustment had already occurred in Tanzania *prior* to 1984, when Tanzania finally adopted the structural adjustment program proposed by the IMF. The ILO had taken great pains to point this out in two reports (ILO/JASPA 1982; ILO 1988 [written in 1984]), advising government on the pros and cons of the IMF remedies. Notwithstanding that, the government finally acceded to IMF demands, not because it was convinced by the IMF's argument, but to receive the IMF stamp of approval, a requirement these days to achieve a resumption of aid from donors.

The policy changes Tanzania had to accept accelerated the turnaround in the rural-urban gap. Two policies in particular were important in this: devaluation and removal of subsidies on maizemeal. Between 1983 and 1986, the Tanzanian shilling declined from 13 to the dollar to 63 to the dollar. This decline enabled higher prices to be paid to farmers for export crops—the *raison d'être* of the devaluation remedy in developing countries. But devaluation also meant higher prices for the consumers as shilling prices of imports rose. These price increases contributed to the inflation in Tanzania in the last few years (Table 12-1), exacerbating the fall in real wages. Further, in 1985, Tanzania did what at one time was thought unthinkable and completely removed the subsidy on maizemeal, the major staple of the urban population. The price shot up 450 percent, increasing from Sh. 2.5 per kilo to Sh. 13.75 per kilo, and the purchasing power of the minimum wage dropped from 8kg of maizemeal per day to 2kg.

There is no doubt that as the adjustment program proceeds there will be further declines in the value of the minimum wage and further increases in food prices. To what avail? What do such huge shifts in relative prices achieve? And what are their social and economic implications? The answers to these questions require answering a series of prior questions: What is the rationale for structural adjustment programs? How far does the Tanzania situation correspond to this? And what is the expected outcome of structural programs compared to the actual?[7]

As we had noted at the start of this paper, the rationale for structural adjustment programs in Africa is the alleged existence of urban bias and the presumption that urban bias is wrong. This is the model that certainly guided

7. In keeping with the theme of the paper, the analysis here is confined to the distributional consequences of adjustment programs. For the pros and cons of devaluation—usually a key component of adjustment packages—see Van Arkadie (1983); Green (1983); Singh (1986); Jamal (1986); and Loxley (1986a). From a wider angle, see also Sharpley (1985) and Stewart (1986).

the IMF, though it is quite evident that no particular analysis was made of the Tanzanian case to establish its relevance. It was simply assumed that there was urban bias in Tanzania in the early 1980s, just as allegedly there was in most African countries. In fact, the Tanzanian situation at this time was quite different. Wages had been falling catastrophically, and food and export crop prices were rising since at least the mid 1970s. In other words, all that the structural adjustment remedy was supposed to accomplish had already happened.

Turning now to the last question—the expected outcome of structural adjustment programs versus the actual outcome—the expected outcome is predicated on the massive shifts in relative prices in favor of rural areas. In consequence, agricultural output should increase and migration slow down. What has been the actual outcome? It is too soon to say anything definite about output, although it would be surprising if it did increase to the extent hoped for by the Fund and its supporters. But given the oft-repeated point that in the typical African economy the constraint to output these days is not prices, but by the physical difficulty of growing and marketing agricultural crops, the lack of tools and fertilizers, and the breakdown of weighing scales, processing plants, and roads, increases in output are unlikely.

As for migration, there is no evidence that it is slowing down. Real wages have been falling for at least a decade, so one would expect trends to manifest themselves. To press the point, since in the last few years income differentials have gone in favor of the rural areas, migration should have reversed itself if orthodox theories are to be believed. There is no sign of this, and the reason is quite simple: migrants come to town for whatever cash income they can earn to supplement total family income. Thus, a migrant's decision is not made in terms of moving a whole family—in which case comparisons of expected income in rural and urban areas would be relevant—but in terms of moving one member of a settled family. The decision is based on the supplement to family income to be expected from migrating to town or staying on the farm. This decision still goes in favor of the urban areas, more so because a migrant can expect to add cash to his family's income.

The above discussion suggests that more and more we have to see African families as conglomerates that pursue diversified survival strategies. This was always so, but the economic crisis has intensified these tendencies. At least in the urban areas, survival strategies have given rise to structures that are fundamentally different from those that one assumed up to now. All families now straddle rural and urban sectors, formal as well as informal, and wage as well as nonwage. Only thus can we understand figures like those in Table 12-1. If the wage has fallen to 20 percent of its level and can buy only a few days' requirement of food for an average family, why is it that we do not see increasing malnutrition in urban areas? Why, with such a massive redistribution of income to rural areas, has there been no social turmoil? The answer stems from the fundamental transformations that have occurred in African economies in the last decade.

That hard-won structural characteristic of African countries—a stable wage-earning class—has disappeared, with families having to resort to diverse strategies to ensure survival. Three particular types of responses can be discerned: (1) grow food crops in urban areas, (2) allow informal trading activities by family members, and (3) make trips back to rural areas to collect food from the family farm.[8] Each urban family has become more rural than before by increasing its ties to the rural areas and undertaking garden farming on household plots. Each normally wage-earning family has become more "informal" as members have extended their activities into the informal sector. Thus, there has been a fusion of sectors—rural/urban, formal/informal, wage earner/farmer. The "side activities" that urban families now undertake quite likely contribute the bulk of their total income and explain why there is no obvious evidence of malnutrition in urban areas despite falling wages.

The "conglomeration" of African urban families thus understood also explains the lack of social unrest despite a massive redistribution of income in favor of the rural areas. If urban family members have lost, those operating in the informal sector have gained. Hence, gains and losses stay within the same family. If urban families thus do not protest rising food prices, it is because the beneficiaries are their own rural kin. If rural extensions of urban households cannot help out with cash, they can at least be cajoled into materializing a *debe* (can) or two of maize during the city folks' periodic visits to the family farm. Further, urban families do not protest rising food prices because they themselves have become subsistence farmers.

One point should be noted, however: While it is true that urban families have not suffered as much as implied by wage statistics, there is no doubt they have suffered considerable losses in their nonfood consumption. Unfortunately, the structural adjustment programs now in operation in Africa offer the prospect of more of the same because of their emphasis on devaluation to catch up with the real exchange rate. In consequence, urban incomes will fall even further, and urban areas will suffer further deindustrialization. Two outcomes that will not occur: labor markets will not clear, and migration will not stop. If unemployment and migration were to be cured by falling wages, that should have happened a long time ago with the catastrophic fall in urban incomes.

8. See Jamal (1985) on the case of Uganda.

CONCLUSION

All African countries have at some time or other been classified as urban bias economies, with urban wage earners posited as the main beneficiaries of this bias. That is still the operative model of African economies for most analysts. Indeed, the structural adjustment programs that aim to shift relative prices in favor of the agricultural sector are based on this perception of African economies.

We have shown with the case of Tanzania that the objective situation of most African countries is now totally different from that which existed even up to a few years ago. In the decade after independence the notions of urban bias and labor aristocracy had perhaps some relevance. The famous—or infamous—rural-urban gap has disappeared, as has the wage-earning class as a distinct entity. Economies have become fused, with distinctions such as rural/urban, formal/informal, and wage earners/farmers rendered increasingly redundant as each family has extended its outreach in the quest for basic survival.

The central problem is that the structural adjustment programs now in force in Africa take scant notice of these new structural characteristics of African economies. Given that urban wages have fallen and prices shifted in favor of rural areas, these structural characteristics actually resemble those envisaged by the structural adjustment programs. Yet there is no evidence that two of the more important objectives of structural adjustment programs have been attained in consequence, nor much hope that they will be attained in the future despite the likely further declines in urban incomes. Unemployment has not fallen in response to falling wages and migration has not stopped—let alone reversed itself—in response to the turnaround in the rural-urban gap. The only hope for African countries is that the third of the major objectives of structural adjustment programs—an increase in agricultural production—will be fulfilled as a result of the shift in prices in favor of the rural areas. The signs thus far are not encouraging.

V SEEKING A SOLUTION

In the final part of the book, five authors attempt to move us toward a solution to the debt crisis, which has become in effect a development crisis. In Chapter 13, Representative Bruce Morrison indicates what is perhaps the greatest barrier to achieving a policy solution—the absence of a meaningful debate in the United States over the role of the multilaterals. If a solution is to be reached, it will require concerted action by the largest creditor country (which, ironically, is also the largest debtor country). Congressman Morrison's call for using the General Capital Increase of the World Bank as a vehicle to debate international adjustment and development policies is a bold and refreshing initiative.

Chapters 14 and 15 seek to move us forward with specific proposals. In Rudiger Dornbusch's view, the evidence is clear that structural adjustment programs have not rejuvenated growth, and the debt service problem is, if anything, more serious in 1988 than it was previously. His solution is both radical and conservative: radical in that it involves a de facto moratorium on overseas payments, and conservative in that in lieu of foreign exchange banks would receive local currency with which they could invest domestically. This emphasis upon the private multinational sector is abandoned in Osvaldo Sunkel's proposal in favor of a National Development Fund, into which debt service obligations would be paid. Along with this reallocation of resources from foreign banks to domestic investment must go a reevaluation of development strategy, Sunkel argues. However, the new strategy he has in mind would bear little resemblence to the priorities implicit in the standard structural adjustment programs.

William Darity, Jr. offers a more dramatic solution in Chapter 16: debt forgiveness and tight regulations imposed upon international banks in their operations (the latter suggestion being at odds with the recommendations of Sacks and Canavan in Chapter 5). Incorporating some aspects of the Darity proposal in another form are the far-reaching suggestions of Michael P. Claudon, which incorporate the issues raised by most of the authors; indeed, his ideas can be viewed as a synthesis of the seminar's discussion of policy (though not necessarily a synthesis with which all would agree). The essential elements of the proposal include accepting that some bank losses must be absorbed by the public sector in creditor countries (taxpayer bailout), recognizing that debts will not be paid and an ordered debt forgiveness plan is required, and instituting safeguards that the current situation will not arise again.

Taken together, these proposals provide a way forward, and represent variations on a single theme: Something bold must be done if the indebted countries of the Third World are not to sink into a morass of intensifying poverty and the financial system is not to suffer a depression that will affect masses of people throughout the world.

13 FACING THE REALITIES OF THE DEBT CRISIS

Representative Bruce Morrison

It is educational to see how the debt issue has and has not been presented in the context of Congress and the U.S. political system. My experience with the debt problem tells a bit about the growth of—importance may be too strong a word—recognition within the Congress of the issue. I shall then examine current actions that are being taken, both in terms of the proposed innovations in the trade legislation Congress passed and the debate over the General Capital Increase (GCI) for the World Bank.

I was elected to Congress for the first time in 1982. My background is that of a legal aid lawyer. I am not a banker, not an economist—which will become evident, I suppose, as I proceed. I came to the Banking Committee not because it deals with Third World debt and banks, but because it has a subcommittee on housing, which addresses the critical problem of housing in the United States. The Banking Committee's first item of business after I became a member was IMF replenishment, on which we held hearings in early 1983. That process was enlightening. It is important to step back and realize the extent to which we have all become victims of word games and have failed to come to grips with the real problems. We have failed to acknowledge the problem or consider the range of solutions. The Banking Committee was treated to presentations, primarily from commercial banks, with the message

This chapter is a lightly edited version of the closing address delivered at the First Annual Conference on North-South Political-Economic Policy Issues, sponsored by the Geonomics Institute, Middlebury, Vermont, April 30, 1988. No effort has been made to conceal the informality of the oral presentation.

that we were dealing with a short-term liquidity problem, not a solvency problem or a fundamental dilemma. It was argued that the solution was short-term bridge financing and some economic reforms—structural adjustments, if you will—which would lead to a reemergence of high rates of growth and voluntary lending. This was, of course, in the midst of worldwide recession.

Following such testimony was a period of recovery, with a relatively high rate of growth in the United States and moderate rates elsewhere in the world. It is important to consider whether the rhetoric of the period was based on excessively optimistic assumptions. A number of us, feeling perhaps that all was not as it seemed, were skeptical and suggested two lines of questioning: How did we get into this circumstance in the first place, and do these numbers really work, can these countries really pay?

The first round of answers to such questions was essentially a rejection of the question: None of your damn business. We were lectured that our questions were impertinent, that we did not understand, that we ought to mind our business, which was merely to appropriate the necessary funds. The IMF replenishment was a commitment the United States had made, we were told, a multilateral agreement being presented to Congress as a formality. This view changed a bit over the course of debate when it became obvious that it was not a winning strategy in terms of votes. Eventually the administration was slightly more forthcoming and assured us all would be okay if we just plowed ahead. I daresay that I, as a new member of Congress, and also my colleagues—including Chuck Schumer from New York, who was one of the people asking a lot of questions—were novices; we clearly did not approach the issue with great expertise.

The rejection of our questions also induced rejection of examining whether all the lending in the 1970s had made any sense in the first place—whether the commercial bank lending binge in the developing world had ever had a fundamentally sound economic basis. That was the second question for which we received no answer. But I think those were and are the important questions, and they remain the questions we face now.

I would suggest that the central problem, the one we must solve before we come up with The Solution, is that we are lying to ourselves (or, if one is outside the system, being lied to). We have lied to ourselves about the scope, severity, and risks of the problem. We must recognize that there *will* be losses, and we must address who will bear them, who will decide who will bear them, and how they will be distributed over time. There are choices with respect to costs and burdens that are better or worse, depending on your point of view, choices that involve public debate, not the narrow interests of private banks or the private economy.

The myth the Reagan administration propagates is that this is a matter to be resolved by a mechanism that is allegedly a marketplace but is not a marketplace; interests are alleged to be private when they are in fact quite public, which leaves the public sector—Congress in particular—in a relatively noninfluential position, not because the issues are unimportant to our constituents, but because someone decided that the best way to serve certain interests at risk in the process was to pretend they were private matters not to be interfered with by Congress. This is the context in which the debate has moved to the present time.

The Banking Committee was dragged kicking and screaming through the IMF replenishment episode. I confess to having sold my vote in exchange for a housing bill, as did most Democrats that year, which explains why there was any IMF approval at all in Congress. Subsequently, a number of us were concerned about the issue and began to focus on it more actively, particularly Senator Bill Bradley, who, more effectively than anyone on the American political scene, has defined to Americans the costs in terms of debts that could not be serviced. I think the observations he made a few years ago are still critically important to recall, for they address how we can solve the problem within a political context.

One problem is the mismatch between the global economic situation and the nation-state political processes that must address the problem. In many ways, I feel schizophrenic. If I am in a meeting at which a global perspective is taken and a very careful and appropriate analysis of the problem from the global perspective is presented, I am struck that there are no votes for solutions from this perspective. It is difficult to explain the global perspective in terms that are helpful in organizing a domestic political majority (referring to members of Congress, not individual voters), which is a problem I assume occurs in all industrialized countries, as well as developing countries, whose perspective is not global, but nation-state.

According to Senator Bradley, from a domestic standpoint the debt crisis is first and foremost a problem of banks with insured deposits in the United States that have significant exposure to Third World loans. There was a time, say 1982, when we did not realize the full implications of the issue—for example, what insured deposits meant. It had been a long time since many banks failed. Banks began to fail again in 1982 and 1983, but the implications had not caught the public consciousness. Today it means something to say, "insured deposit banks are in trouble, or at risk, and might fail." Therefore, issue number one is that the taxpayer stands ultimately behind the banks with exposure. Banks have reduced their exposure since 1982 and are now better able to take a hit, for the ratio of these loans to capital is lower than it was, and precautions have been taken against default to a significant degree. To that extent, the problem is somewhat less severe now, but there is no question that there are banks, such as Manufacturers Hanover, that do not have the capital to withstand a reasonable scenario of default or moratorium from a number of the major countries. Related to exposure are financial security and stability. The problem is not just that the taxpayer might not pay, but also that we cannot sustain collapse by our largest financial institutions without effects rippling through the economy, which is clearly a legitimate concern.

The second issue relates to the trade bill that Congress passed and the President vetoed.[1] From 1981 to 1985, the loss in dollars in the balance of trade to Latin America was greater than the loss in trade to Japan. A significant trade surplus, which has become a significant trade deficit, arose from structural adjustment. This change in policy orientation in Latin America resulted in a decline of imports and import substitution and was not the result of export promotion. Our government has encouraged export promotion, which has had a very clear effect in terms of the U.S. Treasury. The reason our debt proposal is in the trade bill, aside from the convenience of having a vehicle to bring the issue forward, is because Third World debt is probably the largest contributor to the U.S. trade deficit (second only to the domestic budget deficit). Although Third World debt is far more important than other issues raised when the trade bill is discussed, other issues are more politically appealing. You can scarcely find in any article of the bill provisions or effects of the debt, even though as a dollar issue it is probably more important than the rest of the bill put together. The White House would not bother to veto the bill over the Third World debt issue, although it did threaten to at one point, and the President did cite our debt provision as one of just six provisions he objected to in his veto message.

Third is the issue of political civility. There is in Latin America a significant and very promising growth in democratic regimes. There is also less tolerance of human rights abuses and growth in the number of Latin Americans who participate in determining their political and economic systems. I have always taken such measures to be significant foreign policy goals of the United States. The ability of democratic regimes to function is very much related to their ability to deliver in terms of economic well-being for their populations. If fledgling democratic regimes fail to deliver economically—especially in Latin America, with its long history of military takeovers—we reasonably cannot expect democracy to spread or flourish. Regimes trying to

---

1. President Reagan eventually signed the trade bill on August 23, 1988. The bill, as signed, contains the identical language with respect to Third World debt that was in the bill the President initially vetoed and which Representative Morrison discusses here.

establish democratic traditions in the major countries of Latin America are unlikely to succeed without economic growth. You can interpret it as just a defense against the leftist extreme, but I believe it is a defense against the extremes on both sides, in the hope that the political systems will evolve into truly open and successful economies, which is unlikely if they are threatened by the debt problem.

I do not naively say that debt relief would produce dramatic growth, and democracy would then be easy to sustain. We face difficult challenges no matter what actions we take, but I think it is the difference between some and none in terms of chances. If the problem is not alleviated, there is no chance of long-run political stability. If some pressure is diffused, then there are reasonable prospects for the growth of democracy, which will also stimulate other important elements of free activity in the economic sphere. Central to a solution, however, is determining how burdens will fall and how choices will be made.

When I was in Chile, I had an interesting conversation on human rights and economics with a businessman who supported the Pinochet regime. Regarding the problem of human rights abuses, he said, "I will concede that people may be tortured or imprisoned without charge; I know of no one personally, but I will assume that it does happen. But the one thing I want to stress is that when actions are taken to improve the situation, I do not want to upset the economic model that we have here. This government has the economics right." (No pun intended.) I asked him what it meant to have the government economic model "right." He answered, "The right balance between public and private." I took a deep breath and asked, "Where is that written? Where is it written that we know the correct balance of these questions of equity and efficiency and long-run versus short-run benefits?"

My sense is that political scientists, economists, and all the rest of us have been debating those questions in every country around the world for at least a century, and yet he was saying, "Get it right." Without democratic processes in the countries involved, who will decide how to allocate the burdens of these problems? Without democratization there is no long-term credibility for U.S. policies; we cannot mobilize support for policies in the United States unless there are democratic governments with legitimacy, and hard choices should be made in accordance with the preferences of those who have to live with them. That sounds idealistic, but it seems to me the only way for development to function with real grass-roots support.

The costs borne by developing countries are important and affect U.S. resolve to generate a solution to the debt problem. The major reason there has been no significant breakthrough on the debt problem is the policy of the

Reagan administration, which is the policy of Treasury Secretary James Baker. We wind up playing word games that affect reactions of the World Bank, the IMF, and commercial banks. The debate is often downright silly. I will recount an example of this from hearings before our subcommittee. David Mulford, the Assistant Secretary to Mr. Baker, testified before us on the Mexican bond plan, praising the reductions in the stock of debt and interest service costs (before the actual auction took place, of course). I asked, "Does that mean you are supportive of mechanisms that lead to debt relief?" He said no. I then asked, "Won't banks take losses not only when they buy this debt, but also, if they tendered their debt, when they mark down the value of what they tendered on their books?" Again, he said no, but that some would have a reduction in profits. I do not repeat this exchange to make fun of Mr. Mulford, although the temptation is great. I repeat it because this is the level to which we have sunk in the U.S. political process when discussing such issues; we are playing word games over issues that are extraordinarily important to the future of all debtor countries.

And yet, the preservation of mythology seems to be central to the Baker policy, which is never to admit there is a significant problem of payment. It is a "muddling-through" policy that never acknowledges that people are going to suffer losses. I think the most important step we can take is to break through that mythology, to begin recognizing that losses are there. It is critically important to identify the real losses, which means, at least for the political process in the United States, the risk to the taxpayer, the loss of jobs affected by the trade imbalance, and the national security concerns prompted by political stability in Latin America. We are talking about real concerns and real costs. Who within the U.S. political process would say it is more important for the banks to get paid 100 cents on the dollar than for debt problems to be solved? In that context, it seems to me, virtually no one votes for the banks.

That is not to say this is solely a matter of bank bailout; rather, it is a matter of letting the banks take their losses. It is important to examine the origin of the problem, to return to the great boon in banking and development, the recycling of petrodollars, the Walter Wriston (with some help from Henry Kissinger) gift to the world. Accepting the notion that commercial bank lending was the magic wand of development did no one a favor. I question whether commercial banks are the appropriate vehicle for development finance at all; I do not think they are equipped for it. They mismatched short-term lending to long-term needs, which was fine for trade, but not for development. Problems were inherent in the lending from the outset.

In the course of getting from there to here, bankers made a lot of money. They tend not to remind us of the extraordinary amounts earned on these loans and restructuring fees. Although profits have been whittled down and spreads are relatively small now, stockholders did not do badly either during the period of lending. It is not a matter of taking revenge on the banks, but we need not weep for them; the last thing we need is to feel sorry for them. Some U.S. political leaders have very much encouraged such sympathy.

As an aside, I have never understood why the developed world thought it in its interest to help OPEC finance its cartel prices of oil, which is essentially what the recycling of petrodollars involved. It was deemed appropriate to allow OPEC to shift its credit risk to U.S., European, and Japanese banks, a choice we did not have to make, one that in effect facilitated the raising of oil prices by OPEC. Public policy allowed the accumulation of Third World debt such that commercial banks took risks, profits were made as a result of those risks, and the risks have now come home to roost.

I think banks do recognize that losses must be sustained. They may need help, certainly in regulatory terms, to make it easier, and there is interest from creditor country governments, including the United States, in providing that help. But it will take leadership. It is a unilateral disarmament problem, one that will not be solved without political leadership, which takes us back to getting the executive branch of the government to admit that we need more than a "muddling-through" approach like the failed Baker Plan. Everyone in the world knows the Baker Plan does not hold the answer, everyone, that is, except Mr. Baker—and he too probably knows it, but just will not admit it. Someone has to be clever enough to write a new Baker Plan that Mr. Baker can introduce to get himself off the hook, but I do not think that will happen before the election. The issue is what the next U.S. administration is willing and able to do, which brings us to two further issues: (1) what we did on the trade bill and what we hope to accomplish, and (2) where that leaves us with respect to the General Capital Increase.

A little over a year ago, I filed a bill (similar bills were filed by Representative John LaFalce of New York and Senator Paul Sarbanes of Maryland) proposing U.S. negotiation with other OECD countries for the creation of a multilateral debt facility. The idea is simple and does not originate with me or the other authors of the legislation, but with Peter Kenen. It can be structured in a variety of ways, but the facility fundamentally involves creation of a new multilateral institution limited to treating commercial debt. The official debt is a different problem that requires a different solution (which the trade bill addresses). It would be a public-sector, nonprofit institution that is problem-oriented, not a speculator looking to make an arbitrage profit.

The underlying philosophy is the notion that this is a problem with implications reaching far beyond the debtor-creditor relationship between the banks and the countries. It is a public-sector problem that needs a public-sector response. The function of the institution would be to buy the loans from the banks. Determining the price to be paid is a challenge yet to be resolved.

As a benchmark, one has the current secondary market, though it is not a perfect guide. I think a solution can be found through negotiating the price. The purpose is to buy the loans at a market-driven discount price and in exchange give the banks cash or a cash equivalent through the use of an instrument that can solve some of the bank's regulatory problems, something that can be written down over time so that losses can be absorbed slowly. The instrument would have to be such that it could be sold at any time in a market at par to get liquidity, because that is what the banks need. Banks could exit with reduced losses, and taxpayers will absorb part of those losses, because the government will get less tax revenue from banks that have reduced profits. That is a taxpayer bailout, according to Baker, and constituted his major criticism of the idea. Of course whenever the banks take these losses, and surely they will, the taxpayer must inevitably absorb part of the loss through reduced taxes paid to the government.

A major issue is whether banks will voluntarily participate. That depends on the attractiveness of the regulatory relief compared to what would happen if they held their debt, and the extent to which banks that do not participate are forced to mark down these loans without getting the regulatory relief. There is an appropriate and perhaps escalating collection of carrots and sticks to use to induce participation.

The second purpose of the institution is to provide the benefit of the discount to developing countries by passing it on in whatever form of reissued security the institution chooses. Beyond that, the purpose is also to provide a mechanism for restructuring the obligation in a way that is more appropriate to the long-term development strategies of the country. People talk a lot about "new money," but if new money means commercial bank lending, they are talking about something that does not exist, and perhaps never will exist. New money in the form of less money to pay out every year is just as good—in fact, it is better because, in addition to being the same amount, you never have to pay it back. A reduction of $5 billion or $3 billion or even $1 billion a year in debt service payments is better than an equivalent loan of new money of the same amount. So, it seems to me that any new money, except for lending by the multilateral institutions, would have to come from such an institution. There is a lot of flexibility here if one wants to use it, a variety of ways to use the restructuring process as an incentive for countries to reevaluate development strategies. There are also options that Rudiger Dornbusch (Chapter 14) and

Osvaldo Sunkel (Chapter 15) suggest that could be incorporated, since they are consistent with the intent of the debt strategy in the trade bill.

This multilateral institution does have a conditionality role. Debt relief alone will not solve the problem. Countries have to make productive use of the resources that are saved by not having to make interest payments or they will not grow. The difference between the conditionality, if one wants to call it that, involved in this debt facility and what we have had up to date is that it has a longer-term restructuring development focus and is positive as opposed to negative; it involves relief of a burden and is directing that relief in investment-oriented ways. That has a lot more positive possibilities than the policy that has characterized the structural adjustment process to date, which was squeezing and then squeezing a little harder to see if you could send out more dollars to your creditors.

How does one pay for such an endeavor? This depends exactly on who holds the paper that will be sold, the extent to which the new multilateral serves as a brokerage function, and the extent to which it serves as an institution that buys and holds. At the extreme, I point out that we can capitalize the World Bank an additional $75 billion, which has been decided and achieved already, with relatively modest paid-in capital. This level of financial commitment could tackle the problems of even the most troubled countries. The 25 percent of the GCI allocated for structural adjustment lending would go a long way toward establishing the new facility, provided the facility passes off the restructured obligations to a secondary market and does not try to hold all the debt by itself. Thus, it is not a problem that requires taxpayers of developed countries to contribute more than they currently do.

What does this all mean with regard to the World Bank and the General Capital Increase? Within the trade bill there is a provision calling for a study to address the problem of official debt. The study is based on the fundamental proposition of a distribution of a new issue of Special Drawing Rights (SDRs) of the IMF, which would be allocated based on various official debtors' indebtedness and inability to pay. It targets those countries with very high levels of official debt compared to their GNPs, and it is intended to be a mechanism by which the SDRs can be used as a vehicle for debt repayment. It is essentially a debt cancellation or debt forgiveness scheme, presented in a way that does not undermine the official rhetoric with respect to whether or not such forgiveness is granted. The study has not generated much controversy because there is a fairly widespread belief that significant restructuring of official debt, especially in Africa, is absolutely necessary. The problem has not drawn much attention in the U.S. political context because it addresses the African problem rather than the Latin American problem, and the U.S. government is far more focused on the latter. A growing group within the U.S. Congress sees the problem of official debt in Africa to be as important as commercial debt, but the two problems need to be pursued on different tracks because each has different political constituencies and unique problems. For example, how commercial debt and the fight with banks will be handled is a significant factor that is not relevant to the official debt.

The General Capital Increase is the next step after having the trade bill passed. The facility that I described was laid out in the trade bill, and the Secretary of the Treasury was directed to enter into discussions with OECD countries about it. However, as a result of a compromise in the Senate, the Secretary was given the opportunity to make a finding. Were he to find that the proposal depreciated the debt, he could decline to enter into those discussions. I assume that Secretary Baker had the letter already written, and we would have received it shortly thereafter had the President signed the trade bill.[2] But it was also a recurring obligation; the next administration would be required to consider the trade bill again within twelve months after it originally passed. It would have moved the process forward to put it on the desk of the next Secretary of the Treasury. We are back to the GCI.

Whether or not the facility proposal moves forward, and it may not because of the "escape hatch" that may be utilized by the Treasury Secretary. I hope the idea of debt relief will be incorporated into the legislation authorizing the GCI. The General Capital Increase is a significant new commitment being asked of developing countries for Third World development, and it is rather bizarre that the request is proceeding as if there were no questions about what ought to be done. The approach is similar to the IMF increase in 1983, with officials saying, "Yes, we are concerned about debt, and yes, there are these questions of development, but we need this money." It is not just the Jim Bakers or the Barber Conables of the world who deserve the blame for this; developing countries have also contributed to the problem.

The governments of developing countries have treated the GCI as needed resources and have not used it as a vehicle for debate. It is as if they believe they will not get the money unless they are respectful and do not make a fuss. A fuss *should* be made about how the money will be used, to what extent the capital increase is related to any relief from the debt problem, and to what extent the funds are going to be used in the structural adjustment process (25 percent of the GCI is slated for structural adjustment lending). The lack of

---

2. At the time of publication, the trade bill had been signed into law and Secretary Baker had left the administration. He was to be succeeded by former Senator Nicholas Brady, to whom the mandate to initiate multilateral discussion to create a debt facility now applies.

discourse is unfortunate; people want these issues to be debated in a constructive way. The GCI should not be allowed to pass on the notion that it is necessary and therefore cannot be held up.

Why is this a legitimate debate? First, World Bank and regional development bank resources are being laundered to pay current interest. Balance of payments lending is really debt finance, and it extends to project lending as well. Fast-disbursing project lending is simply more money to be paid back to the banks, and so there is no question—and no question in the figures—that the World Bank and other multilateral institutions are taking up an increasing share of the burden, which amounts to a taxpayer bailout. The taxpayer bailout has the multilateral development banks pick up the slack from the commercial banks and pay the money back, in effect turning a commercial debt into an official debt. The situation is similar to the first round of the debt crisis (1982-1983), when private obligations of industries within countries were nationalized as a result of strong-arm tactics by banks.[3]

In practice, the Third World debt is being socialized when the World Bank and the Inter-American Development Bank pick up these obligations, which raises the issue of whether or not we are going to bail out the banks. That debate ought to be carried on with respect to the General Capital Increase because we need a debt strategy not just a GCI. The World Bank, without any legislation in Congress, is certainly in a position to devise a debt strategy, but it has yet to do so.

There is another reason why this is a legitimate debate and why a debt strategy is necessary before $75 billion in new capital is committed to the World Bank. What about the World Bank's credit standing? What about its ability to collect its debts? Such questions are rarely discussed, as if the seniority of official debt implies that somehow it will always be paid. The African case is a prime example that this is not true. If this problem is not addressed at some point, the World Bank will stop being paid and will face a deterioration of its loan portfolio. We should not throw $75 billion more into the ring unless we have a plan to avoid deterioration of the World Bank's credit standing. Once again, the taxpayers of developed countries have a legitimate interest in asking for a realistic debt strategy.

The interests of LDCs and taxpayers in the developed countries overlap on this point. It is a somewhat dangerous road to walk, because it stirs up anti-foreign feelings and opposition to appropriations of any kind for the World Bank or other multilateral institutions. On the other hand, debate over the GCI is a vehicle through which one could put pressure on those who want to see it

3. See the discussion of this point in Chapter 3 by Weeks.

enacted—banks and developed world governments. We need meaningful political discussion or perhaps even political confrontation. There is always the possibility of the major debtors refusing to cooperate, which would force confrontation and debate. However, there is very little evidence of that occurring.

There is another possibility: Use such debates about World Bank funding as a vehicle to force the issue. This is a real political opportunity, an opportunity we must seize, for it will not come again soon. The GCI is essentially a request for time, five or six years during which the World Bank can continue muddling through. The debt collapse may come before then, the moratorium may come before then, the concerted action may come before then. We should act now. I hope people will see the debate over the GCI not as a terribly dangerous attack on the World Bank, but as an opportunity to put political pressure on those who could virtually overnight change the terms of the debate. I shall put my energy over the next few months into that effort, and we shall see what happens, if I have any allies. I hope those concerned about the issue, those eager for new terms of the debate, will support this effort.

14 FROM ADJUSTMENT WITH RECESSION TO ADJUSTMENT WITH GROWTH

Rudiger Dornbusch

Where does the debt problem stand today, and how does structural adjustment fit into it? I consider these questions in two ways. First, I review the belief in 1982 about the debt problem, that it would go away by itself. How have views changed now that we have reached 1988 and know the debt problem is alive and well? Second, what are the good stories one might tell today, and why are they not really right? I then will address how the "generic" solution would work, focusing specifically on a cure for Mexico. I conclude that recycling of interest payments with massive structural adjustment is probably the best business proposition on the debt front today.

Why was the debt problem of 1982 different from that of the 1930s? Why did we believe we could solve the crisis in 1982 when the problems of the 1930s had resulted in a major worldwide debt crisis, with countries going into moratoria and suspending debt payments for ten to fifteen years? We can return to IMF literature to uncover the issues that were on people's minds and lips in

This chapter is a lightly edited version of the keynote speech delivered at the First Annual Conference on North-South Political-Economic Policy Issues, sponsored by the Geonomics Institute, Middlebury, Vermont, April 28, 1988. No effort has been made to conceal the informality of the oral presentation.

1982. We must consider the following commonly held beliefs to determine the ways in which they were wrong.

1. The world economy was in an unusually poor situation from the point of view of debt service.
2. The debtor countries were extraordinarily mismanaged, and just shaping them up would do much to put them back into a position of debt service.
3. If one did not collaborate with the system of adjustment and rolled-over debts, then the return to voluntary lending somewhere down the road was quite inconceivable.

THE WORLD ECONOMY

In August 1982, when Mexico went into moratorium, the world economy was quite obviously in the worst possible shape for debtor countries. Interest rates had reached 18 percent for federal funds, the highest level in recorded history—and those were *real* interest rates. Any debtor country that had interest payments geared to short-run interest rates inevitably had a skyrocketing—doubling, tripling—of interest payments in dollars. At the same time, the world recession, the worst since the 1930s, meant that export demand for manufactures from developing countries had declined, and the real prices of commodities, chief exports for many of the debtor countries, had fallen dramatically. Debtor countries were squeezed between the sharp increase in interest payments and the large decline in export earnings available to make those payments. Inevitably, the money was not there, and Mexico was the first to announce a moratorium.

If you examine the history of the Mexican moratorium, your hair will stand on end. The moratorium was on and off for three months, and every time Silva Herzog was about to board a plane to Washington, someone would come up with $100 million, they would cancel the plane, and then start the whole process over a month later. In any event, Mexico did go into moratorium during this significant deterioration of the world economy.

From the 1982 perspective, it was easy to say the situation *had* to improve: record-high interest rates could only come down, and record-low (since the 1930s) commodity prices could only go up. In fact, commodity prices were certain to increase because they are highly cyclical, declining sharply in real terms during a recession and recovering very sharply when demand in the world economy picks up again. Every recession is followed by a recovery, which means growth in demand for manufactured exports, and, more importantly, rising real prices of commodities, resulting in rising export earnings with which to pay the interest. The world economy, then, had a very good story: The situation was so bad, it inevitably had to get better.

With regard to debtor countries, there had been exemplary mismanagement. If you made a list of all the things you should not do as an economist, all had been done. In Argentina, the real exchange rate had been overvalued by 50 percent, almost as much as we have experienced under the Reagan administration. Capital flight totaled $30 billion; the central bank borrowed in New York and gave the money to locals, who were taking it back to Miami. In Mexico, the story was very much the same. In the middle of a large increase in revenues prompted by world oil price increases, the Mexican government ran a current account deficit that exceeded the increase in oil revenues by enough to produce a debt crisis. Every debtor country had a story of exchange overvaluation, capital flight, excessive consumer goods imports, and large budget deficits, which exacerbated the difficulties. Debtors had a wonderful time because exchange rate freezes were used to stop inflation, and real appreciation offered a standard of living people were not earning but financing by borrowing abroad.

With hindsight, all of this was quite apparent in 1982. It was quite clear that if debtor countries got their acts together, then debt service would be much easier, exchange rates would be more realistic, and, as a result, export earnings would increase, and overly large imports and budget deficits would be contracted, thus reducing financial instability. The list of all the good things that could be accomplished was endless, and included cutting the inflated public sectors, where governments had entered into so many kinds of productive activities that the Brazilian government even owned perfume parlors and motels. In short, the 1982 story—adjustment in debtor countries—implied moving them into a better position for debt service.

The third argument, very persuasive, is that any debtor country faced a choice: It could collaborate with the banks, the IMF, and the U.S. Treasury in keeping its debts current, borrowing some of the interest owed, or it could walk out. Nobody actually said you could walk out, but everybody said, "Imagine what would happen if you walked out." Anyone who walks out offends the world capital market and thus would have a very hard time coming back. Two or three years later, everyone would remember the country that did not even discuss servicing its debt, that suspended debt service entirely. Such countries could not attract new lending. Developing countries need external resources to finance development, resources that supplement domestic saving to finance high rates of investment, one of the basic sources of growth. If one walks away from the world capital market, closing that source of financing, one is condemned to much poorer performance; the long-run consequences for external financing would be very negative.

Because of the three persuasive arguments, all the debtor countries stayed in the game and entered into the process of rescheduling that now has become so familiar. Every year, one goes to Washington, stops at the IMF, gets an adjustment program, goes across the street, gets a structural adjustment loan, stops at the Treasury, gets the blessing, takes the shuttle to New York, and talks to the banks about the fact that one quarter of the money has to come from them (the other quarter comes from the IMF and the World Bank, and the other half has to be earned with trade surplus and good conditionality). The process has been underway for the past five years. One can now question if we have in fact observed what was believed in 1982.

1. Has there been the anticipated return to voluntary lending, with banks calling Brazil and Mexico saying, "We have not made a loan to you for a long time; could we come over and discuss one of those good loans we used to make in the 1970s?"
2. Has streamlining policies in debtor countries, to the extent that it has happened, in fact made it much easier to service these debts, and has it enhanced financial stability, as was believed in 1982?
3. Has the world economy done its part through strong growth, declining interest rates, and a recovery of real commodity prices?

The fact is that none of these three has happened, and as a result the debtor countries today look worse than they did in 1982. Debt ratios today are higher than they were in 1982. In 1982, people said, "After five years of adjustment, you will be reducing your debt ratios because you will be reducing your interest payments and your output will be growing; debt ratios will be lower." But today debt ratios are much higher than in 1982 on any conceivable criterion. With regard to financial stability, inflation is much higher today than in 1982 in virtually all debtor countries; in fact, we are seeing the reemergence of a long-extinct species: hyperinflation. Although hyperinflation had not been seen for forty years, it has reemerged in Latin America as a byproduct of the debt crisis. If we look at per capita income growth, the 1982 argument was that debt service was not inconsistent with moderate progress in the debtor countries (on the contrary, some said). In truth, per capita income has fallen sharply, and, if one excepts Brazil, the capital income in Latin America is 10 percent lower than it was in 1980.

Thus, on any of a number of criteria, debtor countries have not done so well: they are poorer debtors today than in 1982; voluntary lending is more remote than it was even in 1982; and the world economy, while it has been basically okay, has not made debt service much easier. I want to address each of these points because it is important to look ahead and consider whether any of the three is likely to change.

The world economy did everything that was promised when we look at GNP growth of industrialized countries. The 1982 expectation was that growth would average 2.5 to 3 percent over the next five years. In fact, output growth has been more than 3 percent, more than the IMF forecast in 1982. On that basis, debtor countries have experienced larger growth in their manufactured exports and in fact have expected to experience real commodity price increases. The latter has not happened; real commodity prices, until late last year, continued to fall year after year, until they reached the 1930s level in 1987. That is a particularly important factor for those countries with a heavy concentration in exports of primary commodities. Even though the world economy was recovering for those countries—the Philippines, Peru, Bolivia, and those in Central America—export revenues declined, and subsequently their ability to service debts became precarious. The outlook deteriorated for those countries after 1982. Even today, though we have had some increase in real commodity prices over the last year, it has been so moderate that the levels are still below 1982.

The third element, real interest rates coming down from the very high levels of the U.S. monetary contraction and inflation-fighting, has in fact occurred. But rates did not decline as much as was anticipated in 1982. The 1982 story was that inflation-fighting inevitably would succeed, and interest rates by now would fall to 1 or 2 percent. Although inflation-fighting has succeeded, real interest rates have averaged more than 4 percent since 1982, and that more-than-4 percent is far higher than the average of the last sixty years. Nobody could guess in 1982 how high real rates would continue to be; even today there is a real chance they will start going up again.

So, the world economy did not quite do its thing, particularly on the interest rate side, which of course is central for debt service. Nor did it perform with regard to commodity prices, which are central for a large number of small countries and for those with low per capita income levels. Beyond that, it is a special story. If you talk about oil, Mexico in 1986 experienced a 50 percent decline in oil prices; but on the other side is Brazil, the importer of oil, which has the advantage of so large a decline in oil prices. The only systematic factors we can retain are interest rates, nonoil commodity prices, and growth in the world economy.

POLICY ADJUSTMENT

The second element of the 1982 list was policy adjustment—shaping up the debtor countries to put them into a better position of debt service. What went wrong? The 1982 story was very plausible: there were large budget deficits, overvalued exchange rates, and an excessively large public sector, all of which cried out for shaping up. The expectation was that if you shaped up, financial stability would follow, ability to service debts by exports would be greater, and, with the public sector reduced, more efficient industry would mean better use of resources. In short, everything should look much better. In fact, everything looks much, much worse. For all of Latin America, growth rates are just about the opposite of what they were over the last thirty years. If for per capita they were plus three, now they are minus three. If for inflation they were twenty, now they are 100.

In retrospect, nobody should have said that adjustment was such a joyful activity. If we take a drunkard and say, "Good news: We are going to sober you up," nobody would expect him to report for a job at Citibank in a clean shirt the next morning. Sobering up is a very hard exercise, made more difficult because rather than having external resources to assist the adjustment process, debt service meant that resources were going out, putting extra strain on the adjustment. The extra strain was felt in two areas in particular. First, to gain external competitiveness and have an increased level of exports, countries had to have large real depreciation—in fact, all the debtor countries had real depreciation on the order of 40 or 50 percent. To have an effective real depreciation, one must cut the real wage. Selling more abroad means people are willing to work for less. Real depreciation is not something mystic, it is essentially putting domestic labor on sale, which has two effects: (1) the reduction in domestic costs in terms of dollars means increased export potential, increased export volume growth, and (2) the problem of people who earn lower real wages spending less on domestic goods and services when the purchasing power of labor is cut. A slowdown or recession of domestic activity is the inevitable counterpart of the large and rapid real-wage cutting that was experienced there.

The second strain from sobering up results from the attempt to cut wages in a situation of indexation and even more from the budget consequences of the turnaround on debt service. Until 1982, debtor countries did not experience much inflation because they did not print money to finance budget deficits—they borrowed in New York. On the import side, borrowing provided the resources, and the home economy was never touched by recession; everyone felt better. After 1982, the resources to service the debts had to be found. There are three ways of doing that: (1) raise taxes, which was as unpopular as it is here, (2) cut current expenditures, which was as impossible as it is here, and (3) cut investment spending in the public sector, which was done on a massive scale. Latin American debts were basically serviced by not investing. Governments would cancel investment projects and use the resources to make the external payments. To turn the pesos into dollars, a large depreciation would follow.

Another source of financing was printing money. Starting in 1982, there was no more external financing of budgets; financing shifted to the home scene. Countries with domestic money markets, like Brazil, started issuing domestic debt to get the currency with which to service the external debt. The growth in external debt was replaced by a mushrooming of domestic debt. Countries that did not have a capital market, like Argentina and to some extent Mexico, simply issued money, and wound up with even larger inflation. How extreme was the inflation experience? Bolivia at one end went to 5000 percent inflation per year and only stopped the hyperinflation by stopping external debt service. The conditions of the government finance changed, as they no longer had to print money to pay the interest. Argentina only went to 3000 percent inflation at the peak, but is almost back to that level this year. Brazil made it to a high of 1200, which it may repeat. Mexico had an exceptionally high inflation rate, 18 percent in December alone. Inflation is not the result of domestic mismanagement, where governments suddenly have been seized to do a lot of spending, but rather occurs because those governments used to borrow and now must pay interest. They do not have the taxes with which to pay, they do not have the option of expenditure cuts, so what does not come out of investment cuts basically comes out of printed money, or the "inflation tax."

Printing money has made Latin America financially very unstable and has aggravated the problem of debt service by bringing about capital flight. For every dollar of interest that is being paid, there is fifty cents of capital flight because of the financial instability it induces. How can a country sustain capital flight? Only by having a large current account surplus, which means either that people do not consume or do not invest, the government does not invest, private firms take their money abroad and do not invest, and the workers' real wage is cut to generate the trade surpluses to earn the dollars to finance the capital flight. That is essentially what Latin America and the Philippines have been experiencing. Over the last five years, in an attempt to cope with the debt problem through domestic adjustment, governments have muddled through a process they expected in five to seven years would have basically disappeared, with countries back to borrowing normally, somewhat more washed and well-behaved, somewhat chastened by the experience, but basically back to the 1970s. Today, we are further away from the 1970s than ever, and one must ask what comes next.

One could say, "Well, let's start all over again with the world economy. Can we tell a good story this time?" We cannot tell a good story. The expectation is for a slowdown in the world economy. The U.S. budget is going to be cut with little offset through European expansion; Japan is helping with its growth, but not enough to make up for Europe's lack of growth. The restraint on world growth will come inevitably in the United States. A big, strong, sustained world growth of the measure one could predict in 1982 is very unlikely today. I am not saying we will have another Great Depression, but 2.5 percent growth per year on average is probably optimistic; there will not be a world boom that will make this debt problem go away.

REAL COMMODITY PRICES

We know today that for structural reasons real commodity prices are permanently lower than they were in the 1960s and 1970s, partly because of high real interest rates, partly because to earn the foreign exchange with which to service debts, all debtor countries had large real depreciation, which made them much larger exporters of all their goods, competitively lowering real commodity prices. The low real price of commodities is thus a byproduct of the attempt to service debts. We also have agricultural policies in the United States and Europe that lower the real prices of agricultural commodities. There will be some increase inevitably on the commodity side, but one cannot expect too much.

In 1973, we had a wonderful year of 5 percent interest rates and 12 percent inflation, which is what every debtor wants: the debts melt away because the real interest rates are negative. There is very little expectation of that in the future, and the opposite is in fact expected. The Federal Reserve is itchy every morning, saying, "Is inflation coming? Should we raise interest rates to kill it before it comes?" A possible scenario for the U.S. economy is a recession induced by tight money and high real interest rates. No one is willing to predict that the Federal Reserve will preside over a debt liquidation by high inflation and easy money. Thus, the world economy, even if I slightly overstate the case (I do not think I do), is not going to make a major difference to the debt crisis. Optimistically, you can say there will be no decisive change; very optimistically, you can say we are going to have high real interest rates, with the result that all debtor countries will walk away from the debts.

FURTHER ADJUSTMENT

We can say, "For the last five years, you guys have not been doing the push-ups right, and now we are really going to start adjustment. We want serious liquidation of public-sector enterprises. We see budget deficits—they must go. The real exchange rates are not right—you must depreciate more. And we want you to export more to and import less from the United States, so that you get more dollars with which to pay your interest." Well, that advice is not exactly what people have in mind. On the trade side, we certainly already feel that the developing countries (at least the debtors) are doing much too well on their exports. When Mexico tries to export to the United States, sixteen lawyers approach every carload to find out if there is possibly a bit of dumping involved. We want them to open their markets to imports from us, which means they will not have the foreign exchange to pay interest, because they are using the foreign exchange to buy our goods. We do not have a persuasive story of adjustment not having been tried seriously, and another round of adjustment should start to put those countries in a better position to service. In fact, we are observing already in Latin America that governments are moving to the left simply as the economies deteriorate socially, politically, and economically under the weight of the adjustment process. They are experiencing high inflation. The situation is getting unsettled, polarized, and it is very difficult to believe that there is a new age of adjustment to pay the debt around the corner.

VOLUNTARY LENDING

We say, "Well, the story is not good, but if you do not hang in, you can never borrow again." That line of thinking provokes laughter in Latin America because governments realize they are running trade surpluses, and if they stop paying interest, that is the amount of extra goods they could have every year. If they are told to look down the road to 1992, when surely they will want to be borrowing in the world capital market, those countries say, "All we see is that the commercial banks are trying to get out rather than in." Even countries that have always serviced their debt and are paying back principal, like Colombia, cannot roll-over the principal of their debt. When they tried last time, the banks would not touch it. Voluntary lending does not exist, and a massive attempt is underway by commercial banks to reduce Latin American exposure independently of what the particular country is doing, because what counts is the total exposure, not where you have it. Nobody in Latin America believes that voluntary lending is something to worry about and work for. There is now great awareness of the history of the last debt crisis, when, under pressure, governments walked away.

During the 1930s debt crisis, governments could return to the capital market the moment they defaulted on the old loans. When a banker says, "If you default, I will never lend to you again," he or she is not really serious. In uncertain times banks only lend to those who do not need money. Someone who has defaulted and as a result has no debt left is a wonderful credit risk, and that temptation is inevitably there. The best evidence is the case of Mexico. In 1944, after thirty years of not paying a penny—always talking, but never actually paying a penny—the government talked to the bankers and said, "Good news: We will pay you off twenty cents on the dollar, no arrears." The bankers said, "Wonderful, we will take it." Five years later, the commercial banks had already loaned a billion dollars to Mexico; nine years later came the first Mexican bond issue in New York, oversubscribed. Within the next four months, there were eleven more bond issues. It does not take long to reenter the world capital market if the prospects look good. At that time, the Mexican government was extremely conservative, the budget was balanced; the story was investment, and everybody wanted a piece of it. Everybody looked back and said, "Yes, they did have a terrible government, but the guys we are dealing with now are really wonderful." Exactly the same happened with Brazil and every other debtor country. Today we do not really have a convincing story, one that says, "Let's go on because we have the Baker Plan, which is a wonderful way of dealing with this problem."

ALTERNATIVES

What are the alternatives? One can say, "We have to do something about the debt problem that is market-based. We do not believe in big, decisive, comprehensive institutional moves." Anyone favoring market-based approaches would say, "We have two on the shelf, one of which is debt-equity swaps. We have five years of experience with swaps, and the evidence is that in most cases the debt-equity swaps finance investment that would have taken place anyway." For the central banks, dollars that they would have otherwise received do not actually arrive, and there is a cost of financing the pay-off of the external debt in the budget. There will no doubt be debt-equity swaps, but they will be small and will be targeted to those investments that governments actually think they would not otherwise obtain, and that they want badly enough to use budget subsidies to attract. That tendency is quite clear in Mexico, for example, where debt-equity swaps have been suspended except for very special circumstances. In Brazil, a big debt-equity swap program is underway, though primarily because it is the biggest lever for corruption ever seen. I do not believe that debt-equity swaps will be major; they will be small and interesting, but not decisive.

A second possibility is the Mexican Morgan-style buyback operation. Buybacks were very popular in the 1930s and 1940s. Argentina bought back its entire external debt, which was selling at a discount even though the government was regularly paying interest. It was selling at a discount because Argentina was located in Latin America, and creditors thought anyone who lived there in the end probably was not going to pay. The Argentinians used that advantage to retire their whole debt through buybacks. Why not have that today? Banks sell out on a voluntary basis, countries reduce their debt on advantageous terms, and everyone is ahead. The problem with buybacks is very simple: you need money to do it. And the debtor countries, since they cannot even pay interest, certainly cannot buy back the debt. For buybacks to be attractive, the discount must be really large. But if you have a lot of money, the discount will not be large unless you are particularly vicious. Thus, the only way a good buyback situation arises is if the creditors believe they will not get a penny and the country is full of money and can actually retire the debt. Very tough to do, certainly, for example, in Mexico. Porfirio Diaz said that Mexico was so close to the United States and so far from God. That is not a situation where you depress your discount maximally by adverse behavior. I conclude that market-related mechanisms, while they do occur, are going to be in the $10 billion range, far from the $100 billion debt of Mexico and Brazil.

That leaves two options. One is the institutional approach, the facility proposed by Peter Kenen a number of years ago, that appears in the trade bill by the grace of the House Banking Committee. Jim Robinson of American Express, to the consternation of his banker friends, has advocated it. Many people like the idea because they see the debt trading at large discounts in the secondary market and want to capture that discount. They propose that the banks sell their claims to a facility at a discount and turn around and pass those discounts on to the debtor countries as debt relief. The problem is the taxpayers have to guarantee the operation. If it is successful, the banks have a safe asset where previously they had a crummy one, debtor countries have debt relief where they did not before, and, if everything goes well, all the taxpayer is doing is guaranteeing the reduced debts. Reduced debts make payment much more likely, and, because we helped out, the debtors will not be nasty; all is well.

Is this scenario likely? There are a couple of snags that essentially condemn the approach. First, any bank would try and hold out if such a scheme emerged. Anyone who holds out can go to the debtor country and say, "Now that everybody has given you debt relief, there must be a lot of money around to pay me everything you owe me." Second, the free-rider problem requires a facility to use carrot-or-stick mechanisms to make the banks sell. "Carrot" means if you sell, we are going to give you wonderful tax breaks on your losses; "stick" means if you do not sell, we will make your life miserable by capital requirements. Congress is very reluctant to do this to the banks.

There is a more workable plan in which debtor governments decide to pay their interest obligations in domestic currency, which cannot be converted and expatriated, but can be invested without any restrictions. The result would be to revitalize investment. In the case of Mexico, for example, the trade surplus would disappear and be replaced by an equal increase in investment. The banks, which now get the pesos, will immediately scurry to buy equity, to buy land, to buy real estate, or to make loans that create an investment climate. Private Mexican investors would say, "Well, the peso is not going to collapse because we do not have to pay interest in dollars." Capital flight would return. What follows is a stimulation of economic activity in Mexico; everyone would want a piece of the action. As private capital returns, reversing capital flight, the central bank has enough dollars to actually pay the banks interest in dollars. And we have a paradox: If the banks want the money in dollars, they cannot have it, and capital goes out of Mexico. If the banks are willing to take it in pesos, then in fact they can get it in dollars—perhaps not all, perhaps not immediately, but quite rapidly.

THE CASE OF MEXICO

What are the preconditions for something to work in the way I have described? I think in Mexico, where the budget today is balanced, they actually exist to a high degree. If you look at the raw budget numbers, they show a deficit of 17 percent, but that is only because the nominal interest payments on the large domestic debt are inflated by a 200 percent inflation rate. If you make the inflation adjustment on interest payments as we do here, then the budget in Mexico is balanced. It means the government is collecting enough in taxes to pay the creditors in pesos the full interest they are owed. The government frees through taxation enough resources to tell the creditors, "Here, you can take all this—and I earned it without inflation." What happens today is that the creditors take the money and say they would like dollars. As a result, there is a large trade surplus; exports are high because the real exchange rate is depreciated, and imports are low, which finances the outflow of the dollars earned through the budget.

The alternative is investment that increases sharply as the creditors put $10 billion into Mexican investments of all kinds. Mexican firms import American goods, so the trade surplus disappears. Previously, the trade surplus was needed to pay interest, but under my plan the trade surplus is used to buy American capital goods so that extra resources are available to the Mexican economy to start a process of growth. Let this happen for three, four, five years, and Mexico will be back where it was in the 1950s or 1960s, a country without inflation, with steady 7 to 8 percent growth and private-sector investment. As the economy grows, there is plenty of money around to pay off the bank loans, which over time will come to look very small. In the end, I think it is the only feasible way to solve the debt problem for a large country like Mexico.

Is the domestic macroeconomic situation in Mexico such as to make this scenario plausible? If you look at the Mexican economy, there are three concurrent problems. The first is the high inflation that is the counterpart of large real depreciation to cope with the debt crisis and the large collapse of oil (which meant 30 percent reduction in export revenues). Last fall, inflation was running at 200 percent and sharply accelerating. Since January, the government has introduced a stabilization program of the kind Israel, Argentina, and Brazil entertained over the last three years. Israel was successful, Argentina and Brazil were not. The Mexicans went to each of the three countries, looked carefully at what had happened, and said, "We conclude that these programs fail when there is not very tight fiscal discipline accompanying the price-wage exchange rate freeze that puts an end to inflation." So, they postponed for a year and a half stopping inflation until the budget was in a sufficiently strong position that, from the budget side, there was no inflationary pressure. The government was actually retiring debt. They reached that point last year. Their budget is totally sound, even on a sustainable basis, because the improvements were made by closing public-sector firms, raising taxes, and broadening the tax base, all measures that are not emergency taxation that might disappear in a year or two. On the budget side, everything has succeeded.

How well have they done on disinflation? If you look closely over the last month, inflation now is already less than 20 percent, and less than 10 percent per year for producers' prices. For the moment at least, the price-wage exchange rate freeze system is working extremely well. It has reduced inflation, even for those prices that are not actively controlled. The real exchange rate is still in a very good position; even though there is a little bit of inflation, the real exchange rate is at the same level as when oil was $6—and oil is already $13. On that side, everything is safe. The problems are essentially the problems of adjusting from a stabilization to a growth scenario.

A huge budget action of the kind Mexico has undertaken means an enormous restraint on demand and little growth. Mexico has had recession rather than growth over the last five years. Real interest rates are extremely high—40 percent—because inflation has stopped, and the government has not allowed sharp money growth to bring rates down. The economy is in a precarious situation because there is too much monetary and fiscal tightness to make this disinflation program stick. Until the election in July, policy is unlikely to change because inflation is the main problem. After July, however, life has to normalize, and the country will need growth. Looking ahead, the issue facing the Mexican government is not success on the disinflation program—there is every reason to believe it will work because the budget is in such a wonderful position—but how to return to growth.

The serious problem of growth in Mexico, or in any country where you have stabilization, is that everybody now says the fundamentals are right and they are just waiting for the boom, which would justify making the investments everybody thinks are totally appropriate, given that everything is all right. It is a very classic coordination problem, with everyone saying, "After you." And if everyone says, "After you," we will not see much action. What can the government do? Well, they cannot go out and spend because then the fundamentals are gone. They can call people and say, "Why don't you spend?" And receive the answer, "Yes, we are actually thinking of it. We think the fundamentals are right, we are just waiting." Everyone is waiting.

The country cannot afford to wait because the sociopolitical fiber is being tested by these very tight monetary and fiscal policies. Something has to happen. The debt problem is on people's minds. They say, "Imagine we had growth. Growth for a year and a half would mean that the current account surplus that we have today, with which we can pay all the interest and retire debt, would go away. High investment would mean large capital goods imports. Increased imports and reduced exports mean there is no more money to pay the interest on the debt, and then we have the rescheduling confrontation that will not go well, and then people say we need a real depreciation, and then capital flight starts, and then we are back to where we were last year." An essential element in moving from stabilization to medium-term growth is the resolution of the debt problem. If we solve the debt problem in the recycling manner that I have suggested, then of course everything adds up. Why? Because starting a month from now, all the banks would be running around Mexico pushing loans. It would be exactly the coordinating device that gets investment moving, while at the same time removing the external balance constraint and the expectation that there could be yet another large depreciation because the debt problem is inconsistent with growth.

Looking at the Mexican economy, the number-one problem is to bring a very rapid solution to the debt crisis.   The solution must be non-confrontational because of Mexico's proximity to the United States. It must also be sufficiently conservative so that the United States can regard it as a reasonable settlement that in the end gives creditors the very best chance to get all their money, every penny, while at the same time assuring that Mexico resumes growth in a way that is sustainable and stable.

Could Mexico possibly accomplish this? You might say, "You've seen one Latin American country, you've seen them all," but, on close inspection, Mexico is very different. Between 1956 and 1976, Mexico actually had a fixed exchange rate on the dollar and very low inflation.   In fact, Mexico is traditionally a country of financial stability. The events of the last ten years wreaked havoc with the country, partly because oil wealth was so poorly digested, partly because financial instability led to $40 billion of capital flight, and partly because the oil collapse exacerbated the problem. But a history of financial stability is there. The budget efforts can survive if there is strong, decisive, rugged action that turns from the debt crisis to a growth scenario. If that does not happen, then within a year there will be real depreciation, and the Mexican political system will then open up.

The Mexican case is interesting because in the end all the illusions about miracles are off the mark. The adjustment actually is being done the hard way, by closing public-sector firms, by pulling a Reagan-style affair on AeroMexico to break the unions, and by balancing the budget and putting an extra 2 percent in for safety. When adjustment has been substantially completed, as in Mexico today, the next question is where the growth comes from. And if it does not come very, very fast, then there is a terrible problem. Growth today in Mexico is inconsistent with debt service. Everybody knows it does not add up after all the adjustments are done, and that means the onus falls on the United States, on the creditors, to find a way of first having growth in Mexico, and then debt service.

15 FROM ADJUSTMENT AND RESTRUCTURING TO DEVELOPMENT

Osvaldo Sunkel

It is necessary to understand both the present and the past when considering the restructuring of developing economies. It is essential to go back in history before moving forward because, as I have argued since 1984 (Sunkel 1984; Sunkel 1985; Griffith-Jones and Sunkel 1986), the debt crisis is no mere financial phenomenon, but the culmination of a profound development crisis that was emerging in Latin America already by the late 1960s. What is needed, therefore, is not just a solution to the debt crisis, although this is a necessary condition, but a renewed development effort to overcome this double crisis.

I must emphasize that I do not subscribe to the now prevailing view of Latin American development that condemns all that happened there from the 1930s to the 1970s as a monumental failure. That is a seriously misleading interpretation, because Latin America during the 1950s and 1960s became semi-industrialized, highly urbanized, and partially modernized. Relatively modern states evolved out of rather primitive nations, and that can hardly be described as a failure.

This positive historical process of economic and social change was brought about by the breakdown of the old regimes established in the nineteenth century, which crumbled under the effects of the Great Depression and its

The opinions expressed in this paper are strictly personal and should not be attributed to the institutions with which the author is associated.

aftermath, including World War II. The Depression weakened the power of the landed oligarchies and the related commercial and financial interests linked to international primary commodity trade, commerce, and banking. In its stead gradually emerged a new political coalition of social groups that had been struggling against the old regimes: industrialists, middle classes, professional groups, and organized labor.

That coalition sustained an exceptionally rapid and intense development process during the 1950s and 1960s. The way in which the coalition articulated political interests and economic development was basically through a very active role of an expanding state apparatus. As a consequence of the substantial decline in the power of the old elites, such new political groups were able to use the state to tax away the surplus generated in the foreign-trade sector, which was achieved through various means, including exchange rate manipulation, increased taxation, and eventually through the nationalization of certain primary export activities.

During subsequent decades, the state and the public sector grew considerably and took on a large number of important new functions:

1. The state increased its role as an investor, playing a substantial role in the creation of the transportation, communication, and energy infrastructures, and thereby preparing the way for industrial development.
2. The state created public enterprises in areas in which the private sector was not interested, willing, or able to invest, such as iron and steel, machinery, and petrochemical industries.
3. The state provided capital to finance private entrepreneurs through institutions like the Corporación de Fomento de la Producción in Chile, Banco Nacional do Desenvolvimento in Brazil, and Nacional Financiera in Mexico. These powerful financial and technical state agencies were designed to promote and support industrialization and agricultural modernization in the private sector.
4. The state, to complete the demands and interests of the political coalition behind this new role, also established in some cases, and significantly increased in others, the basic social services of an incipient welfare state: education, health, social security, and housing. The middle classes and the organized urban labor force benefited greatly from this process.

With significant differences among countries, this was an extremely successful program, one which brought about a high rate of economic growth, industrialization, and modernization both in relation to past history and contemporary world experience. However, a number of serious problems began to surface by the late 1960s, as was amply recognized in the critical literature of the period—from the right (neoliberal), left (dependency), and center (more of the same development, with some changes in emphasis).

The policy of industrialization was from the beginning proposed with the explicit aim of exporting manufactures, because specialization in the exportation of a few primary commodities led to stagnation, external vulnerability, instability, and an asymmetric relationship with developed nations. But the actual process of industrialization emphasized import substitution rather than exports of manufactures. Although this was initially justified both on the grounds of the development of infant domestic industry and the negative conditions prevailing until the late 1950s in the world market, those conditions changed in the 1960s, and the emphasis should have shifted more decisively to exports of manufactures.

The increasing taxation of the primary-export sector also started to reach its limits. Taxation made that sector less profitable and therefore lacking in new investments and technology, which contributed to the balance of payments problem. It was also generating a growing structural fiscal crisis, as revenues extracted from the export sector failed to increase sufficiently to match the increasing public expenditures of a state pursuing the development policies mentioned before. At the same time, some of these expenditures ran out of control. Rising expenditures should have been limited and rationalized, and a very substantial transformation of the taxation structure should have taken place to radically increase the reliance on domestic revenues. But it was, of course, easier and politically more expedient to continue spending and depend on taxation of exports, inflation, and, later, external financing. Multilateral and bilateral development assistance and foreign private direct investment provided funds up to the 1970s, and then when borrowing on the international private financial market boomed.

A social crisis was also in the making because the process of fast economic growth was highly inequitable, generating both affluence and poverty, particularly among the fast-growing number of the displaced rural population that moved into urban slum areas with precarious employment conditions. While this process of massive transfer from rural to urban poverty might be considered to have some positive aspects, it was nevertheless a dreadful accumulation of visible absolute and relative poverty.

Under the growing weight of these problems, the political coalition that underpinned development policies began to break down, particularly in growing marginal (or so-called informal) sectors, which did not claim much benefit from the model of growth. In response to accumulating sociopolitical and economic tensions and contradictions, various attempts at more or less radical reforms of a socializing character occurred in the late 1960s and early 1970s in Chile, Jamaica, Argentina, Bolivia, and Peru. These were put forward as progressive solutions to the dead ends reached by the import substitution industrialization model based on a populist sociopolitical coalition. These attempts at further socializing the development process aimed at changing its capitalist nature and solving its structural problems. They all failed, partly for political reasons, partly because of the tremendous disorganization of the economy, which was brought about by essentially populist policies and the reactions of the middle classes against structural reforms and partly by external pressures.

In the 1970s, a radically conservative, neoliberal reaction in economic policy took place in several countries, which moved in the opposite direction, liberalizing the economy, reducing the role of the state, opening up the economy to foreign trade, finance, and investment, and relying on the market mechanism rather than planning. Other countries continued to practice the development policies of the 1960s. The new international financial situation permitted both the liberalization policies and the continuation of the development policies without having to undergo fundamental structural changes, which included reform of manufacturing sectors to be able to export (Brazil did achieve this); formulation of policies in the social sector to alleviate poverty and under- and unemployment; and adoption of measures to overhaul the tax system, overcome the fiscal crisis, and introduce greater rationality and efficiency.

Structural transformation was already necessary in the late 1960s and is even more necessary now. Latin America ran heavily into debt everywhere, even in the oil-exporting countries where financial resources increased enormously, because it had accumulated great economic and social imbalances during its rapid and profound economic development process. The financial abundance and permissiveness made it possible to postpone structural readjustment during the 1970s, because almost anything could be financed borrowing from the quickly expanding private international banks.

In summary, there was a very positive development process in the postwar period, but that process began to show serious flaws, requiring reorganization and reorientation. A number of the elements that are part of the structural adjustment programs proposed now are therefore necessary. But I am very wary of the general approach or philosophy that accompanies them, which is a revulsion against everything that went before. This attitude is incorrect and very costly indeed, as shown by some of the most extreme examples, namely the countries of the Southern Cone. The programs are largely an ideological cover for neoliberal reform rather than policies for the resumption of a genuine economic and social development effort.

Once the debt situation erupted in 1982, an additional financial crisis was created on top of the development crisis that had been looming since the late 1960s. The most damaging consequence of the debt crisis is a reversal of Latin America's financial relationship with the developed world. Until 1982, the rest of the world transferred savings to Latin America, which allowed it to invest more than what it was able to save. Since 1982, Latin America has been transferring to the rest of the world around 3 or 4 percent of its GDP, which means a very large proportion of its savings. Therefore, the adjustment programs have meant a substantial reduction of investments. This reversal of the international transfer process has been going on now at a rate of around US$30 billion per year, totaling nearly US$150 billion over the last five years.

Thus, a large proportion of the savings of the Latin American countries is being shipped abroad, and this has been occurring without any significant change in the adjustment policies that have been followed over the last five or six years. Such adjustment policies have in fact made it possible to enforce an unacceptable situation in which developing countries are contributing to finance developed countries. The transfers mean that there is a fundamental contradiction between achieving reasonable rates of economic growth and servicing the debt. To service the debt, Latin America as a whole has had to reduce its investment rate from about 23 percent before 1982 to around 16 percent since.

This is a recipe for stagnation that must end. The end is not likely to be initiated from abroad because there is no expectation that the international economy will improve dramatically in the near future. There is general agreement about the things that will not happen: the world economy and international trade will not soon start growing to renew their lending; foreign private investment is not coming back soon; interest rates are not coming down; and international cooperation and assistance policies have been more or less abandoned.

So what are the scenarios for the next few years? One is to continue debt service for a few years, stop when it becomes impossible, and then begin payments again, as during the last years. This stop-go debt-service situation has led to a continuing deterioration of the debtor countries. After six years of drastic adjustment policies and oppressive external debt negotiations, the indebtedness besetting most Latin American countries continues to increase. A precarious external balance has been struck at the cost of utter internal imbalance. In the short term, the result has been a sharp and steady contraction of economies (leaving substantial unused production capacity), drastic cutbacks in imports, and an accentuation of inflationary pressures.[1]   In the medium term, we have seen a serious degradation in the employment situation, real wages, social services, and the distribution of income. Over the longer term, the consequence will be a severe deterioration in the capital accumulation process, with negative effects on productive and technological capability as well as economic and social infrastructure.

A further macroeconomic imbalance is involved, that of the public sector, which has to generate a surplus of income over current expenditure to cope with domestic and foreign public debt servicing. This burden has increased sharply as the state has assumed many a private debt and as, during external debt renegotiations, the state has been forced to accept liability and stand guarantor for private debt servicing. Consequently, the state is in fact responsible for all foreign debt servicing, public and private, unless the private debtors are capable of servicing their debt themselves. In the case of those who are not (which is the general case), the state assumes liability for the debt or has to subsidize private debtors so that they in turn may service their obligations. In short, the state has to make an extraordinary effort to limit its expenditure and increase its income.

As far as public expenditure is concerned, public investment usually suffers the quickest and sharpest contraction, but the contraction soon moves on to the civil service, transfer payments, and subsidies. Social security, public health care, and education, which are major items in public budgets, are frequently those most affected (especially since military expenditures prove quite inflexible).

Concerning revenue, it is very probable that virtually the entire effort is concentrated on indirect taxation, such as VAT or sales taxes, which provide a higher yield over the short term, but directly and regressively affect the majority of poorer consumers. As for public corporations, an effort is made to sell them off to domestic or foreign private interest (the debt-equity swap is being used for this purpose) or to make them self-financing by increasing prices, reducing staff and wages, and introducing various forms of rationalization. The specific aim is to avoid burdening the budget with subsidies, making enterprises pay for themselves, which is no easy task under recessionary conditions.

The purpose of such policies is to generate a surplus on current account available for servicing the foreign debt. The political cost of maintaining the recessive adjustment policies and servicing the foreign debt increases exponentially. The supposed advantages of these policies rapidly fritter away,

1. See the discussion of debt and inflation in Chapter 14 by Dornbusch.

while an alternative policy of economic reactivation of a populist character becomes ever more probable. For want of a better option, sociopolitical pressure inevitably will tend to impose the latter solution, as has already been seen in a number of countries. Nevertheless, given the sharp reduction in imports and the severe external strangulation, an indiscriminate policy of expansion will immediately upset the precarious external balance and bring the threat of runaway domestic inflation. On the other hand, by maintaining recessive adjustment policies, investment and savings necessary for financing increased expenditure is inhibited just when these are needed to stimulate employment and growth without exerting excessive inflationary pressure.

If external conditions, interest rates, trade conditions, exports, foreign demand, foreign investment, and external financing do not improve dramatically—and there is nothing to indicate that this will be the case over the medium term—our countries will continue to be adjusted to a stagnation "equilibrium" with massive underutilization of resources and increasing poverty. Under the most favorable conditions, improving export performance will be a difficult and longer-term task while the economic, social, and political situation continues to deteriorate, especially in those sectors not related to tradeable goods.

I suggest that there is an alternative to these regressive structural adjustment programs and to populist strategies for coping with the crisis: the total or partial suspension of the transfer abroad of internal savings earmarked for debt servicing. Note that I refer to a suspension of the transfer, not an end to the corresponding domestic savings effort. Such a measure would make available a considerable volume of foreign currency, the specific amount depending on the weight of the foreign debt borne by any given country, the proportion of the payment of the debt that the country decided to suspend, and the retaliatory action taken by creditor countries and banks. If, through the interplay of these various factors, it was possible effectively to make available a large part of this potential volume of resources, the resulting capacity to import would allow for an increase of several percentage points in growth of national product, the increase varying by country. Under current conditions, the result of my proposal would be a move from a state of stagnation to one of growth and a recuperation in per capita income.

If an appreciable part of the foreign currency earmarked for servicing the foreign debt was made available for imports, it would make for a considerable increase in investment from the abysmal level to which it has had to adjust, back to about the normal postwar level. Given current idle production capacity, this would generate in turn a steady increase in economic activity, employment, and incomes. Growth would allow for an increase in domestic savings to the extent necessary for financing high priority domestic investments. Bear in mind that a truly Herculean savings task is necessary to compensate not only for the drop in savings brought about by the recession and adjustment policies, but also to replace the considerable contribution made by external savings until 1981. It would be possible to achieve this improvement in the savings-investment equation over the short and medium terms only if all or a substantial part of external debt servicing was suspended. Under present circumstances, an increase in imports is essential if new investment efforts are to have any real and lasting effects. The external restriction on reactivation would be removed over the short term, and the internal restriction on productive capacity and savings would be relieved over the medium term, thus making for sustained growth.

If, conversely, the newly available import margin were to be used to increase consumer expenditure, economic activity would expand over the short term, but no medium term growth could be maintained. We would fall once again on the populist alternative, followed in due time by the recessionary adjustment medicine.

Current policies, both populist and recessionary, are such that they cannot offer any hope of an increase in savings that might possibly lead to increased investment; indeed, they inhibit any such increase in savings. An autonomous increase in investments is required, which would trigger a process of recuperation of economic activity, employment, incomes, and wages. The restriction that hinders such a line of action is debt servicing, which is why such servicing should take second place, until exports and external financing can be brought up to levels that make the servicing charges tolerable.

I stress that suspending or reducing debt servicing should not mean suspending the domestic savings effort. Quite to the contrary, this exceptional savings effort should continue and be entrusted to an institutional body as it were, a national fund for economic and social development. All major groups of society should be democratically represented within such a fund and would be able to direct the national savings drive exclusively to financing priority projects to tackle the most acute short- and long-term social problems and to raise the efficient production of tradeable goods.

My proposal would be the internal technically and politically indispensable complement to the external measure of limiting or suspending debt servicing. It would be a policy that could rally majority domestic support, bringing consensus among entrepreneurs, middle classes, workers, and the marginal sectors. The purpose would be to create a social pact for the reactivation and social development of the economy. Cautious and selective expansion of economic activity would have permanent and positive effects on key economic and social sectors, without major inflationary consequences, all of it aimed at overcoming both the long-term development crisis and the debt problem.

A domestic effort of such proportions should arouse sympathy in the international community, particularly among those actors not directly affected by the total or partial suspension of debt-servicing payments. One would hope that a development-oriented program would have a positive effect on the governments of industrialized countries and international organizations and even lead to a new form of international cooperation.

Even the most affected party in this proposal, the banks, could be positively associated with it by participating in the investment ventures launched by the national fund for economic and social development, part of a gradual repayment of the principal of the debt owed to them, duly discounted according to the values prevailing in the secondary market. Banks could even be offered some interest payments in return for contributing new funds to the investment effort and to the export drive. Instead of the present debt-equity swaps, with their highly negative characteristics, banks could be offered attractive debt-investment and debt-export swaps, which would be a contribution to the solution of both the debt and development crises.

We are currently engaged in an international "negative-sum game" situation in which almost everyone loses or, at the very least, ceases to win. The debtor countries, more particularly their poorer classes, are those most affected. But the creditor countries also lose, or cease to win. The sharp reduction in the imports of the debtor countries affects the exports of the creditors and the income and employment of hundreds of thousands. Likewise, there is a reduction in direct investment and private loan financing opportunities, as profit and interest remittances from debtor countries are restricted. The reduction in domestic economic activity and in international trade, investments and financial flows has a further recessive effect on the world economy and contributes to instability and uncertainty.

In the industrialized countries, individuals and groups of importance are expressing increasing dissatisfaction with official policy toward developing country debt. Latin America must advance concrete proposals and sound technical and political arguments to support and fortify this dissatisfaction. Discussion and the resulting internal political pressure in industrialized countries could be crucial in changing official stances.

On the other hand, Latin America will have to develop a credible negotiation position to threaten important institutions and groups with considerable costs. Without hard pressure and negotiating positions, or at least a credible threat, there can be no negotiation. Without such attitudes, Latin America will not be taken seriously, or even be considered, except when yet another financial crisis in an important country of the region forces the centers of international financial power to react to defend their own interests, with all the serious consequences that this has been having and continues to have for the peoples of Latin America.

16 IS TO FORGIVE THE DEBT DIVINE?

William Darity, Jr.

Why not call the whole thing off? The lingering external debt crisis of the developing countries lingers into the late 1980s with no apparent resolution in sight. Formal repudiation is not in the offing; Brazil's moratorium on payments was a short-lived attempt at temporary repudiation. The precise points of leverage that preclude national leaders of debtor LDCs from declaring their government's refusal to continue to service foreign claims are not known with certainty. Bulow and Rogoff (1988) recently have shown that it is misleading to argue that leaders fear that their nation's credit reputation will be tarnished so badly that their respective regimes will be barred permanently from access to international credit markets. After all, reputations can change with regimes.

Bulow and Rogoff contend that the leverage must be more substantive than fear of lost reputation; instead, it must encompass the possibility that a nation's creditors can expropriate assets held abroad or the prospect of outright military intervention. Indeed, the former point of leverage for the creditors is reinforced by what Horn and I have called the bankers' "true insurance": their possession as liabilities the deposits of the elites of developing nations, in large part via episodic capital flight (Darity and Horn 1988: chapter 5). Such liabilities could be impounded if any government of a debtor nation undertakes formal repudiation or nonconciliatory default (see Kaletsky 1985). Repudiation only becomes likely with the rise to power of revolutionary regimes with

233

leaders uninterested in protecting funds placed abroad by elites as deposits in multinational banks.

If the debtor LDCs will not repudiate, then why not have the governments of the creditor nations' banks simply declare the loans forgiven? Would that not effectively put an end to the crisis? There would be no more rounds of rescheduling, no more nervousness about whether Argentina would go into default on its entire debt, no more worry about whether 10, 20, 30, or 40 percent of Peru's export earnings would ever service a single year's interest obligations to the multinational commercial banks, and indeed, no more conferences on the debt crisis. Why not, as Bulow and Rogoff suggest, simply forgive and forget? An obvious consequence of a declaration of forgiveness, if it were feasible, would be the necessity of the creditor institutions writing down their loans at substantial losses. U.S. banks, specifically the money center banks, have moved recently to build loan loss reserves, particularly against their claims on Latin nations. But the U.S. (and British) bank loan loss reserve ratios on LDC debt of 25 to 30 percent are still well below the 70 percent ratio being maintained on LDC loans by continental European banks (Truell 1988c: 2), suggesting much greater vulnerability to a complete write-off of the loans for U.S.-based banks.

There is even speculation that if the money center banks were compelled to write-down their loans partially to the discounted values at which the Latin debt sells on the secondary market, at least one of them, Manufacturers Hanover, would be bankrupted (Bailey and Hill 1988: 1). In fact, Standard and Poor downgraded the creditworthiness of Manufacturers Hanover and four other money center banks at the start of February 1988, explicitly because of "concerns over the five banks' loans to Latin American and other less developed countries, low equity-capital levels and an increasingly competitive operating environment" (Truell 1988d: 3). Correspondingly, by February 1988, corporate bond offerings for the money center banks were being sold at the highest margin of yield or spread over U.S. Treasury issues with similar maturity dates relative to the bond issues of other major corporations. The yields required by investors to purchase big bank bonds were so high at the start of 1988 that they were approaching the characteristics ascribed to junk bonds (Winkler 1988: 14).

A further consequence of forgiveness of LDC debts would be to call into question the legitimacy of other assets held by the commercial banks. If sovereign or semi-sovereign loans are to be forgiven, why not also forgive the loans made by U.S. banks to troubled farmers, homeowners, and independent petroleum producers? Debt forgiveness targeted in one direction toward one set of borrowers opens up an unsettling Pandora's box of possibilities for questioning the entire set of contractual relationships between creditors and debtors. The *differentiae specifica* for forgiveness of the obligations to one set of borrowers and not another—particularly if both sets of borrowers have been overextended by the bankers' overlending—is not obvious.

Indeed, there *is* a subversive school of thought that says that the big banks' managers have no one to blame but themselves for this precarious situation. It includes a quite diverse array of scholars, ranging from two University of Pennsylvania finance professors, Guttentag and Herring (1985), to the scion of financial liberalization, Ronald McKinnon (1984). These parties agree that major banks have a tendency to herd in their lending decisions and periodically to overlend. This being the case, why not let them suffer the effects of writing off the Latin loans in full? After all, this is the same community of commercial institutions that made loans to Panama and is now unclear with whom to negotiate with over debts that are now in arrears (see Bennett 1988: A8, and Truell 1988b). These are the same institutions that paid their executives large bonuses in 1987 despite huge losses for all the money center banks (Bailey and Guenther 1988: 34). Why not go ahead and let one or two of these big banks go under? Would this not bring much needed discipline to the banking industry and winnow away the most imprudential and inefficient enterprises?

The essential question is: Do we wish to protect the innocent from the repercussions of developing country loan-induced failure of a major bank? Recall that the upstream linkages of a bank as relatively small as Penn Square in Oklahoma were so significant as to have adverse repercussions on Continental Illinois when the former failed. And when the latter failed, U.S. bank officials were so nervous about the potential systemwide effects, they moved to prevent Continental from closing its doors. Can the system handle the closing of, say, Manufacturers Hanover and Bank America? One can only speculate at the downstream linkages of these large banks. While they are not innocent—nor are most of their institutional depositors (often other banks)—the impact of failures of banks of this magnitude certainly would have an adverse effect on the fiduciary soundness of many regional and local banks, which would in turn undermine the security of thousands, perhaps millions, of everyday deposit holders with branch banks. The fundamental fear is that the collapse of a big bank will engender generalized financial collapse and economic and social chaos. It is already apparent that the Federal Deposit Insurance Corporation (FDIC) does not have adequate insurance funds to protect all insured depositors who could be threatened by a proliferating bank panic (Bailey and Hill 1988: 1), a panic supposedly rendered impossible by the very existence of the FDIC.

But without significant forgiveness of the extant debt—without a requisite modicum of divinity—the LDCs will retain intolerable repayment burdens. The officials of the nations that contracted such enormous external debts, now estimated to be close to $390 billion for the Latin American region alone, were not innocents either. But the brunt of the burden of repayment does not fall on them. Rather, it falls on the masses of their relatively impoverished fellow citizens who must endure a litany of policies that frequently spell recession in the name of expanded export earnings, coupled with the clubbed hand of the IMF.

The difficult task is to drastically relieve the LDC debt burdens without inducing financial collapse. There is an additional task, however, that receives considerably less attention in conversations about how to manage the debt crisis. Because the banks get into these types of situations routinely, how do we prevent them from producing a new international (or domestic) debt crisis at a later date?[1] Relief from debt burdens for LDCs requires some mode of debt forgiveness. Certainly such forgiveness is not part and parcel of the banks' tactic of building up loan loss reserves. As Tarshis has observed recently, "From the standpoint of the debtors, they face just as much pressure when creditor banks add to their reserves as they would have faced with no such action. Their debt remains unchanged . . ." (Tarshis 1988: 12).

Sale of debt on the secondary market de facto can amount to partial forgiveness, given the magnitude of the discounts at which the debt is selling at present, if countries can buy back their own debt at the discount. As of late 1987, one dollar of debt from Venezuela, Chile, and Mexico was selling for fifty to sixty cents, while the debt of Bolivia was selling for ten to fifteen cents per dollar (Bridges 1987: 12). But the secondary market for debt remains relatively thin. Banks are unwilling to unload large portions of their claims on the resale market, for such dumping would presumably drive prices down even further.[2] To the extent that Folkerts-Landau (1985) is correct in his claim that the spreads offered developing country borrowers by the banks did not incorporate risk of default (or repudiation or forgiveness), then resale of the loans at very sharp discounts, understandably, would be a most unattractive option.

1. And presumably it must be a later date. U.S. commercial banks are so deep into the phase of revulsion from easy lending that they have become tight-fisted with all manner of borrowers, especially local businesses. See, for example, Apcar and Brown (1988: 1 and 18), and Ladendorf (1988: H1 and H4).
2. See the discussion of the secondary market in Chapter 3 by Weeks.

Folkerts-Landau's evidence that the spreads offered by commercial banks to LDC borrowers did not include default risk is the following: (1) spreads over LIBOR on loans to nonoil developing countries generally stayed at less than one-half percentage point above rates paid by industrial country borrowers between 1974 and 1983, although the debt crisis was apparent by early 1982; (2) the difference between the spread paid by developing country borrowers with a rescheduling and the spread paid by industrial country borrowers was less than one percentage point until 1981, when it rose to one and one-half percentage points; (3) generally, the rate of interest on loans to nonoil developing countries has been less than that charged to major U.S. corporations; and (4) interest rates in the multinational bank loan market generally have been less than rates on international bonds (1985: 332-335). Folkerts-Landau contends that the latter must have default risk incorporated into the returns they promise, given the familiar history of actual bond defaults.

Debt-equity swaps,[3] to the extent that the property obtained by the creditor is valued at less than the contractual value of the initial debt, have a similar flavor of resale of the debt at a discount. This is essentially a scheme that constitutes an *ex post* collateralization of uncollateralized loans, typically accompanied by a change in ownership. As Helpman (1987) points out, debt-equity swaps can amount to schemes of partial forgiveness of the debt, and complete forgiveness in the special case "in which a positive amount of debt is exchanged for zero equity" (1987: 2).

Tarshis (1988: 13) is skeptical about the enthusiasm of the bankers for such schemes:

> . . . just as it would be amazing to find banks offering to forgive even 30 percent of their claims as creditors, so it would be surprising for these creditors to take an equity interest in return for surrendering their status as creditors. Who wants, anyway, to become a part owner of a corporation in a country that cannot gain access to the foreign exchange it needs for the service of its debt? And with the banks eager to keep the discounts on their debt-claims low, and with debtor countries not at all ready to give their creditors too generous a serving of equity, the process of bargaining should be quite a spectacle!

After all, ownership rights to Pemex (the Mexican national oil company)—or anything else of genuine substance, for that matter—were not part and parcel of the offerings made available to creditors by the Mexican government under the terms of the plan they established with Morgan Guaranty for debt-equity swaps.

---

3. An example is the recent arrangement between Morgan Guaranty and Mexico involving U.S. bonds as debt-backing. See the ensuing discussion.

The plan appears likely to fall far short of reducing the Mexican government's estimated external debt of more than $53 billion by the initially projected $10 billion. As of late May 1988, the plan had achieved an actual reduction in Mexico's external debt of less than $1.5 billion (Truell and Moffett 1988: 4). If anything, the banks may hunger for rights to public-sector enterprises that they believe will be more efficient and profitable under private control.[4] But one wonders how often other Third World governments will follow the Chilean regime's lead in privatizing a public-sector company and then exchanging it in a debt-equity swap, as it did in giving American Express a stake in Soquimich (Bridges 1987: 18).[5]

What about the U.S. Congress simply declaring that all debts of developing country borrowers to U.S. money center banks are now null and void? This would be the purest form of forgiveness. The total of U.S. banks' claims on the developing world were estimated to be $84.8 billion in June 1987, $56.1 billion of which was owed to the nine money center banks (Truell 1988a: 20). If Congress could wipe out the claims of U.S. banks overnight, it would amount to a rather healthy cup of absolution. Of course, the banks would be likely to rush to the courts as did various offended parties upset by the abrogation of the gold clause in the 1930s in the United States. If the legislature was to prevail, debts would have to be written down. To protect the financial system from collapse, the Federal Reserve could run an intensive monetary expansion or, more directly, simply create deposits at the endangered institutions. Recall that one of the proximate, although not fundamental, factors in the emergence of the debt crisis was the Fed's contractionary, disinflationary policy between late 1979 and 1982 that induced a recession in the United States. The Fed simply could take the opposite step and induce an

4. Robin King made the following related points to me in correspondence dated May 2, 1988:
"a. [I]t is currently illegal under U.S. law for U.S. banks to own corporations that are actually productive. They changed the law last year to allow for temporary (five to ten years, I think) ownership of companies that were formerly public-sector enterprises and that are in the process of privatization via debt-equity swaps, but the bank is still required to sell off the investment after a certain amount of time . . .
"b. Based on interviews I did with bankers in Mexico last summer, the foreign bankers are interested primarily . . . in projects that produce foreign exchange, not pesos.
"c. The Mexican-Morgan bonds were/are known as *tortibonos internacionales*. *Tortibonos* are Mexican food stamps (short for tortilla-bonos, or tortilla bonds). A result of the Salomon Brothers memo/prospectus, maybe."
5. Debt-equity swaps may be no more than an exit route from the market in LDC debts for "smaller" banks (see Truell 1988c: 2). These banks are not small, and, given the unbridled swath of acquisitions being cut by the regional banks, now often dubbed "super-regionals," some may not be smaller than the money center banks in the near future.

inflationary expansion to offset the potential destabilization of the banking system.

The legal capability of Congress to declare the debt forgiven would rest on the whims of the judiciary. But there are other major types of forgiveness schemes that are less murky from a judicial standpoint. One scheme advanced by American Express would create a new institution or corporation to purchase LDC debt from the banks, presumably at a discount, and then arrange renewed debt service on terms adjusted for such a discount (see Bartels 1988). This is, however, a less promising route toward genuine forgiveness because the banks have a right of refusal of sale of the debt at discounts they view as unacceptably large. The scheme could be workable if the new institution was designed to operate at a substantial loss, in which case it could buy up the debt at face value and forgive it partially or in its entirety. Here the true spirit of magnanimity would be abroad, for both debtors and creditors would be forgiven their indiscretions. In short, the banks would not even get their hands slapped for their imprudential lending.

In an alternative scheme, Tarshis would rely on existing institutions, the central banks of each of the creditor nations, to function as the agent that purchases the debt and then eliminates some percentage of it, perhaps 100 percent, for each country (1988: 23-27). Tarshis' forgiveness also is universal in spirit. He would compensate the commercial banks by having the central banks directly create additional deposits for them. Then the world could get back on the path toward a condition where the developed countries could sell their exports to the debtor countries without endangering the latter's capacity to repay the debt. The debtors would not all be scrambling against one another for market shares merely to earn foreign exchange to meet debt obligations.[6] Trade and growth could proceed with a certain cosmopolitanism lacking on the debt-driven scene prevailing today.

Perhaps it does make sense to spread forgiveness all around in heaping doses to resolve the existing crisis. Forgiveness and inflation in the creditor countries might turn the trick of relieving debt burdens and preventing financial collapse. But that still leaves open the question of how to prevent the recurrence of such circumstances in the future. In fact, although the bankers are in a phase of revulsion from lending to Latin America (and Sub-Saharan Africa, for that matter) they apparently are shifting their focus toward Asia rather than

---

6. Although, as Robin King observes, "Instead, the scrambling of the LDCs will be replaced by MDCs scrambling to capture market shares for their exports."

pulling back entirely (Riding 1988a).[7] Bankers are always looking for customers. They will seek new ones when the enchantment of older customers fades. It is simply the nature of the banking beast.

Unless one accepts the position that the debt crisis was due primarily to bad policies in LDCs and unforeseeable external shocks (see Sachs 1987-1988), then major responsibility must be given to the natural practices of commercial banks. To keep a debt crisis from reoccurring bankers must be deprived of what they consider their normal freedoms. This is certainly not an opportune time to cave in to the bankers' clamor to repeal the Glass-Steagall Act, which separates commercial and investment banking (see Axilrod 1988; Litan 1988). It is not wise, in such a turbulent financial environment, to permit deposit-taking institutions to move freely into participation on securities markets. Current conditions suggest the contrary. It may be time to reevaluate Glass-Steagall with an eye toward strengthening it—to restore its effectiveness in light of the potential circumventing operations of commercial bank holding companies and to overcome its failure to reach the offshore operations of the commercial banks.

It may even be appropriate to contemplate such "impractical" but "ideal" (Axilrod 1988: 61) proposals as the old Henry Simons radical-conservative proposal of imposing 100 percent reserve requirements on deposit-taking institutions. Regulators would then have to be vigilant in ensuring that the managers of such institutions do not devise new labels for accounts that would permit depositors' funds to be used as a basis for lending.[8] Their source of profit would be the fees charged to depositors for the service of holding their accounts in secure fashions. This is tantamount to making commercial banks behave like medieval goldsmiths. Such institutions would not require deposit insurance, for customers would only need adequate legal recourse from fraud.

For those bankers who really want "the adventure of banking"—which so many seem to want—they could operate institutions that made loans but obtained their funds exclusively by issuing equity in their operations. Such institutions should not receive public-sector insurance, because they would be in a sense true venture capital operations. Under the scheme they would be truly free—free of the mundane retail banking duties, free to do investment banking with minimal supervision, and free to shoulder the high risks and to reap the high returns.

7. See Chapter 4 by Lissakers and Chapter 5 by Sacks and Canavan, where it is argued that a general pull-back has occurred.

8. One evasion that regulators would have to be alert about is the relabeling of depositors' accounts as equity accounts.

While making investment banking a venue for unparalleled excitement, commercial banking should be made as boring an enterprise as many of us grew up believing it was before adulthood shattered our illusions. Now we know that bankers are not reluctant to part with *our* money. In fact they will part with our money *before* they actually receive it, because their loans are many multiples of deposits in place, as well as anticipated deposits. If commercial banking can be transformed into a truly dull activity, it would be an outcome of the international debt crisis that is truly divine. It will be a moment for the angels of finance, rather than the demons.

17 FOREIGN LENDING AT THE BRINK

Michael P. Claudon

Is the world debt situation a temporary liquidity problem or a debt crisis of major proportions? Wringing our collective hands over the U.S twin deficits (federal government budget and trade) is very much in vogue of late. These deficits are highly visible, close to home, and relatively easy to perceive. LDC debt, by contrast, is a distant, poorly understood problem between some tiny countries and isolated U.S. banks. In the halls of Congress and on Main Street USA, global debt is viewed as a curiosum, unrelated and nonthreatening to American economic well-being, that will sort itself out in time.

Nothing is further from the truth. Over 1,500 U.S. banks (more than 10 percent of total U.S. banks), operating in every state of the union, extended loans either directly or indirectly to Latin America. Bank income statements and balance sheets are losing credibility. Bank stocks have been consistently selling on Wall Street for less than their stated book value, making it harder for them to acquire new equity capital and also harder for them to satisfy the financing needs of a robust U.S. economy. The debt problem is a profound social and economic crisis that has already taken a huge toll on U.S. real incomes, jobs, exports, and banks. It has fostered austerity, strangled economic development, and caused incalculable political, human, and economic misery in the Third World.

Muddling through on a case by case basis promises dire consequences for U.S. commercial banking institutions, and for the global economy as well.

243

The post-World War II economic boom is over. Global growth in the 1990s is unlikely to match that of the 1950s and 1960s. Continuation of balance of payments and market liberalization conditionality policies will not contribute to enough meaningful growth in the South to offer a reliable debt resolution. Structural adjustment, as traditionally conceived and executed by the multilateral institutions (the IMF and the World Bank), needs to be reassessed and redirected in light of the realities of the next decade. The IMF and World Bank need to review and redirect lending programs to promote growth and development rather than focus singularly on balance of payments and internal relative price issues.

LDCs must develop a growth strategy for the 1990s consistent with anticipated globally declining growth rates and the South's long-term basic needs. Above all, LDC domestic investment spending must be dramatically increased, its targeting and sequencing brought into greater harmony with individual economies, and its pace, scope, and timing improved. Countries in the South must develop industrialization strategies consistent with their own needs and resource-labor mixes. Unfortunately, new lending from banks of the North, desperately needed to service debt and finance internal growth, declined precipitously after 1983, until by 1986 it had completely dried up. The debtors lost creditworthiness in the banks' eyes. Here is strong evidence of how fruitless efforts to devise credit packages between the banks and debtor countries have been.

Executing such a growth strategy is all but impossible until developing debtor countries' interest liabilities are comfortably within net export earnings. The $30 billion to $50 billion in desperately needed financial resources currently being transferred to the North each year are quickly depleting investment spending and debtor LDC growth potential. Although each country's situation tends to be unique, all debtors share one common need: interest liabilities must be discounted to the minimum politically feasible levels. The key element in resolving the crisis is that private banks and multilateral agencies officially and explicitly recognize that their loans will not be completely repaid.

In this chapter, I argue that some form of public intervention is an essential ingredient of a long-term resolution strategy because private banks are unlikely to voluntarily accomplish the requisite debt-discounting. The policy change must come from Washington in cooperation with other OECD country governments, the IMF, and the World Bank.

ORIGIN

When and why did foreign loans "go bad?"

> The International Monetary Fund (IMF) was about to convene its annual meeting in Toronto, Canada, when, in August 1982, Mexico shocked the financial community by declaring itself unable to meet its debt service obligations. Brazil and a host of other major borrowers quickly followed suit. Those declarations pushed the world banking system to the brink of financial chaos. Foreign lending was on trial.[1]

University of North Carolina economist William Darity, Jr. has argued persuasively that the debt explosion and LDC overborrowing may not have been totally benign. Did private banks of the North, especially large U.S. money center banks, push bad loans on LDCs? Did they offer credit lines at interest levels unsupported by prudent risk analysis? Did they imprudently lengthen maturities and offer unjustifiably large loans? In other words, have the big banks victimized themselves by making absurd lending decisions and advancing credit to foreign borrowers having less than a prayer of repaying?

> . . . [B]ankers as loan pushers become active door-to-door salesmen (albeit in pinstripe suits). They persuade borrowers to agree to credits when borrowers have no thoughts of obtaining a loan at all, or at least not a large one. Moreover, from this perspective, in euphoric times (such as the late 1970s and very early 1980s) banks will sell loans to borrowers in regions they [the banks] customarily leave alone.[2]

The early phases of explosive private bank lending to developing countries were intoxicating for all participants. The loans promised handsome returns to banks in the North and much needed development funds to LDCs of the South. A life-threatening post-party hangover began with Mexico's default in August 1982, and it continues unabated today.

LDCs' external debt increased 400 percent between 1972 and 1979, primarily in the form of loans from private banks. However, largely because of success-ful export programs and low interest rates, only fifteen developing countries were in arrears on payment of external debt in 1975. By the end of 1981, thirty-two countries were having problems making payments on time. Disaster struck in 1982 when U.S. interest rates, and subsequently those charged on commercial bank loans to LDCs, skyrocketed. The twenty-four major debtor

1. Claudon (1985: xix).
2. Darity and Horn (1988 xii).

LDCs shipped $37 billion in interest payments, money desperately needed for local development, to the U.S. and Europe that year. U.S. banks alone had lent $99 billion, 149 percent of their total worth, to these countries. Argentina, Brazil, and Mexico borrowed $52.4 billion, 84 percent of the banks' worth. Incredibly, these three countries had managed to borrow $31 billion from the nine largest U.S. money center banks. Worse yet, these same banks lent $60.3 billion, 222 percent of their combined worth, to all non-OPEC LDCs.

Interest Rates

When debt servicing problems first emerged, interest rates were significantly lower than they have been in recent years. In the United States, where most LDC debt is held, nominal interest rates rose faster than inflation rates, resulting in a significant upward trend in real interest rates applied against most LDC debt. U.S. money center banks responded to the trend and increasing volatility of U.S. interest rates with floating rates of interest on debt extensions, rather than on continuing the practice of having a fixed rate of interest apply during the term of a loan.[3] Bankers insisted on passing the interest rate risk of financial intermediation from lender to borrower. The LDCs, however, could not afford to absorb interest rate volatility during the protracted upswing of interest rates in the United States.

Dollar Appreciation

Real U.S. interest rates rose relative to real interest rates in other industrialized nations, causing significant appreciation of the U.S. dollar against other major currencies. Since most commodity prices in world markets are quoted in terms of dollars, appreciation in exchange markets increases the real cost of commodity purchases by countries whose currencies have depreciated against the dollar. Such cost increases tend to dampen commodity demands over an extended period of time, which can either depress commodity prices or prevent them from rising further.

An LDC's ability to meet its external debt servicing obligations is first and foremost constrained by its net export earnings, particularly when the debt is denominated in foreign currencies (mainly the U.S. dollar). LDCs tend to concentrate on raw materials and agricultural exports, commodities whose

3. See the discussion of the impetus to floating rates in Chapter 9 by Epstein.

markets are insensitive to falling prices. When the dollar pricing of commodities is depressed by dollar appreciation, the value of LDCs' net exports often declines, even when the volume of net exports rises. Accordingly, a rising dollar in currency exchange markets increases the difficulty of LDC debt servicing. Indeed, increased strength of the U.S. dollar in the early 1980s triggered widespread defaults on LDC debt held by American banks.

Rescheduling Debt Defaults

Every one of the banks appearing in Table 17-1, and each of the countries in Table 17-2, was in dire straits in 1982, especially after Mexico's default was quickly matched by Brazil and Argentina. U.S. banks, the IMF, the World Bank, and the United States government have responded to chronic post-1982 reschedulings, interest payment moratoria, and growing threats of debt repudiation with a case by case crisis management posture. Regional policymakers have tried most of the orthodox approaches to balance of payments and debt management. Every combination of muddling through, debt rescheduling, and North-inspired LDC austerity has been tried.

Rescheduling LDC debt added accrued interest on default to the principal amount due, causing the total volume of outstanding LDC debt to rise, even though no additional funds were advanced to LDCs. U.S. interest rates have declined significantly from their peak in 1981, but interest payments due on LDC debt have remained very high because of the rising amount of debt incurred from rescheduling. Moreover, while the dollar's foreign exchange value has declined substantially since 1985, commodity prices have not rebounded much from previously depressed levels. As a result, a number of LDCs have and are facing annual interest obligations substantially in excess of their net export earnings.[4]

Years of negotiations and myriad structural adjustment programs have produced little beyond a widening feeling of debt fatigue. With few exceptions, orthodox policy has barely held impending political, social, and financial disaster at bay. Debtor LDCs are now facing interest payments greatly in excess of their net export earnings. Debt repudiation, defaults (such as Brazil's unilateral suspension of interest payments on some commercial bank loans in 1987), and a debtors' cartel are looming on the horizon. U.S. banks have been

---

4. In several widely publicized cases, the net export positions of LDCs are valued at slightly more than half the annual interest due on debt.

Table 17-1. Exposure of U.S. Banks to Six Troubled
Developing Countries, 1984

($ Billions, Percent)

Institution	Total Loans	Total as a Percent of Stockholders Equity[a]
Bank of America	7.8	150.9
Citicorp	12.5	206.7
Chase Manhattan	7.4	212.7
Manufacturers Hanover	7.8	268.5
Morgan Guaranty	4.9	143.3
Continental Illinois[b]	2.4	129.9
Chemical	4.6	196.7
Bankers Trust	3.3	177.6
First Chicago	2.4	126.9
First Interstate	1.5	70.8
Security Pacific	1.6	88.8
Wells Fargo	1.7	129.8
Nine Money Center Banks	53.2	179.2

a. Includes common and preferred.
b. Continental Illinois has since gone bankrupt.

Source: Pool and Stamos (1987: 82).

accumulating loan loss reserves to help cover possible defaults, if and when they begin. Some banks have been able to unload their LDC loans, albeit at discounts ranging from as high as 40 percent of loan face values. Perhaps banks' creative financial gymnastics can hold off the crisis for awhile, but stopgap strategies affect symptoms, not causes. They certainly do not make banks or business communities they serve any healthier.

The popular view notwithstanding, developing debtor countries will not (and cannot) trade their way out of debt troubles. Most large debtors realized substantial export gains during the early 1980s, but debtors' export growth rates turned negative in 1985, reaching over 4 percent per year by 1987. The very success of these export drives has begun to work against the LDCs. The United States has been running a $13 billion annual trade deficit with Latin America since 1982. The Omnibus Trade Bill bristles with new impediments to expanded LDC exports to the United States, their largest customer. Latin American commodity imports have been cut in half since 1981.

Table 17-2. Financial Resource Balance

($ Billions, Percent)

Latin America		Financial Resource Balance Compared to War Reparations of Germany and France		
Year	Total[a]	Country/Period	Balance/GNP	Balance/Exports
1978	10,327	Germany (1925-1932)	2.5	13.4
1979	6,628	France (1872-1975)	5.6	30.0
1980	5,070	Latin America (1982-1985)	5.3	32.5
1981	5,582	Argentina	5.6	38.2
1982	-22,419	Brazil	3.3	28.9
1983	-38,537	Chile	4.8	21.7
1984	-38,345	Colombia	0.1	1.1
1985	-39,627	Costa Rica	6.3	16.7
		Ecuador	3.8	16.5
		Mexico	7.4	40.0
		Peru	1.7	9.4
		Uruguay	0.4	1.7
		Venezuela	11.7	42.3

a. A negative entry means that financial resources are flowing from South to North.

Source: Devlin (1987).

The danger in the present situation is that banks and LDCs can fall into a war of attrition, grinding each other down in an effort to gain a negotiating advantage. At some point, that struggle could turn into a mutual suicide pact, crippling both banks and LDCs (Robinson 1988: 7).

A POLICY PROPOSAL[5]

The future is not bright if debt rescheduling and muddling through continue to be the only financial tools used to address the LDC debt problem.[6] The

5. This proposal was originally conceived by Robert A. Jones, Chairman of the Board, Geonomics Institute for International Economic Advancement.
6. The rescheduling of LDC debt must not always mandate repayment of principal. In most instances, paydowns on LDC debt are completely beyond any possibility. Indeed, it is the inability to service interest payments on LDC debt, not the impossibility of paying down LDC debt, that has required many large banks to write off LDC debt from their balance sheets and reported income.

situation promises to worsen through time and portends a banking crisis (or collapse). To make matters even worse, there appears to be a widespread notion that LDCs must somehow reduce their national debt when industrialized countries are not expected to reduce theirs (and, in fact, sometimes continue to rapidly expand their national debt because of fiscal deficit financing). Demands from international lending organizations that LDC governments raise taxes and cut government spending are not only politically unacceptable, but they smack of imperialism. Demands for tighter fiscal policy, greater wage restraint, and lower inflation are intended to raise the LDC net export earnings to service huge interest liabilities, and to achieve this end by limiting LDC living standards. If IMF and World Bank conditionality demands were fully met, an economic crisis might be temporarily averted, but only at the expense of creating a much more damaging political crisis.

Now is the moment to consider bold, new, comprehensive policy initiatives involving some form of debt service forgiveness, or some sort of new international institution that can ameliorate the current exposure situation. It should also provide adequate new lending to LDCs so they can regain their prior growth levels, and facilitate adjustment of debt service requirements so as to guarantee these will remain within debtors' net export earnings.

Given the benefit of hindsight, it appears now that competition among major banks for LDC loan business encouraged them to overlook prudent lending standards. Credit became excessively available to LDC officials who had seemingly insatiable desires to employ more capital within their countries. LDC external debt volume increased much too rapidly relative to financial resource constraints. It soon became very difficult for many LDCs to meet their debt service obligations, their debt in terms of interest payments, and the contractual reductions in outstanding principal.

U.S. bank reclassification of LDC debt to nonperforming loans has seriously impaired the capital position of large money center banks. Write-downs of the LDC debt have also begun to reduce the general level of depositor confidence in the American banking system. In the equities market for bank stock (shares) there are daily rumors about whether all problem loans of large banks are being rigidly monitored by banking regulators or properly reported on accounting statements released by the large banks. In some instances, there is speculation that proper reporting of problem loans might result in write-offs that could exceed the capital position of several large banks.

U.S. thrift and banking institution regulators have long been concerned about potentially inadequate funding for deposit insurance programs. If the officials administering these programs were to ask Congress for full funding of potential deposit insurance liabilities, the huge sum likely to be requested would shock and frighten the American people. If funded by Congress, it would greatly enlarge the federal government deficit. It is therefore suspected that banking regulators do not want to force large banks to write down all LDC debt that might be questionable, or the related reduction of bank capital might further scare depositors and create a need for emergency funding of deposit insurance programs.

Underlying Assumptions

LDC interest payments on debt must be reduced to within reasonable net export limits or debt rescheduling will continue to inflate the principal on which interest is payable and will soon push interest defaults up to 50 percent on interest due. Achieving a reduction in interest payments will avert a crisis and stabilize the debt situation. The only way to achieve lower interest payments is to substantially reduce the interest rate applied to LDC debt.

THE PROPOSAL

The interest rate reduction can be initiated by the U.S. Congress in the following manner:

1. Congress can enact a law authorizing the U.S. Treasury to guarantee LDC debt held by American banks. Under such a law, American bankers could petition the Treasury for the LDC debt guarantee provided that a petitioning bank agrees to price the guaranteed debt according to a legislated formula. The formula would allow pricing of guaranteed debt at about one percentage point more than the average cost (excluding administration and marketing) of demand deposit funds at an average bank. Under present circumstances, the intent of the pricing formula would be the calculation of a lending rate of 5 percent, perhaps as much as 5.5 percent. The formula might also include marginal as well as average cost and all or part of savings passbook account cost.
2. Congress can direct current and supplemental funding of international lending organizations to assume roughly half of the interest payments due on guaranteed LDC debt. Such funding could reduce interest rates payable on LDC debt to 2.5 percent, which should reduce LDC interest payment liabilities comfortably below net export levels. Congress should extend discretion to administrators of this funding. Such power to fund or not fund

guaranteed LDC interest payments should not be linked with any demands on LDCs regarding fiscal and other governmental policies. Instead, the discretion to fund should be based on debt-level monitoring of each LDC. The interest program enables LDCs to pay down debt, but this should not be a condition of funding. Debt levels should be allowed to increase, but only if interest payments remain comfortably within net export values. Congress might want to give administrators additional authority to vary the interest funding proportion based on general financial criteria it establishes.

3. Bankers who successfully petition the Treasury for a loan guarantee will be able to reclassify loans back to a performing status, which of course helps boost reported profits and the capital position of the bank.

EVALUATION

Most of the initial congressional reaction to the proposal is likely to be negative. Members of Congress may be politically uncomfortable with proposals appearing to remove the American bank stockholder's loss risk from the LDC debt crisis. Yet Congress, through its funding of international lending organizations, is already helping the bank shareholder, albeit only temporarily, according to this analysis. In effect, there is currently public intervention in the debt crisis on a massive scale through the World Bank and the IMF. But this intervention is poorly planned and leads to no solution. The proposal outlined in this chapter would not initiate public intervention—intervention is rampant—it would result in effective intervention.

Moreover, while the public may view the suggested legislation as a bank bailout, the Washington banking lobby will initially react very negatively to the proposed reduction of LDC lending rates from prime-plus to a percentage point above their lowest cost of funds. Obviously, potential interest earnings of participating banks will be reduced, but not as much as will occur without some resolution to the LDC debt crisis. If the banking lobby is vocal this may be to the good, for the legislation will look to the public less like a bailout for large banks.

If there is no protection for large banks in the form of a guarantee, it can be argued that Congress will be forced to bail out the Federal Deposit Insurance program (and the bank shareholder) for a considerable sum of money. Of course, the public might well complain about funding LDC interest payments on debt. Yet if all defaults are permitted, the American public will be the biggest loser of all, and at a very hefty price. The legislation might appear one-sided in favor of LDCs, but it is not. Administrators' financial oversight responsibility to the interest funding holds an enormous club over LDCs, one which should be used with proper discretion for benefit to all concerned. Threats of debt boycotts are currently very serious, but would surely vanish under the suggested plan.

The capital strengthening of the banking system achievable through reclassification is precisely what is needed now. Such banking benefits should be provided at the cost of strict loan reviews by the Federal Reserve System prior to Treasury action on the guarantee. Through a strict loan review, all nonperforming and questionable loans could be properly accounted for, perhaps offsetting much of the benefit to bank capital structures provided by the loan guarantee. Such loan review nonetheless will help restore public confidence in the banking system.

It is doubtful that banks holding LDC debt will refuse to apply for the federal guarantee. The cost of applying a lower lending rate is far less than the cost of default, and the interest cost is likely to be offset by profits accrued from loan upgrading. In addition, with a government guarantee, bankers could probably issue marketable LDC certificates from a pool of LDC debt. Such an underwriting would broaden LDC debt ownership and, more importantly, provide American bankers with a needed new source of liquidity.

BIBLIOGRAPHY

Addison, Tony, and Lionel Demery. 1986. "The Impact of Liberalization of Growth and Equity." International Employment Policies Working Paper 4. Geneva: ILO. Mimeo. World Employment Programme Paper (September).

Aguilar, Adolfo. 1987-1988. "Mexico: The Presidential Problem." *Foreign Policy* (Winter): 53.

Altimir, Oscar. 1984. "Poverty, Income Distribution, and Child Welfare in Latin America: A Comparison of Pre- and Post- Recession Data." In Richard Jolly and Giovanni Andrea Cornia, eds., *The Impact of World Recession on Children*. Oxford: Pergamon Press.

AMEX Bank Review. 1988. "Japan as Global Creditor: A Changing Profile" (March 24).

Apcar, Leonard M., and Buck Brown. 1988. "Branch Bullying: Small Texas Towns Are the Latest Victims of Big Banks' Crisis." *Wall Street Journal* (May 25).

Arellano, Jose Pablo, and Joseph Ramos. 1987. "Case Studies: Chile." In Donald R. Lessard and John Williamson, eds., *Capital Flight and Third World Debt*. Washington, DC: Institute for International Economics.

Arkadie, Brian van. 1983. "The IMF Prescriptions for Structural Management in Tanzania." In K. Jansen, ed., *Monetarism, Economic Crisis and the Third World*. London: Frank Cass.

Avramovic, Dragoslav. 1987. *Economic Growth and External Debt*. Baltimore, MD: Johns Hopkins University Press.

Axilrod, Stephen. 1988. "Let's Go Slow in Repealing the Glass-Steagall Act." *The International Economy*, vol. 2: 2 (March/April).

Bailey, Jeff, and Robert Guenther. 1988. "Top Bankers Received Healthy Bonuses, Despite Firms' Record Losses in 1987." *Wall Street Journal* (March 29).

Bailey, Jeff, and G. Christian Hill. 1988. "Federal Fiasco: Banks and S&Ls Face New Wave of Failures as Regulators Goof Up." *Wall Street Journal* (March 25).

255

Bailey, Norman A., and Alfred J. Watkins. 1987. "Mexico's Dilemma." *New York Times* (December 29).

Balassa, Bela. 1981. *Structural Adjustment Policies in Developing Countries.* World Bank Staff Working Paper 464. Washington, DC: World Bank (July).

Balassa, Bela, et al. 1986. *Toward Renewed Economic Growth in Latin America.* Washington, DC: Institute for International Economics.

Barrett, Anthony. 1985. "Regional Variations in the Determinants of Debt Repayment Problems." Presented at the meetings of the North American Economics Association, New York (December).

Bartels, Andrew H. 1988. "A Comprehensive Framework for Relieving LDC Debt Burdens." Mimeo prepared for "The Economy in the 90's: New Voices, New Proposals." LBJ School of Public Affairs, University of Texas at Austin (April 15).

Barzel, Yoram. 1982. "Measurement and the Organization of Markets." *Journal of Law and Economics* 25: 27-48.

Bates, Robert H. 1981. *Markets and States in Tropical Africa.* Berkeley, CA: University of California Press.

Bauer, Peter Tamàs. 1981. *Equality, the Third World, and Economic Delusion.* London: Weidenfield and Nicolson.

Becker, D., J. Frieden, S. P. Schatz, and R. L. Sklar. 1987. *Postimperialism: International Capitalism and Development in the Twentieth Century.* Boulder, CO: Lynne Rienner.

Becker, Gary. 1965. "A Theory of the Allocation of Time." *Economic Journal* 65: 493-517.

Bell, Daniel. 1988. "Some Simple Predictions About Planet Earth in 2013." *Washington Post National Weekly Edition* (February 22).

Bennett, Robert A. 1988. "Banks Tread Cautiously on Panamanian Arrears." *New York Times* (March 10).

Berg, E. J. 1966. "Major Issues of Wage Policy in Africa." In A. M. Ross, ed., *Industrial Relations and Economic Development.* London: MacMillan.

Bird, Graham. 1984a. "Relationship, Resource Uses, and the Conditionality Debate." In Tony Killick, ed., *Adjustment and Financing in the Developing World: The Role of the International Monetary Fund.* Washington, DC: IMF.

Bird, Graham. 1984b. "Balance of Payments Policy in Developing Countries." In Tony Killick, ed., *The Quest for Economic Stabilization.* London: Overseas Development Institute.

Bitterman, Henry J. 1973. *The Refunding of International Debt.* Durham, NC: Duke University Press.

Block, Fred. 1977. "The Origins of International Economic Disorder: A Study of United States International Monetary Policy from World War II to the Present." Berkeley, CA: University of California Press.

Bogdanowicz-Bindert, Christine A. 1986. "The Debt Crisis: The Baker Plan Revisited." *Journal of Interamerican Studies and World Affairs* 28, 3 (Fall).

Bornschier, Volker, and Christopher Chase-Dunn. 1985. "Transnational Corporations and Underdevelopment." New York, NY: Praeger.

Bradley, William (Senator). 1986. "A Proposal for Third World Debt Management." U.S. Senate Mimeo (June).

Brett, E. A. 1985. *The World Economy Since the War: The Politics of Uneven Development*. New York, NY: Praeger.

Bridges, Tyler. 1987. "Chile Cuts $2.3 Billion of Red Ink by Turning Debt into Investment." *Christian Science Monitor* (December 10).

Bulow, Jeremy, and Kenneth Rogoff. 1988. "Sovereign Debt: Is to Forgive to Forget?" Mimeo. Graduate School of Business, Stanford University (February).

Canak, William L. 1988. "Debt, Austerity, and Development in the New International Division of Labor." In William L. Canak, ed., *Lost Promises: Debt, Austerity, and Development in Latin America*. Boulder, CO: Westview Press.

Carr, Barry. 1986. In Barry Carr and Ricardo A. Montoya, eds., *The Mexican Left, the Popular Movements, and the Politics of Austerity, 1982-1985*. San Diego, CA: Center for U.S.-Mexican Studies, University of California, San Diego.

Carvounis, Chris. 1984. *The Debt Dilemma of Developing Nations: Issues and Cases*. Westport, CT: Quorum Books.

Christian, Shirley. 1988. "Argentina's Economy Seen as Out of Control." *New York Times* (April 18): D14.

Claudon, Michael P. 1985. *World Debt Crisis, International Lending on Trial*. Cambridge, MA: Ballinger Publishing.

Cline, William R. 1972. "Potential Effects of Income Redistribution on Economic Growth." New York, NY: Praeger.

Cline, William R. 1982. "Can the East Asian Model of Development Be Generalized?" *World Development*, vol. 10, no. 2.

Cline, William R. 1984. *International Debt: Systemic Risk and Policy Response*. Washington, DC: International Institute for Economics.

Coase, Ronald. 1960. "The Problem of Social Cost." *Journal of Law and Economics* 25: 27-48.

Cohen, Roger. 1988. "Wavering Leadership in Brazil Renders Any Economic Improvements Unlikely." *Wall Street Journal* (April 6).

Collet, Merrill. 1988. "Pacemaker '88: Carlos Andres Perez." *South* (January): 30.

Corbo, Vittorio. 1985. "Reform and Macro-Economic Adjustment in Chile during 1974-1984." *World Development* 13: 3 (August).

Corbo,V., M. Goldstein, and M. Khan, eds. 1987. *Growth-Oriented Adjustment Programs*. Washington, DC: IMF and the World Bank.

Corden, Warner Max. 1984. "Booming Sector and Dutch Disease Economics: A Survey." *Oxford Economic Papers*, 36, no. 3 (November).

Cornia, G. A., R. Jolly, and F. Stewart, eds. 1987. *Adjustment with a Human Face*. Oxford: Clarendon Press.

Cortazar, Rene. 1986. "Employment, Real Wages and External Constraint: The Case of Brazil and Chile." International Employment Policies Working Paper 8. World Employment Programme Paper. Mimeo. Geneva: ILO (October).

Cortes, Rosalia, and Adriana Marshall. 1986. "Salario Real, Composicion del Consumo y Balanza Comercial." *Desarrollo Economico* 26: 72-88.

Damm, Kenneth. 1982. "The Rules of the Game: Reform and Evolution in the International Monetary System." Chicago, IL: University of Chicago Press.

Darity, William Jr., and Bobbie L. Horn. 1988. *The Loan Pushers: The Role of Commercial Banks in the International Debt Crisis*. Cambridge, MA: Ballinger Publishing.

Demery, Lionel, and Tony Addison. 1987. "The Alleviation of Poverty Under Structural Adjustment." Washington, DC: World Bank.

Deppler, Michael, and Martin Williamson. 1987. "Capital Flight: Concepts, Measurement and Issues." *Staff Studies for the World Economic Outlook.* Washington, DC: IMF (August).

Devlin, Robert. 1987. "Economic Restructuring in Latin America in the Face of Foreign Debt and the External Transfer Problem." *CEPAL Review* 32. Washington, DC: CEPAL (August).

Diaz-Alejandro, Carlos. 1985. "The Early 1980s in Latin America: The 1930s One More Time?" Paper prepared for the Expert Meeting on Crisis and Development in Latin America and the Caribbean, ECLAC, Santiago, Chile (April 23-May 3).

Dietz, James L. 1987. "Debt, International Corporations, and Economic Change in Latin America and the Caribbean." *Latin American Perspectives* 55: 508-515.

Dillon, K. B., C. M. Watson, G. R. Kincaid, and C. Puckahtikon. 1985. "Recent Developments in External Debt Restructuring." Occasional Paper 40. Washington, DC: IMF.

Donovan, David J. 1982. "Macroeconomic Performance and Adjustment Under Fund Supported Programs: The Experience of the Seventies." IMF Staff Papers (June 29), pp. 171-203.

Donovan, David J. 1984. "Nature and Origins of Debt-Servicing Difficulties." *Finance and Development* (December).

Dornbusch, Rudiger. 1986. "International Debt and Economic Instability." *Debt, Financial Stability, and Public Policy.* Kansas City, MO: Federal Reserve Bank of Kansas City, pp. 63-86.

Dutt, Amitava K. 1984. "Stagnation, Income Distribution and Monopoly Power." *Cambridge Journal of Economics* 8: 25-40.

ECLAC (Economic Commission for Latin America and the Caribbean). 1985. *External Debt in Latin America: Adjustment Policies and Renegotiation.* Boulder, CO: Lynne Rienner.

ECLAC (Economic Commission for Latin America and the Caribbean). 1986. *Debt, Adjustment, and Renegotiation in Latin America: Orthodox and Alternative Approaches.* Boulder, CO: Lynne Rienner.

ECLAC (Economic Commission for Latin America and the Caribbean). 1987. "Preliminary Overview of the Latin American Economy, 1987" (December 31).

Edwards, Sebastian. 1984. "LDC Foreign Borrowing and Default Risk: An Empirical Investigation." *American Economic Review* (September): 726-734.

Ellis, Frank. 1982. "Agricultural Price Policy in Tanzania." *World Development,* vol. 10.

Ellis, Frank. 1983. "Agricultural Marketing and Peasant-State Transfers in Tanzania." *Journal of Peasant Studies,* vol. 10.

Ellis, Frank. 1984. "Relative Agricultural Prices and the Urban Bias Model: A Comparative Analysis of Tanzania and Fiji." *Journal of Development Studies* 20: 3

Estado de Minas. 1987. *Dieese acha Pequeño Novo Piso Salarial.* Bello Horizonte: Estado de Minas (November).

Feder, Gershon, and Richard Just. 1977. "A Study of Debt Servicing Capacity Applying Logit Analysis." *Journal of Development Economics:* 25-39.

Feder, G., R. Just, and K. Ross. 1981. "Projecting Debt Service Capacity of Developing Countries." *Journal of Financial and Quantitative Analysis*: 651-659.

Feinberg, Richard. 1987. "Multilateral Lending and Latin America." *World Economy* 10: 205-218.

Feinberg, Richard, and Valleriana Kallab. 1984. "Adjustment Crisis in the Third World." Washington, DC: Overseas Development Council.

Ferrer, Aldo. 1984. "Spreading the Burden of Debt." *South* (July).

Ffrench-Davis et al. 1985. Deuda Externa, Industricional y Ahorro en America Latina. Coleccion Estudios. Santiago: CIEPLAN (September).

FIBGE (Fundacao Instituto Brasileiro de Geografia e Estatistica). 1987. *Anuario Estatistico do Brasil, 1986*. Rio de Janeiro: FIBGE.

Fields, Gary S. 1984. "Employment, Income Distribution and Economic Growth in Seven Small Open Economies." *Economic Journal* (March).

Fishlow, Albert. 1985. "The State of Latin American Economics." *Economic and Social Progress in Latin America, 1985 Report*. Washington, DC: IDB.

Folkerts-Landau, David. 1985. "The Changing Role of International Bank Lending in Development Finance." *IMF Staff Papers*, vol. 32 (June).

Fox, Jonathan. 1987. "Popular Participation and Access to Food: Mexico's Community Supply Councils, 1979-1985." In Scott Whiteford and Ann Ferguson, eds., *Food Security and Hunger in Central America and Mexico*. Boulder, CO: Westview Press.

Foxley, Alejandro. 1982. *Latin American Experiments in Neoconservative Economics*. Berkeley, CA: University of California Press.

Foxley, Alejandro. 1987. "The Foreign Debt Problem: The View from Latin America." *International Journal of Political Economy* 17 (1): 88-116.

Foxley, Alejandro, and Dagmar Raczynski. 1984. "Vulnerable Groups in Recessionary Situations: Case of Children and the Young in Chile." *World Development* 12: 3.

Frank, Charles R., and William R. Cline. 1971. "Measurement of Debt Servicing Capacity." *Journal of International Economics:* 327-344.

Frenkel, Roberto, and Guillermo O'Donnell. 1979. "The Stabilization Program of the International Monetary Fund and Their Internal Impacts." In Richard R. Fagan, ed., *Capitalism and the State in U.S.-Latin American Relations*. Stanford, CA: Stanford University Press.

Fröbel, F., J. Heinrichs, and O. Kreye. 1985. *The New International Division of Labour: Structural Unemployment in Industrialized Countries and Industrialization in Developing Countries*. Cambridge, MA: Cambridge University Press.

Furtado, Celso. 1987. "Transnationalization and Monetarism." *International Journal of Political Economy* 17 (1): 15-44 (Spring).

Garcia, Norberto E. 1987. "Remuneraciones, Precios e Importaciones de Bienes, Ecuador, 1970-82." *Politica Salarial, Inflacion y Restriccion Externa*. Santiago: PREALC-OIT.

Garcia, Norberto E., and Victor Tokman. 1985. "Acumulacion, Empleo y Crisis." *Investigaciones Sobre Empleo*. Santiago: PREALC.

Garcia Perez, Alan. 1985. Inaugural Address. *Foreign Broadcast Information Service, Daily Report*. Latin America (July 29): J3-J24.

Garten, Jeffrey E. 1982. "Rescheduling Sovereign Debt: Is There a Better Approach?" *World Economy* 5 (3): 279-290 (November).

Geller, T., and Victor Tokman. 1986. "External Debt Crisis and Latin American Development Rethinking: Theories and Practice." Geneva: ILO.

Ghai, Dharam. 1987. "Economic Growth, Structural Change and Labour Absorption in Africa: 1960-1985." Mimeo. Geneva: UNRISD (December).

Ghani, Ejaz. 1984. "The Effects of Devaluation on Employment and Poverty in Developing Countries." World Employment Programme Working Paper, WEP2-32, WP.57: 7-12 (November).

Glassman, Debra. 1985. "Determinants of Debt Rescheduling of Less-Developed Countries: An Exploratory Analysis." Presented at Meetings of the North American Economics Association, New York (December).

Glyn, A., A. Hughes, A. Lipietz, and A. Singh. 1988. *The Rise and Fall of the Golden Age*. Cambridge, England: Cambridge University (March). Unpublished.

Golden, Tim. 1988. "Glory Days over for Ecuador's Tough-Guy Leader." *Miami Herald* (February 5).

Goodhart, Charles. 1988. "The Foreign-Exchange Market: A Random Walk With a Dragging Anchor." LSE Finanical Markets Group Discussion Paper.

Green, Reginald H. 1983. "Political-Economic Adjustment and the IMF Conditionality: Tanzania 1974-1981." In J. Williamson, ed., *IMF Conditionality*. Washington, DC: Institute for International Economics.

Green, Reginald H. 1986. "Stabilization, Adjustment and Basic Needs in Sub-Saharan Africa: Annotated Jottings Towards an Agenda." Geneva: ILO.

Griffith-Jones, Stephany. 1984. *International Finance and Latin America*. London: Croom Helm.

Griffith-Jones, Stephany, and Osvaldo Sunkel. 1986. *Debt and Development Crises in Latin America: The End of an Illusion*. Oxford: Clarendon Press.

Grindle, Merilee. 1988. "The Response to Austerity: Political and Economic Strategies of Mexico's Rural Poor." In William L. Canak, ed., *Lost Promises: Debt, Austerity and Development in Latin America*. Boulder, CO: Westview Press.

Grinspun, Bernard. 1984. "Support Us Debtor Nations." *Euromoney* (October).

Guitian, Miguel. 1980. "Fund Conditionality and the International Adjustment Process." *Finance and Development* (December).

Guitian, Miguel. 1982. "Economic Management and International Monetary Fund Conditionality." In Tony Killick, ed., *Adjustment and Financing in the Developing World: The Role of the International Monetary Fund*. Washington, DC: IMF.

Guttentag, Jack, and Richard Herring. 1985. *The Current Crisis in International Lending*. Washington, DC: Brookings Institution.

Haignere, Clara S. 1983. "The Application of the Free-Market Economic Model in Chile and the Effects on the Population's Health Status." *International Journal of Health Services* 13 (3): 389-405.

Hakkert, Ralph, and Frank Goza. 1988. "Demographic Consequences of Austerity Policies in Latin America." In William L. Canak, ed., *Lost Promises: Debt, Austerity and Development in Latin America*. Boulder, CO: Westview Press.

Hardy, C. S. 1982. *Rescheduling Developing Country Debts, 1956-1981: Lessons and Recommendations*. Washington, DC: Overseas Development Council.

Helleiner, Gerald K. 1985. "Balance of Payments Experience and Growth Prospects of Developing Countries: A Synthesis." Mimeo prepared for UNCTAD Balance of Payments Adjustment Project.

Helpman, Elhanan. 1987. "The Simple Analytics of Debt-Equity Swaps and Debt Forgiveness." Mimeo. Tel Aviv University (September).

Hewko, John, and Jorge Chediek. 1988. "Economic and Political Awakening of Argentina's Peronists." *Wall Street Journal* (March 11): 23.

Hirschman, Albert O. 1981. *Essays in Trespassing: Economics to Politics and Beyond.* Cambridge, MA: Cambridge University Press.

Hollihan, Michael. 1988. "Ecuador's Free-Market Experiment Takes Wrong Turn." *Wall Street Journal* (April 8): 17.

Hyden, Goran. 1980. *Beyond Ujamaa: Underdevelopment and an Uncaptured Peasantry.* London: Heinemann.

Hymer, Stephen. 1972. "The Internationalization of Capital." *Journal of Economic Issues* 6: 91-111.

IDB (Inter-American Development Bank). 1985. *Economic and Social Progress in Latin America.* Washington, DC: IDB.

IBRD (International Bank for Reconstruction and Development). 1981. *Accelerated Development in Sub-Saharan Africa: An Agenda for Action.* Washington, DC: World Bank.

IBRD (International Bank for Reconstruction and Development). 1985. *World Development Report.* Washington, DC: World Bank.

ILO (International Labour Organization). 1964. "Methods and Principles of Wage Regulation." Report for the Second Africa Regional Conference. Geneva: ILO.

ILO (International Labour Organization). 1967. "Report to the Government of the United Republic of Tanzania on Wages, Incomes and Prices Policy." Turner Report I. Geneva: ILO.

ILO (International Labour Organization). 1975. "Report to the Government of Tanzania on the Past, Present and Future of Incomes Policy in Tanzania." Turner Report II. Geneva: ILO.

ILO (International Labour Organization). 1976. *Employment, Growth and Basic Needs: A One World Problem.* Geneva: ILO

ILO (International Labour Organization). 1986. *Report of the Director General to the 12th Conference of American States Members of the International Labour Organization.* Montreal: ILO.

ILO (International Labour Organization). 1988. *Distributional Aspects of Stabilization Programmes in Tanzania.* Geneva: ILO.

ILO/JASPA (International Labour Organization/Jobs and Skills Programme for Africa). 1978. *Towards Self-Reliance: Development, Employment and Equity Issues in Tanzania.* Addis Ababa: ILO/JASPA.

ILO/JASPA (International Labour Organization/Jobs and Skills Programme for Africa). 1982. *Basic Needs in Danger: A Basic Needs Oriented Development Strategy for Tanzania.* Addis Ababa: ILO/JASPA.

ILO/PREALC (International Labour Organization/Programa Regional del Empleo para America Latina). 1986. *Creation of Productive Employment: A Task that Cannot Be Postponed.* PREALC Working Paper, no. 280. Santiago: ILO/PREALC.

IMF (International Monetary Fund). 1959. "International Reserves and Liquidity: A Study by the Staff of the International Monetary Fund." Washington, DC: IMF.

IMF (International Monetary Fund). 1985a. *Summary Proceedings of the Fortieth Annual Meeting of the Board of Governors.* Washington, DC: IMF (October 8-11).

IMF (International Monetary Fund). 1985b. "Fund Supported Programs, Fiscal Policy, and the Distribution of Income." Prepared by Fiscal Affairs Department, approved by Vito Tanzi. Washington, DC: IMF (April 23).

IMF (International Monetary Fund). 1985c. *International Financial Statistics: 1984 Yearbook*. Washington, DC: IMF.

IMF (International Monetary Fund). 1986. *World Economic Outlook*. Washington, DC: IMF (April).

IMF (International Monetary Fund). 1987. *World Economic Outlook*. Washington, DC: IMF.

IMF (International Monetary Fund). 1988. *World Economic Outlook*. Washington, DC: IMF.

Islam, Shafiqul. 1988. "Breaking the International Debt Deadlock." *Critical Issues* 2. Council on Foreign Relations Publication.

Jamal, Vali. 1982. *Rural-Urban Gap and Income Distribution: The Case of Tanzania*. Addis Ababa: ILO.

Jamal, Vali. 1985. *Structural Adjustment and Food Security in Uganda*. World Employment Programme Working Paper. Geneva: ILO.

Jamal, Vali. 1986. "Economics of Devaluation: The Case of Tanzania." *Labour and Society*. World Employment Programme Working Paper (September).

Jamal, Vali, and John Weeks. 1987. "Rural-Urban Income Trends in Sub-Saharan Africa." Geneva: ILO.

Jamal, Vali, and John Weeks. 1988. "The Vanishing Rural-Urban Gap in Sub-Saharan Africa." *International Labour Review* 127: 3.

Jamal, Vali, and John Weeks. Forthcoming a. "Rural Urban Income Trends in Sub-Saharan Africa." *International Labour Review*.

Jamal, Vali, and John Weeks. Forthcoming b. *Africa Misunderstood: Or, Whatever Happened to the Rural-Urban Gap?* London: Rutledge.

Johnson, G. G. 1985. "Formulation of Exchange Rate Policies in Adjustment Programs." Occasional Paper 36. Washington, DC: IMF.

Joint Economic Committee. 1986. "The Impact of the Latin American Debt Crisis on the U.S. Economy." A staff study prepared for the Joint Economic Committee, Washington, DC (May 10).

Joint Ministerial Committee of the Board of Governors of the World Bank and the International Monetary Fund on the Transfer of Real Resources to Developing Countries. 1987. "Protecting the Poor during Periods of Adjustment." Washington, DC: World Bank.

Jolly, Richard, and Giovanni Andrea Cornia, eds. 1984. "The Impact of the World Recession on Children." *World Development*. Washington, DC: UNICEF (March).

Kaletsky, Anatole. 1985. *The Costs of Default*. New York, NY: Priority Press.

Kaufman, Henry. 1986. *Interest Rates, the Markets, and the New Financial World*. New York, NY: Times Books.

Kaufman, Robert. 1986. "Democratic and Authoritarian Responses to the Debt Issue: Argentina, Brazil and Mexico." In Miles Kahler, ed., *The Politics of International Debt*. Ithaca, NY: Cornell University Press.

Kenen, Peter B. 1984. "Comments on the Debt Crisis." Working Party on the Future of International Bank Lending. Institute of International Finance. Mimeo (January 31-February 1): 36-37.

Killick, Tony. 1984a. *International Monetary Fund and Stabilization.* New York, NY: St. Martin's Press.

Killick, Tony. 1984b. *The Quest for Economic Stabilization.* New York, NY: St. Martin's Press.

King, Robin A., and Michael D. Robinson. 1988. "The Economic Impacts of International Debt Rescheduling." Presented at the Eastern Economic Association Meetings in Boston. (March 10-12).

King, Robin A., and Michael D. Robinson. Forthcoming. "Debt Rescheduling: Postponing the Crisis?" In K. Fatemi, ed., *International Trade and Finance: A North American Perspective.* New York, NY: Praeger.

Klein, Emilio, and Jose Wurgaft. 1985. "La Creacion de Empleo en Periodos de Crisis." *Investigaciones sobre Empleo.* Santiago: PREALC.

Korner, P., T. S. Geromass, and T. Rainer. 1986. *The IMF and The Debt Crisis: A Guide to the Third World Dilemma.* London: Zed Press.

Kraft, Joseph. 1984. *The Mexican Rescue.* New York, NY: Group of Thirty.

Ladendorf, Kirk. 1988. "Austin Banks Tighten Requirements for Loans." *Austin-American Statesman* (April 17).

LAM (Latin American Monitor). 1987. *Mexico 1987: Annual Report on Government, Economy, and Business.* London: Latin American Monitor, Ltd.

Lancaster, Kelvin. 1966. "A New Approach to Consumer Theory." *Journal of Political Economy* 74: 132-157.

Landell-Mills, Pierre. 1981. "Structural Adjustment Lending: Early Experience." *Finance and Development* 18:4.

Lever, Lord H. 1983. "The International Debt Threat: A Concerted Way Out." *Economist* (July 9).

Lewis, William A. 1950. "The Industrialization of the British West Indies." *Caribbean Economic Review.*

Lipton, Michael. 1977. *Why Poor People Stay Poor: Urban Bias in World Development.* London: Temple Smith.

Lipton, Michael. 1984a. In Gerald M. Meier and Dudley Seers, eds., *Pioneers in Development.* World Bank Publication. New York, NY: Oxford University Press.

Lipton, Michael. 1984b. "Urban Bias Revisited." In John Harriss and Mick Moore, eds., *Journal of Development Studies* 20: 3 (April).

Litan, Robert. 1988. "What Reforming Glass-Steagall Will Bring." *International Economy* 2: 2 (March/April).

Loxley, John. 1984. *The IMF and the Poorest Countries.* Ottawa: North-South Institute.

Loxley, John. 1986a. "Alternative Approaches to Stabilization in Africa." In Gerald K. Helleiner, ed., *Africa and the IMF.* Washington, DC.

Loxley, John. 1986b. *Debt and Disorder: External Financing for Development.* Boulder, CO: Westview Press.

Lustig, Nora. 1980. "Underconsumption in Latin America." *The Review of Radical Political Economics* 12: 35-43.

Marcussen, Henrik Secher, and Jens Erik Torp. 1982. *The Internationalization of Capital: The Prospects for the Third World.* London: Zed Press.

Marshall, Adriana. 1988. "The Fall of Labor's Share in Income and Consumption: A New 'Growth Model' for Argentina?" In William L. Canak, ed., *Lost Promises: Debt, Austerity and Development in Latin America.* Boulder, CO: Westview Press.

Martin, Edward M. (former Chairman of the Development Assistance Committee). 1985. "Jobs and Other Basic Human Needs." *Twenty-Five Years of Development Co-operation.* Paris: OECD (November).

Martine, G., I. C. Neiva, and M. Macedo. 1984. "Migracao, Crise e Outras Agruras." Paper Presented at the Fourth National Meeting of ABEP, Aguas de Sao Pedro.

Mayo, A., and A. Barrett. 1980. "An Early-Warning Model for Assessing Developing Country Risk." In S. Goodman, ed., *Financing and Risk in Developing Countries.* New York, NY: Praeger, pp. 91-107.

McFadden, D., R. Eckaus, G. Feder, V. Hajivassilov, and S. O'Connell. 1985. "Is There Life After Debt? An Econometric Analysis of the Creditworthiness of Developing Countries." In G. Smith and John T. Cuddington, eds., *International Debt and the Developing Countries.* Washington, DC: World Bank.

McGranaham, D. V., E. Pizarro, and C. Richard. 1985. *Measurement and Analysis of Socio-Economic Development.* Geneva: United Nations Research Institute for Social Development.

McKinnon, Ronald. 1984. "The International Capital Market and Economic Liberalization in LDCs." *Developing Economies,* vol. 22 (September).

Merrill Lynch. 1988. "Multinational Banks: Foreign Lending Survey Results" (February). New York, NY: Merrill Lynch.

Moffitt, Michael. 1983. *The World's Money: International Banking from Bretton Woods to the Brink of Insolvency.* New York, NY: Simon and Schuster.

Morawetz, David. 1981. "Why the Emperor's New Clothes are not Made in Colombia. World Bank Publication. New York, NY: Oxford University Press.

Moreira, Marcilio Marques. 1986. "The Brazilian Quandary." Twentieth Century Fund Paper. New York, NY: Priority Press.

Morgan Guaranty Trust Company of New York. 1983. *World Financial Markets* (June).

Morss, Elliot R. 1984. "Institutional Destruction Resulting from Donor and Project Proliferation in Sub-Saharan African Countries." *World Development* 12: 4 (April).

MTTS (Ministerio de Trabajo y Servicios Sociales y Direccion General de Estadistica y Censos). 1986. *Encuesta Nacional de Hogares, Empleo y Desempleo.* San Jose, Costa Rica: MTTS.

Nashashibi, Karim. 1980. *A Supply Framework for Exchange Reform in Developing Countries: The Experience of Sudan.* Washington, DC: IMF.

Ndulu, B. No date. "Stabilization and Adjustment Policies and Programs: Country Study 17—Tanzania." Helsinki: Wilder.

Nelson, Joan. 1986. "The Diplomacy of Policy Based Lending in Between Two Worlds: The World Bank's Next Decade." Washington, DC: Overseas Development Council.

Neu, Carl R. 1979. "The International Monetary Fund and LDC Debt." In Lawrence Franko and Marilyn J. Seiber, eds., *Developing Country Debt.* Oxford: Pergamon Books.

North, Douglass C. 1981. *Structure and Change in Economic History.* New York, NY: W.W. Norton.

North, Douglass C. 1984. "Government and the Cost of Exchange in History." *Journal of Economic History* 44: 255-264.

North, Douglass C., and Robert Thomas. 1987. "Institutions and Economic Growth: An Historical Introduction." Paper prepared for the Conference on Knowledge and Institutional Change, sponsored by the University of Minnesota (November 13-15, 1987); also presented at the Tulane University Murphy Institute of Political Economy (Spring 1988).

Nyilas, Jozef. 1982. *World Economy and its Main Development Tendencies.* Hague: Martinus Nijhoff.

Officer, Lawrence. 1982. "The Differential Use of IMF Resources by Industrial, Other Developed, and Less Developed Countries: A Historical Approach." *Journal of Developing Areas* 16: 3 (April).

Overseas Development Council. 1988. *Agenda 1988, Growth Exports and Jobs in a Changing World Economy.* Rutgers University New Brusnwick, NJ: Transaction.

Pastor, Manuel, Jr. 1985. "The Effects of IMF Programmes in the Third World Debate and Evidence from Latin America." Occidental College. Mimeo.

Pastor, Manuel, Jr. 1987. *The International Monetary Fund and Latin America: Economic Stabilization and Class Conflict.* Boulder, CO: Westview Press.

Payer, Cheryl. 1975. *The Debt Trap.* New York, NY: Monthly Review Press.

Payer, Cheryl. 1982. *The World Bank: A Critical Analysis.* New York, NY: Monthly Review Press.

Pearson, Lester B. 1969. *Partners in Development, Report of the Commission on International Development.* New York, NY: Praeger.

Petras, James, and Howard Brill. 1986. "The Effects of IMF Programs in the Third World: Debate and Evidence from Latin America." *World Development* 15: 249-262.

Pfeffermann, Guy. 1986. "Poverty in Latin America: The Impact of Depression." Washington, DC: World Bank.

Pollack, M., and Uthoff. 1984. *Costa Rica: Evolucion Macroeconomica, 1976-1983.* Monografias sobre empleo, no. 50. Santiago: PREALC.

Pool, John, and Steve Stamos. 1987. *The ABCs of International Finance.* Boston, MA: Lexington Books.

Portes, Alejandro, and Michael Johns. 1988. "The Polarization of Class and Space in the Contemporary Latin American City." In William L. Canak, ed., *Lost Promises: Debt, Austerity and Development in Latin America.* Boulder, CO:

PREALC (Programa Regional del Empleo para America Latina). 1985. *Beyond the Crisis.* Santiago: ILO

PREALC (Programa Regional del Empleo para America Latina). 1986. *Ajuste y Deuda Social.* Santiago: PREALC-OIT.

Prebisch, Raul. 1981. *Capitalismo Periférico: Crisis y Transformación.* Mexico City: Fondo de Cultura Económica.

Prieto, Ana. 1986. "Mexico's National Coordinadoras in a Context of Economic Crisis." In Barry Carr and Ricardo A. Montoya, eds., *The Mexican Left, the Popular Movements and the Politics of Austerity.* Monograph 18: 75-94. San Diego, CA: Center for U.S.-Mexican Studies, University of California, San Diego.

Raczynski, Dagmar, and Cesar Oyarzo. 1981. "Por Que Cae la Tasa de Mortalidad Infantil en Chile?" *Estudios.* CIEPLAN 6: 45-84.

Ranis, Gustav. 1984. "Adjustment in East Asia, South Korea and Taiwan." *North-South Roundtable Adjustment with Growth: An Equitable Solution.* UNDP.

Ranis, Gustav, and William R. Cline. 1985. *World Development,* vol. 13, no. 4. Comment by Ranis, Reply by Cline.

Reichman, T. M., and R. T. Stillson. 1978. "Experience with Programs of Balance of Payments Adjustments: Standby Arrangements in the Higher Tranches, 1963-1972." IMF Staff Papers (June 25): 292-310. Washington, DC: IMF.

Rhee, Y. W., Bruce Ross-Larson, Garry Pursell. 1984. *Korea's Competititve Edge: Managing the Entry into World Markets.* Baltimore, MD: Johns Hopkins Press.

Riding, Alan. 1988a. "Brazil's Reversal of Debt Strategy." *New York Times* (February 22): D8.

Riding, Alan. 1988b. "Disillusioned Brazil Awakes from a Dream of Prosperity." *New York Times* (April 18): D14.

Rieffel, Alexander. 1977. "The Role of the Paris Club in Managing Debt Problems." *Essays in International Finance,* no. 161. Princeton, NJ: Princeton University.

Robinson, James D., III. 1988. "A Comprehensive Agenda for LDC Debt and World Trade Growth." *AMEX Bank Review,* no. 13: 7 (March).

Robinson, Joan. 1964. *Economic Philosophy.* Garden City, NJ: Anchor Books.

Rockefeller, Nelson A. 1969. "Quality of Life in the Americas: Report of a U.S. Presidential Mission for the Western Hemisphere." Washington, DC: U.S. Government Printing Office.

Rodriguez F., Miguel A. 1987. "Consequences of Capital Flight for Latin American Debtor Countries." In Donald R. Lessard and John Williamson, eds., *Capital Flight and Third World Debt.* Washington, DC: Institute for International Economics.

Roett, Riordan. 1984. "Democracy and Debt in South America: A Continent's Dilemma." *Foreign Affairs: America and the World 1983,* vol. 62 (February): 695-720.

Roett, Riordan. 1987. "Brazil and the Debt: Will the Cost be Too High?" Paper presented at the Conference on the Latin American Debt: Problems and Policies. Stanford University, Stanford, CA (September 17-19).

Rofman, Alejandro. 1988. "Austerity and Regional Development in Argentina and Latin America," In William L. Canak, ed., *Lost Promises: Debt, Austerity and Development in Latin America.* Boulder, CO: Westview Press.

Rohatyn, Felix G. 1983. "A Plan for Stretching Out Global Debt." *Business Week* (February 28).

Saboia, Joao. 1986. "Tranformacoes no Mercado de Trabalho no Brasil Durante a Crise: 1980-1983." *Revista de Economia Politica* 6: 82-106.

Sachs, Jeffrey. 1987-1988. "Developing Country Debt." *NBER Reporter* (Winter).

Salomon Brothers, Inc. 1985. "Japan: the World's Number One Capital Exporter" (February). New York, NY: Salomon Brothers.

Sanderson, Steven E. 1985. "A Critical Approach to the Americas in the New International Division of Labor." In Steven E. Sanderson, ed., *The Americas in the New International Division of Labor.* New York, NY: Holmes and Meier.

Sargen, N. 1977. "Economic Indicators and Country Risk Analysis." *Federal Reserve Bank of San Francisco Economic Review* (Fall).

Scarpaci, Joseph L. 1988. *Primary Medical Care in Chile: Accessibility Under Military Rule.* Pittsburgh, PA: University of Pittsburgh Press.

SEADE (Fundacao Systema Estadual de Analise de Dados). 1987. *Pesquisa de Emprego y des Emprego, Principais Resultados,* vol. 34. Sao Paulo: SEADE.

Sen, Amartya, K. 1983. "Development: Which Way Now?" *Economic Journal*, vol. 93, no. 372 (December).

SEPLAN (Secretaria de Estado do Planajamento e Coordenacao General). 1986. *Boletim de Migracao, Ano VI*. Porto Velho: SEPLAN.

Sewell, John W., et al. 1988. "Growth, Exports and Jobs in a Changing World Economy." *U.S. Third World Policy Perspectives*, no. 9. Washington, DC: Overseas Development Council.

Sharpley, Jennifer. 1985. "External Versus Internal Factors in Tanzania's Macro-Economic Crisis: 1973-1983." *Eastern African Economic Review* 1: 1.

Shaw, Karen D. 1988. "Capital Adeqaucy Standards May Increase Risk." *American Banker* (February 10).

Singh, A. 1986. "Tanzania and the IMF: The Analysis of Alternative Adjustment Programmes." *Development and Change*, vol. 17.

Smith, A. D. 1969. In A. D. Smith, ed., *Wage Policy Issues in Economic Development*. London: MacMillan.

Solimano, Andras. 1986. "Contractionary Devaluation in the Southern Cone: The Case of Chile." *Journal of Development Economics* 23: 1 (September).

Srinivasan, T. N. 1982. "Why Developing Countries Should Participate in the GATT System." *World Economy* 5: 85-105.

Stevenson, Gail. 1988. *World Bank Policy-Based Lending, 1980-1985: A Review and Evaluation*. Unpublished Ph.D. Dissertation. Washington, DC: The American University.

Stewart, Frances. 1986. *Economic Policies and Agricultural Performance: The Case of Tanzania*. Paris: OECD.

Stewart, Frances. 1987. "Alternative Macro Policies, Meso Policies and Vulnerable Groups." In G. A. Cornia, R. Jolly, and F. Stewart, eds., *Adjustment with a Human Face*. Oxford: Clarendon Press.

Streeten, Paul. 1987. "Structural Adjustment: A Survey of the Issues and Options." *World Development* 15, no. 12 (December).

Subcommittee on Foreign Economic Policy. 1977. Committee on Foreign Relations, United States Senate, *International Debt, the Banks, and U.S. Foreign Policy*. Washington, DC: U.S. Government Printing Office (August).

Sunkel, Osvaldo. 1984. "Past, Present and Future of the International Economic Crisis." *CEPAL Review* (April).

Sunkel, Osvaldo. 1985. *America Latina y la crisis económica internacional: ocho tesis y una propuesta*. Buenos Aires: Grupo Editor Latinamericano.

Tagliabue, John. 1985. "Bundesbank to Loosen Rules." *New York Times* (April 11).

Tarshis, Lorie. 1988. "LDC Debt vs. The Free Rider Virus." Mimeo. Paper presented at the Eastern Economic Association Meetings in Boston (March 10-12).

Todaro, Michael. 1969. "A Model of Labour Migration and Urban Unemployment in Less Developed Countries." *American Economic Review* 59: 1 (March).

Trifari, Sheila, and J. Antonio Villamil. 1983. In William H. Baughn and Donald R. Mandich, eds., "Country Risk Analysis—Economic Considerations." *The International Banking Handbook*. Homewood, IL: Dow Jones-Irwin.

Triffin, Robert. 1978. "Gold and the Dollar Crisis: Yesterday and Tomorrow." *Princeton Essays in International Finance*, no. 132.

Truell, Peter. 1987. "Brazil and Argentina Face Difficulties." *Wall Street Journal* (November 9).

Truell, Peter. 1988a. "Debt Cure Hinges on Reactions to Brazil." *Wall Street Journal* (February 5).

Truell, Peter. 1988b. "Foreign Banks Are Caught Up in Battle Over Panama as Loans Start Falling Due." *Wall Street Journal* (March 10).

Truell, Peter. 1988c. "Mexico's Plan to Lower Debt Seems a Success: But Banks Expected to Swap Far less Than $10 Billion of $53 Billion in Loans." *Wall Street Journal* (February 26).

Truell, Peter. 1988d. "S&P Cuts Debt Ratings of Bank America, Chemical New York, Chase and Two Others." *Wall Street Journal* (February 2).

Truell, Peter, and Matt Moffett. 1988. "Mexico Works on Less Ambitious Plans with J. P. Morgan to Cut Foreign Debt." *Wall Street Journal* (May 25).

UNICEF. 1987. *Ajuste com Dimensao Humana, Parte II da Edicao Completa, Situacao Mundial da Infancia.* Brasilia: Ideal.

United Nations. 1986a. "Definition and Measurement of the Net Transfer of Resources." *World Economic Survey*, Annex III. New York, NY: United Nations.

United Nations 1986b. "The Development Crisis in Sub-Saharan Africa." *World Economic Survey*. New York, NY: United Nations.

United Nations. 1986c. *Economic Recession and Specific Population Groups.* New York, NY: United Nations, Department of International Economic and Social Affairs.

United Nations. 1987a. *Handbook of International Trade and Development Statistics* (1986 Supplement). Conference on Trade and Development. New York, NY: United Nations.

United Nations. 1987b. "The Fast-Growing Developing Countries of the 1980s." *World Economic Survey 1987*. New York, NY: United Nations.

United Nations. 1987c. "Debt, Net Resource Transfers and External Adjustment in Turkey." *World Economic Survey 1987*. New York, NY: United Nations.

United Nations. 1988a. "Report of the Working Group on Human Resource Development." Gerasimos Arsenis, Chairman; Keith Griffin, Rapporteur. United Nations Committee for Development Planning, 24th Session, New York, NY (April 12-15).

United Nations. 1988b. "Report and Recommendations of the Advisory Group on Financial Flows for Africa." *Financing Africa's Recovery*. New York, NY: United Nations (February).

United Nations. 1988c. *World Economic Survey 1988.* New York, NY: United Nations.

van der Hoeven, Rolph. 1982. "Zambia's Economic Dependence and the Satisfaction of Basic Needs." *International Labour Review* 121: 2 (March/April).

van der Hoeven, Rolph. 1987. "External Shocks and Stabilization Policies: Spreading the Load." *International Labour Review* 126: 2 (March/April).

van der Hoeven, Rolph. 1988. "Planning for Basic Needs: Soft Options on Solid Policy." A Basic Needs Simulation Model Applied to Kenya. Aldershot: Gower.

van der Hoeven, Rolph. Forthcoming. "Some Thoughts on Employment and Unemployment in Africa." *Trade and Development*, no. 7. Geneva: UNCTAD.

van der Hoeven, Rolph, and Jan Vandemoortele. 1987. *Stabilisation and Adjustment Policies and Programmes, Country Study 4, Kenya.* Helsinki: WIDER.

Van Roy, Ralph. 1984. "Undocumented Migration to Venezuela." *International Migration Review* 18: 541-557.

Vetter, David M. 1983. "A Evolucao das Condicoes de Saneamento Basico da Populacao Urbana Durante a Decada de 70: uma Analise Preliminar." *Revista Brasileira de Estatistica* 44: 173-174, 181-198.

Walton, John. 1987. "Urban Protest and the Global Political Economy: The IMF Riots." Unpublished manuscript, Department of Sociology, University of California, Davis.

Walton, John, and Charles Ragin. 1988. "Austerity and Dissent: Social Bases of Popular Struggle in Latin America." In William L. Canak, ed., *Lost Promises: Debt, Austerity and Development in Latin America.* Boulder, CO: Westview Press.

Weaver, James H., and Howard M. Wachtel (assisted by Peter Glick and Cameron Duncan). 1984. "The LDCs, the IMF, AID, and the Link Between Them." Washington, DC: The American University, pp. 21 and 23 (August 7).

Webb, Richard H. 1984. "Vector Autoregression as a Tool for Forecast Evaluation." *Federal Reserve Bank of Richmond Economic Review* (January/February): 3-11.

Weber, Max. 1968. *Economy and Society: An Outline of Interpretive Sociology,* vol. 1. Translated by Guenther Roth and Claus Wittich. New York, NY: Bedminster Press.

Weeks, John. 1985a. *The Economies of Central America.* New York, NY: Holmes & Meier.

Weeks, John. 1985b. "The Central American Economies in 1983 and 1984." In Jack Hopkins, ed., *Latin American and Caribbean Current Record.* New York, NY: Holmes & Meier.

Weeks, John. 1988. "Prospects for the Central American Economies Towards 2000." In Michael Conroy, ed., *The Future of the Central Economies.* Paper presented to the Symposium on the Central American Economies, University of Texas at Austin (April 21-22).

Weeks, John. Forthcoming. *A Critique of Neoclassical Macroeconomics.* London: MacMillan.

Whitefield, Mimi. 1988. "Inflation Dictates Brazil's Politics." *Miami Herald* (February 15).

Williamson, John. 1982. *The Lending Policies of the International Monetary Fund.* Washington, DC: Institute for International Economics.

Winkler, Matthew. 1985. "U.S. Financial Firms Grab Growing Share of European Markets." *Wall Street Journal* (February 25).

Winkler, Matthew. 1988. "Some Banks' Debt is Behaving like Junk: Investors are Wary of Latin Loan Exposure." *Wall Street Journal* (February 2).

Wood, Robert. 1986. *From Marshall Plan to Debt Crisis: Foreign Aid and Development Choices in the World Economy.* Washington, DC: World Bank.

World Bank. 1983-1984, 1984-1985, 1985-1986, and 1987-1988. *World Debt Tables.* Washington, DC: World Bank.

World Bank. 1986. *Poverty in Latin America: The Impact of Depression.* Washington, DC: World Bank.

World Bank. 1987a. *World Bank Atlas.* Washington, DC: World Bank.

World Bank. 1987b. *Developing Country Debt: Implementing the Consensus.* Washington, DC: World Bank.

World Bank. 1987c. "Argentina: Economic Recovery and Growth." *World Bank Country Study*. Washington, DC: World Bank.

World Bank. 1988. "Lending for Adjustment: An Update." *World Bank News Special Report* (April).

Wright, Peter. 1980. "World Bank Lending for Structural Adjustment." *Finance and Development* 17: 3.

Zoeteweij, Hubertus. 1985. "Wages in Stabilization and Adjustment Programmes of Developing Countries." Mimeo. Geneva: ILO (November).

INDEX

Adjustment, structural. *See*
    Structural adjustment
Adjustment program, objective of, 28
Africa (*see also individual countries*)
    debt repayments as reparations, 62-
    63
    depression in, 41-42
    GDP in, 10
    intransigence of the debt crisis in,
    30-31
    migration in, 177-89
    output per capita, 8, 9, 10
    perceptions of the debt crisis in,
    203-4
    structural adjustment and, 175-76
    Sub-Saharan
        adjustment policies in, 30-36
        development policies in, 92
        economies of, 30-34
        food supplies in, 92
        growth in, 92
        income per capita, 24

    transfer of financial resources
        and, 14, 15, 16
Agriculture
    growth in, 16
    and pricing policies in Tanzania,
    182-86
American Express, 238
Andean Pact, 61
Argentina (Argentine Republic)
    buyback of debt by, 217
    capital flight from, 24
    debt and, 14 n.16
    debt rescheduling by, 85, 123
    debt service, costs of, 213
    default by, 247
    exchange rates in, 209
    financial resources of, 249
    PBL and, 138
    political change in, 170-71
    productivity per capita, 172
    solvency of, 172
    tariff barriers in, 135 n.1

trade structure of, 4
unemployment in, 26
wages in, 159
Asia
growth in, 9, 16, 91-92
output per capita, 8, 9
Australia
deregulation in, 70
trade structure of, 4

Baker, James A., III, 14, 14 n.16,
78-79, 80, 131, 139, 200, 201,
204
Baker Plan (Initiative), 30, 73, 78-
79, 80, 85, 112 n.8
criticism of, 200, 201, 216
Balance of payments
Kenyan, 38-39
viable, 23 n.2
Bangladesh, trade structure of, 4,
4 n.2
Bank of America, 71, 236, 248
Bank of Boston, loan write-downs
by, 81
Bank of England, 71
Bankers Trust, 248
Banking
merchant, effect of, on foreign
loans, 79
monopoly in international, 49-55,
152-53, 153 n.12
Banking Committee, testimony
before, on the LDC debt crisis,
195-97
Banks, commercial U.S. (private)
and costs of debt relief, 30
effect of debt forgiveness on, 234
effect of writing down LDC debt
on, 250
exposure of, to the Latin American
debt crisis, 243, 247, 248
foreign loans made by, 68
lending policies of, 47

monopoly of, 49-55
program financing by, 133-35
regulations for, and loan policies,
240-41
repercussions of failure of, 235-36
reserve requirements of, 240
responsibility of, for LDC debt
crisis, 235
shortcomings of as sovereign
lenders, 200-201
size of, and competition for
sovereign loans, 76-77
as venture capitalists, 240-41
Bauer, Lord Peter, 6-7
Belgian Congo, wages in, 176
Berg, Elliot, 176
Bias
in debt renegotiation, 153-54. *See
also* Banking, monopoly in
urban, in structural adjustment
policies for Africa, 176-77, 188-
91
Bolivia, 14 n.16, 123
debt service, costs of, 213
discounted debt of, 236
exports from, 211
political change in, 166
unemployment in, 160
Bradley, Senator Bill, 197
Brady, Senator Nicholas, 204 n.2
Brazil, 14 n.16, 123
ability to service debts of, 116,
117
capital flight from, 24 n.3
debt-equity swaps and, 217
debt repayment by, 72
debt service, costs of, 213
default by. *See* Brazil, moratorium
of
development in, 11
effect of oil prices on, 43, 211
exports by, 47 n.9
financial resources of, 249

GDP of, 10
imports into, 135 n.1
loans for, 68
moratorium of, on debt, 75, 80,
   81, 233, 247
PBL and, 138
political change in, 170-71
public health policies in, 157-58
riots in, 161
structural adjustment in, 28
unemployment in, 26, 160
urban migration in, 158
wages in, 159
Bresser-Pereira, Luiz Carlos, 68
Bretton Woods, 44, 52-55,147, 148,
   150
Britain, deregulation in, 70
British West Indies, undervaluation
   in, 127
Burden-sharing, as an element of
   structural adjustment, 104, 105
Burma, growth in, 12 n.12, 17 n.18

Cameroon, growth in, 12 n.12
Canada, deregulation in, 70
Capital flight, 55, 209, 213
   reversing, 218
Capital requirements, and foreign
   loans, 72
Capital strength, banking, and
   divestiture, 81
Caribbean
   output per capita, 9
   political costs of structural
      adjustment in, 165-66, 173-74
Central America, exports by, 47 n.9
Central American Common Market,
   61
Chase Manhattan Bank, 248
Chemical Bank, 248
Chile, 14 n.16, 28, 123
   debt-equity swap in, 238
   discounted debt of, 236

financial resources of, 116 n.12,
   249
perception of the debt crisis in, 199
privatization in, 53-54, 238
public health policies in, 157
unemployment in, 25, 26
wages in, 159
China, People's Republic of
   as a developing country, 4, 6
   growth in, 16, 17 n.18, 126
Citibank (Citicorp), 68, 71, 75, 81,
   84, 248
Coffee prices, 37
Colombia, 14 n.16, 123
   financial resources of, 249
   GDP of, 10
   political change in, 166
   trade structure of, 4
   unemployment in, 25, 26
   urban migration in, 158
Commodity prices, 16, 21, 208-9,
   211
   and the debt crisis, 214
   in Kenya, 37
Conditionality, 56
   devaluation in, 125
   and the disbursement of funds, 97-
      98
   effects of, 153, 154-55, 250
   and a multilateral institution to
      buy back LDC debt, 203
   and PBL, 133, 135-36
   as policymaking, 155
   political consequences of, 167-68
   principles of, 104, 151
   and SALs, 135-37, 145-46
Congress, United States, and the debt
   crisis, 195-206
   proposal for amelioration by, 251-
      53
   repercussions of forgiveness by,
      238-39
Continental Illinois Bank, 248

Costa Rica
  emergency loan for, 57, 61
  financial resources of, 249
  GDP of, 10
  growth in, 99
  public health policies in, 157
  urban migration in, 158
  wages in, 92, 159
Costs
  political
    of the debt crisis, 199-200
    of structural adjustment, 165-74
  transaction, and trade, 143-44
Côte d'Ivoire, 14 n.16, 123
  GDP of, 10
  growth in, 99
Countries
  developing. See Less developed
    countries
  middle income, transfer of financial
    resources and, 14, 14 n.14, 15
CPEs. See Economies, centrally
  planned
Credit, private, and debt, 14. See
  also Banks, commercial U.S.
Creditworthiness
  of U.S. commercial banks, 234
  of the World Bank, 205
Crisis, social, in Latin America and
  Sub-Saharan Africa,, 92
Cruzado Plan (Brazil), 170-71
Currency
  domestic, for debt servicing, 218
  foreign. See Foreign exchange
  reserve, and LDC debt, 43-44

Darity, William, Jr., 245
Debt crisis, 67-68
  contributory causes of, 92, 93,
    207-216
  creditors' responses to, 57-62
  effect of, in the U.S., 197-98
  origins of, 245-49

proportions of, 243-53
solutions for, 244, 251-53
Debt-for-debt swap, 80, 83
Debt-for-equity swap, 80, 216-17,
  237-38, 238 n.5
Debt, LDC
  buyback plans for, 217
  effects of repudiating, 233-34
  forgiveness of, 233-41
  growth of, 152
  perceptions of, in the U.S.
    Congress, 195-206
  as reparations, 41-63
  rescheduling (see also Structural
    adjustment), 123
    Latin American, 247-49
    outlook for, 249-50
  and reserve currencies, 42-49
  and transfer of financial resources,
    12-16
Debtor, motivations of, in the debt
  crisis, 83-84
Debt service
  in domestic currency, 218
  effect of, on the debtor's economy,
    212
  equable, 244
  Latin American, effect of, on world
    financial markets, 227
  as a percentage of GNP, 153-54
  proportions of, 245-46
  proposed moratorium on exporting,
    229-232
  simulation of ability in, 114-18
  structural adjustment and, 105, 107
Default
  effect of
    on the American public, 252-53
    on credit ratings, 216
  imminence of, and structural
    adjustment, 104
  in Latin America, 42
  as a policy, 42 n.3

Deficit
    budget, in Sub-Saharan Africa, 32, 33
    current account, 22-25
    during structural adjustment, 107
Deflation
    in industrialized countries, 22
    and structural adjustment, 61, 105
Deindustrialization
    as a consequence of structural adjustment, in Tanzania, 190-91
    in Sub-Saharan Africa, 34
deLarosière, J., 53
Demography, structural adjustment and, 156-58
Deposit insurance, inadequacy of, 250-51
Depository Institutions
    Deregulation and Monetary Control Act, 70
Depression
    in Africa, 41-42
    in Latin America, 41-42
Deregulation
    in the international financial markets, 69-70
    in Latin America, 27
    in U.S. banking, 70
Destabilization, political
    in Latin America, 225-26
    and structural adjustment, 160-61, 163
Devaluation
    effectiveness of, 126
    as "exchange rate adjustment," 125-30
    in Latin America, 25, 26, 28
    moral issues in, 130
    and structural adjustment, 59 60, 94-95, 106, 107
    in Sub-Saharan Africa, 32-33
    successful, 128-29
    in Tanzania, 188, 190

Development, economic
    discussed, 5-7
    outlook for, in developing countries, 3-19
    and structural adjustment, 223-32
Disclosure, public, of foreign loans, 72
Disinflation, in Mexico, 219-20
Divestiture, from sovereign loans, 75-87
DMEs. See Economies, developed market
Dollar, U.S.
    appreciation of, and debt servicing, 246-47
    depreciation of, and foreign debt, 79-80
    as a reserve currency, 44, 150-51
Dominican Republic
    GDP of, 10
    political change in, 166
    "Dutch Disease" in, 128

Economies
    centrally planned (CPEs)
        growth rate in, 9
        output per capita, 7, 7 n.7, 8
    developed market (DMEs)
        compared with LDCs, 10, 10 n.10
        growth rate in, 9
        output per capita, 7, 8
Ecuador, 14 n.16, 123
    financial resources of, 249
    GDP of, 10
    moratorium on debt service by, 81
    political change in, 166, 173
Efficiency, in structural adjustment, 94
Ellis, Frank, 185
Employment
    declines in, 160
    growth of, in Latin America, 160

in Sub-Saharan Africa, 30, 31
Eurodollars, and program financing, 133-34
Europe, Eastern, 4
output per capita, 7 n.7
Exchange control, as socialized private debt, 53-54
Exchange rates
"adjustment" of. *See* Devaluation
pegging, 129
regulation of, 148
and structural adjustment, 95
and the world economy, 144-45
Exports
and devaluation, 126, 127, 128-29
and economic shocks, 23
and growth, 16
inadequacy of, to finance debt servicing, 248
from Kenya, 36-37
Latin American, 25, 29-30, 47, 47 n.9
and structural adjustment, 94, 95, 99, 107-8
from Sub-Saharan Africa, 33

Falkland (Malvinas) War, 68
FDIC. *See* Federal Deposit Insurance Corporation
Federal Deposit Insurance Corporation (FDIC), 235, 252
Federal Reserve System, 238
loan review by, 253
Finance, international market, and structural adjustment, 67-73
First Chicago Bank, 248
First Interstate Bank, 248
Food
as aid, 101
production of
in Kenya, 37-38
in Zambia, 36 n.12

Foreign exchange
controls on, and structural adjustment, 106
importance of, 28
reallocation of, to stimulate Latin American economies, 229-32
France, reparations paid by, 62, 249
Free market
orthodoxy of, 60-62
and PBL, 138

Garcia, Alan, 119, 167
GATT. *See* General Agreement on Tariffs and Trade
GCI. *See* General Capital Increase
GDP. *See* Gross Domestic Product
General Agreement on Tariffs and Trade (GATT), 149
General Capital Increase (GCI), of the World Bank, 203-6
Germany, reparations paid by, 62, 249
Germany, Federal Republic of
bank regulations in, 82
deregulation in, 70, 71
hidden banking reserves in, 82
and oil prices, 42-43
Ghana
growth in, 99
measure of success in, 93
Glass-Steagall Act, 70, 79 n.1, 240
GNP. *See* Gross National Product
Gold standard, 150-51
Greece, as a developing country, 4
Greenidge, Carl, 125
Gross Domestic Product (GDP)
declines in, 10
growth in, 11-12
and structural adjustment, 99
Gross National Product (GNP)
decline in, in Latin America, 25
growth of, 211

Group of 77, 4
Group of Seven, 19
Growth, economic
  deterrents to, 220
  and development policy, 7-12
  inhibition of, by structural
    adjustment, 105
  in the LDCs, 91-92
  model for, 143-44
  patterns in, 16-18
  per capita, 9
  slowdown in, 10, 21
  and structural adjustment, 60-61,
    110-12, 112 n.8
  in U.S., 46
Guatemala, GDP of, 10
Gulf States, oil from, 47
Guyana
  SALS for, 136
  sectoral adjustment loans for, 137

Haiti, 123, 161
Havana Charter (1948), 149
Health, and public expenditures, in
  Latin America, 157-58
Honduras, 123, 166
Hong Kong
  development in, 11
  growth in, 12 n.12, 17 n.18, 126
Hyperinflation, 210, 213

IDA. See International Development
  Association
IDB. See International Development
  Bank
IFC. See International Finance
  Corporation
IFI. See International Financial
  Institutions
Illiquidity, and sovereign loans, 78
ILO. See International Labour Office
IMF. See International Monetary
  Fund

Immigration, illegal, into the U.S.,
  158
Imports
  foreign currency for, 229-30
  into Latin America, 26-27
  into Sub-Saharan Africa, 34
  substitution in, 95
Income
  declines in, and structural
    adjustment, 158-60
  distribution of, and adjustment
    policies, 35
  per capita, 24
    in Latin America, 24, 159, 165,
    210
  as a measure of development, 3-4
India, growth in, 16, 17 n.18
Industrialization, as a policy, in Latin
  America, 225
Inflation
  domestic, and structural
    adjustment, 95
  and growth, 17
  in Latin America, 24, 26
  in Mexico, 219
  and structural adjustment, 59, 106
  in Sub-Saharan Africa, 32
Institutional Investor, 135
Institution, multilateral, to buy back
  LDC debt, 201-3, 217-18, 239
Institutions, weakness in, and
  structural adjustment, 101-2
Inter-American Development Bank,
  function of, 55
Interest rates, 46, 46 n.8, 48-49
  debt servicing and, 246
  and Eurodollars, 134
  and Latin American debt crisis, 67-
    68, 211, 214
  in Mexico, 220
  proposed regulations on, for LDC
    debt, 251-52, 253
  real, 21-22

and structural adjustment, 97, 108
International Bank for Reconstruction
  and Development. *See* World Bank
International Coffee Organization, 37
International Debt Management
  Authority, 85
International Development
  Association (IDA), 148
International Development Bank
  (IDB), sectoral adjustment loans
  from, 137
International Finance Corporation
  (IFC), 148
International Financial Institutions
  (IFIs), 132
International Labour Office (ILO),
  World Employment Programme, 6
International Monetary Fund (IMF)
  and Africa, 30
  classification of developing
    countries by, 4
  conditionality policies of. *See*
    Conditionality
  economic development and, 5
  and economic restructuring, 92-93
  establishment of, 147
  free market orthodoxy of, 61-62
  function of, 55, 147-48, 151
  postwar lending by, 145
  on privatization, 52
  replenishment funds for, 195-96,
    252
  SDRs of, 43, 150, 203
  and structural adjustment. *See*
    Structural adjustment
International Trade Organization
  (ITO), 147, 149
Internationalization, effect of, 154,
  156
Investment, stimulating, 219
  in Latin America, 229-30
Ireland, per capita income in, 3-4
Israel, as a developing country, 4

ITO. *See* International Trade
  Organization

Jamaica, 99, 123, 173
Japan
  bank regulations in, 82
  as a capital exporter, 69
  deregulation in, 70-71
  hidden banking reserves in, 82
  oil prices and, 42-43

Kaufman, Henry, 71
Kenen, Peter, 201, 217
Kenya
  adjustment policies in, 36-39
  economy of, 39
  employment in, 31
  food production in, 37-38
  GDP of, 10
  revenue in, 31
King, Robin, 238 n.4
Korea, Republic of
  debt of, 43
  development in, 11
  exports from, 99
  growth in, 12 n.12, 17 n.18, 99,
    126
Kuwait, per capita income in, 3

Labor
  devaluation as exploitation of, 130
  effect of structural adjustment on,
    105, 106
  New International Division of,
    148, 154, 156
LaFalce, John, 201
Latin America
  debt crisis in, 67-68, 93
  debt rescheduling in, 247-49
  debt service in, 153-54, 155, 227
    simulation of ability to provide,
      114-18
  default in, 42, 51

deficit in, 24-25
depression in, 41-42
deregulation in, 27
devaluation in, 25, 26, 28
development policies in, 223-26
employment in, 25, 26, 28
exports from, 25, 29-47, 47 n.9
financial resources of, 247, 249
imports into, 26-27
income per capita, 24, 159, 165,
    210
industrialization policy in, 225
inflation in, 24, 26.
investment in, 229-30
market liberalization in, 27-28
migration in, 158
output per capita, 8, 9, 10
and PBL, 138-140
political outlook for, 173-74, 198-
    99, 225-26
population growth in, 56-57
structural adjustment in, 24-30,
    165-74
U.S. policy toward, 198
wages in, 25, 27
LDC. See Less developed countries
Lending
    policy-based (PBL)
        Baker on, 131-32
        focus of, 136, 138
        history of, 131-40
        in Latin America, 138-40
    structural adjustment (SAL) (see
        also Structural adjustment)
        conditionality in, 57
        defined, 132-33
        effects of, 152
        focus of, 136, 137-38, 151-52
        growth of, 136
    voluntary, to Latin America, 215
Less developed countries (LDCs)
    development strategies of, and the
        debt crisis, 92

effect of devaluation on, 125-30
external debt of, 245-46
growth in, 3-19, 91-92, 244
and the international financial
    markets, 71-73
productivity in, 7, 8, 130
transfer of financial resources in,
    12-14
Lewis, W. A., 127
Liberalization (see also Deregulation)
    market, in Latin America, 27, 28
    and structural adjustment, 106, 108
Liquidity
    excess domestic, in Africa, 31
    and PBL, 138
    and sovereign debt, 80-81, 85, 86,
        236, 253
Loan
    forgiveness of, as a policy, 234-35
    policy-based. See Lending,
        structural adjustment
    program. See Structural
        adjustment
    reclassifying, under U.S. Treasury
        guarantees, 252, 253
    sectoral adjustment, 137
    sovereign, 75
        competition in the market for,
            76-77
        divestiture from, 75-87, 80-84
        freezing of, 77-80
        syndication of, 76
        and U.S. capital reserves, 81
        and the U.S. government, 84
    Structural adjustment lending
        (SAL). See Lending, structural
        adjustment

Madagascar, revenue in, 31
Malaysia, growth in, 17 n.18
Malnutrition, and the debt crisis, 92
Manufacturers Hanover Bank, 234,
    235, 248

Market, international financial
  changes in, and sovereign loans,
    68-71, 75
  and public policy, 85
Marshall Plan, 145, 150
Mauritius, growth in, 31, 99
McNamara, Robert, 6
Mexico, 14 n.16
  bond issue of, 85-86, 200
  buyback of debt by, 217
  capital flight from, 24
  debt crisis in, 22
  debt-equity swaps and, 216-17,
    237-38, 238 n.5
  debt-for-debt swap in, 82
  debt service, 213, 218-21
  default by, 75, 77, 208, 216, 247
  discounted debt of, 236
  domestic currency for debt
    servicing, 218-21
  exchange rates in, 209
  exports by, 47 n.9
  financial resources of, 249
  GDP of, 10
  inflation in, 219
  interest rates in, 220
  loans for, 68
  as a member of GATT, 149 n.6
  moratorium on debt service by.
    See Mexico, default by
  oil and, 47, 211
  PBL and, 138
  political change in, 168-69
  riots in, 161
  unemployment in, 25, 26, 92, 160
  urban migration in, 158
  wages in, 159-60
Migration
  in Latin America, 158
  urban, in Africa, 177, 189
Mismanagement, economic, 209
Model, vector autoregression (VAR),
  of structural adjustment, 112,

  114, 116 n.11, 118, 120-122
Morgan Guaranty Bank, 85, 237,
  248
Morocco
  debt and, 14 n.16
  GDP of, 10
  growth in, 99
Mulford, David, 200

New Zealand, trade structure of, 4
Nigeria, debt and, 14 n.16, 15

OECD. See Organization of
  Economic Cooperation and
  Development
Oil prices
  and the international finance
    market, 76
  and the LDC debt, 42-46
  and recession, 68
Oman, growth in, 12 n.12, 17 n.18
OPEC, changing status of, 68-69
Organization of Economic Coopera-
  tion and Development (OECD)
    growth in, 29, 91
    imports into, from LDCs, 127
    lending by, 68, 84-85, 155-56
    and the NIDL, 146
Output per capita, 7-8, 10, 11

Pakistan
  growth in, 12 n.12, 17 n.18, 99
  SALs for, 136
Panama, riots in, 161
Paraguay, GDP of, 10
Paris Club, 104, 105, 109, 155, 155
  n.13
PBL. See Lending, policy-based
Pearson Commission Report, 55
Pemex, 237
Peru, 14 n.16
  debt service
    ability in, 116, 117

moratorium on, 174
economic difficulties of, 100
exports from, 211
financial resources of, 249
political change in, 167
riots in, 161
sectoral adjustment loans for, 137
unemployment in, 25, 26
Petrodollars, recycling of, 43, 76
Philippines, 14 n.16
  debt service, costs of, 213
  exports from, 211
  growth in, 99
Poland, debt crisis in, 68, 77
Policy
  adjustment. *See* Structural
    adjustment, policies of
  development, and growth, 7-12
  incomes and prices, 29
  public
    and the divestiture of sovereign
      loans, 84-86
    and the monopoly of
      international banks, 52
  reform of, and PBL, 140
  social, and development, 6-7
  trade, and structural adjustment, 28-
    29
Politics
  and devaluation, 125, 127-28
  and program financing, 134-35
  and structural adjustment policies
    in Latin America, 165-74
Population growth, 9, 9 n.8, 10,
  156-57
Portugal
  deregulation in, 70
  as a developing country, 4
Pound sterling, as a reserve currency,
  44
Poverty
  and development programs, 6
  and IMF policies, 62 n.32

as a selling point, 6-7
and structural adjustment, 35-36,
  100-101
in Sub-Saharan Africa, 33-34
Prebisch, Raul, 6 n.5
Prebisch-Singer hypothesis, 47
Prices, policies on, 96, 182-86
Privatization
  and bank debt, 53-54
  and structural adjustment, 97
  World Bank and, 52
Program, stabilization, 105
Program financing
  by commercial banks, 133-35
  policy-based lending as, 133
Protection, effects of tariff, 28

Regulation, of banks, and sovereign
  loans, 82
Reparations
  France, 62, 249
  Germany, 62, 249
  LDC debt as, 41-63
Reserves, banking, and divestiture,
  81-82
Resources
  financial
    and debt, 12-16
    of Latin America, 247, 249
  use of, in structural adjustment,
    94, 97
Risk
  accounting for default as, 49-50,
    76-77, 236, 237
  changing perceptions of, 134, 135
  elimination of, by international
    banks, 53, 54-55
Robinson, Jim, 217
Robinson, Joan, 130
Rockefeller Report, 55

SAL. *See* Lending, structural
  adjustment

Sarbanes, Paul, 201
Scandinavia, deregulation in, 70
Schumer, Chuck, 196
SDRs. *See* Special Drawing Rights
SEC. *See* Securities and Exchange Commission
Securities and Exchange Commission (SEC), 86
Security Pacific Bank, 248
Sen, Amartya, 5
Senegal
    SALs for, 136
    wages in, 176
Shock, economic
    effects of, 21-40
    and the international financial market, 76-77
Simons, Henry, 240
Singapore
    growth in, 12 n.12, 17 n.18, 126
    per capita income in, 4
Soquimich, 238
South Africa, as a developing country, 4
Soviet Union, output per capita, 7 n.7
Spain, per capita income in, 3-4
Special Drawing Rights (SDRs), 43, 150, 203
Sri Lanka, growth in, 17 n.18
Stabilization
    in Mexico, 219
    in structural adjustment, 94
Structural adjustment
    and ability to service debts, 114-18
    analysis of economic change and, 112-14
    assessment of, 103-23
    comparison of economic performance and, 110-12
    criticism of, 105
    defined, 58
    definition of successful, 108-10

design of, 102
and development, 223-32
economic climate during, 107-8
effects of, 98-99, 105-8, 114, 175-91, 212-15, 227-29, 247-48
    in LDCs, 227
    modelled, 110-14
    social, 165
financing of, 100
hypothetical problems with, 109
implementation of, 97-98
and incomes and prices, 29
institutions involved in, 145-51
and the international finance markets, 67-73
issues in, 143-45
origins of, 91-93
outlook for, 99-102
policies of, 28-29, 36-40, 58-62, 104-5, 106, 151-53
political unrest and, 160-61, 163
rationale for, 119, 156, 209-10
strategy of, 93-97
trade and, 28-29
World Bank and, 91-102
Subsidy, on foodstuffs, in Tanzania, 188
Switzerland, per capita income in, 3

Tanzania
    employment in, 31
    revenue in, 31
    structural adjustment and, 176-91
    wages in, 33, 176, 178-82, 184, 186-87
Tariffs, trends in, 149. *See also* General Agreement on
Tarshis, Lorie, 236, 237, 239
Taxation
    changes in, and foreign loans, 72-73, 86
    and development, in Latin America, 225

and structural adjustment, 96-97
Taxpayer, U.S., as guarantor of LDC
    debt, 205, 217, 244, 251-52
Tax Reform Act (1986), 72
Tea Prices, 37
Thailand, growth in, 12 n.12, 17
    n.18, 99
Timing, in devaluation, 128-29
Trade
    as a measure of development, 4
    and structural adjustment, 94-96
    transaction costs and, 143-44
Trade Bill, 1988, 198, 201, 204, 217
Trinidad and Tobago, per capita
    income in, 4
Tunisia, GDP of, 10
Turkey
    exports from, 99
    growth in, 12 n.12, 17 n.18, 18,
        18 n.19, 99
    SALs for, 136, 138
    trade structure of, 4
Turner, Professor, 180-82

Uganda, growth in, 12 n.12
Undervaluation
    effect of, as policy, 126-27
    political constraints against, 127-
        28
Unemployment, and wages, 25, 26
United Arab Emirates, per capita
    income in, 3
United Nations
    Committee for Development
        Planning, 5
    Secretariat, 4, 7, 17
United States of America
    as a capital importer, 69
    current account deficit in, 22
    economic development in, 5
    per capita income in, 3
    recovery in, and effect on LDC
        debt, 47

Uruguay, 14 n.16
    financial resources of, 249
USAID, program financing by, 133
U.S. Treasury, as guarantor of LDC
    debt held by American banks, 251

VAR. See Model, vector
    autoregression
Venezuela, 14 n.16
    capital flight from, 24
    discounted debt of, 236
    financial resources of, 249
    oil from, 47
    political change in, 167, 169-70
    unemployment in, 25, 26

Wages
    in Latin America, 25, 27
    policies of, in Tanzania, 178-82
    and structural adjustment, 59, 60
        n.27, 61, 158-60
    in Sub-Saharan Africa, 30, 31
Wells Fargo Bank, 248
Wood, Robert, 152
World Bank (International Bank for
        Reconstruction and
        Development)
    approach of, to development, 56-57
    capitalization for, 203
    creditworthiness of, 205
    on default, 41 n.1
    dependence of, on the U.S.
        taxpayer, 252
    economic development and, 5
    and economic restructuring, 92-93
    establishment of, 147
    function of, 55, 148-49
World Bank Group, 148
World economy, 211
    exchange rates and, 144-45
    and the Latin American debt crisis,
        208-11
    theories of, 146

Yugoslavia, 14 n.16
  as a developing country, 4

Zaire, revenue in, 31
Zambia
  economic difficulties of, 100
  employment in, 31
  food pricing in, 96
  foreign exchange in, 36 n.12
  revenue in, 31
  wages in, 33

ABOUT THE CONTRIBUTORS

William L. Canak is Assistant Professor in the Department of Sociology at Tulane University. He holds a joint appointment in the Roger Thayer Stone Center for Latin American Studies, Tulane University.

Chris Canavan is Director of the Latin America Group at Multinational Strategies, Inc. He was previously employed by the World Bank, Latin America Programs Department.

Michael P. Claudon is President and Managing Director of the Geonomics Institute for International Economic Advancement, and Professor of Economics at Middlebury College.

William Darity, Jr. is Associate Professor of Economics at the University of North Carolina at Chapel Hill, and was a Visiting Scholar, Board of Governors of the Federal Reserve.

Rudiger Dornbusch is Professor of Economics at the Massachusetts Institute of Technology.

José D. Epstein is Professor of Economics and Director, Master of Arts Program in Development Banking, The American University, Washington, D.C. He was Manager of the Plans and Programs Department at the Inter-American Development Bank, Washington, D.C.

Richard D. Fletcher has been Acting Manager of the Plans and Programs Department of the Inter-American Development Bank since March 1986. He served as Deputy Manager of the same department beginning July 1985, and as Deputy Manager for Integration in the Economic and Social Development Department of the Bank from 1980 to 1985.

Peter Hakim is staff director of the Inter-American Dialogue in Washington, D.C. He was formerly Vice President of the Inter-American Foundation and writes frequently on U.S.-Latin American relations.

Barry Herman is an Economist in the United Nations Department of International Economic and Social Affairs. He recently led the staff work for the Secretary-General's Advisory Group on Financial Flows for Africa.

Vali Jamal is Senior Research Economist, Employment Department, International Labour Organization, Geneva. Between 1976 and 1984, he was a member of ILO's Regional Employment Team for Africa—JASPA (Jobs and Skills Program for Africa)—for which he participated in employment-advisory missions to several African countries.

Robin A. King is a Ph.D. Candidate in Economics at the University of Texas at Austin. She previously worked in the International Department of a major regional bank.

Danilo Levi is a Graduate Student in the Department of Sociology at Tulane University. His dissertation research focuses on the relationship of international technology transfers, state policy, and national development.

Robert Liebenthal is Chief of the Policy Analysis and Review Division of the World Bank. Prior to joining the Bank he worked as an economist with the government of Zambia. He has worked in East and North Africa and Southern Europe, and has been a Research Officer at the Institute for Development Studies at Sussex.

Karin Lissakers is a Lecturer at the Columbia University School of International and Public Affairs, focusing on International Banking and Finance. She was formerly the Deputy Director for Policy Planning at the U.S. State Department.

Bruce Morrison serves the state of Connecticut as a Democrat in the U.S. House of Representatives.

Peter Nicholas is an Economist with the Policy Analysis and Review Division of the World Bank, and has written on adjustment and poverty issues. He has worked for consulting firms in the United Kingdom and the United States.

Michael D. Robinson is Assistant Professor of Economics at Mount Holyoke College.

Paul M. Sacks is President of Multinational Strategies, Inc., a New York-based consulting house specializing in political and economic analysis. Prior to establishing this firm, he taught Political Science at UCLA, and was employed by Chase Manhattan Bank and The Conference Board.

Louellen Stedman is an Economist in the Office of International Debt Policy at the U.S. Treasury Department. She was previously a Program Associate with the Inter-American Dialogue in Washington, D.C.

Osvaldo Sunkel, is Advisor to the Economic Commission for Latin America and the Caribbean, Santiago, and Director of *Pensamiento Ibero-americano. Revista de Economía Política,* Madrid. He was a Professorial Fellow, Institute of Development Studies, University of Sussex, from 1975 to 1987, and was associated in various capacities with ECLAC and ILPES from 1955 to 1968 and since 1978.

Rolph van der Hoeven is Senior Planning Officer, Adjustment, at the United Nations Children's Fund (UNICEF). Before joining UNICEF, he occupied various positions in the International Labour Organization (ILO), including Senior Economist, and was responsible for the ILO's work on employment and adjustment issues.

ABOUT THE EDITOR

John F. Weeks is Professor of International Politics and Economics at Middlebury College. He is an internationally recognized development economist with extensive policy-related work in developing countries. He has advised governments or conducted research in Nigeria, Kenya, Somalia, Jamaica, Peru, and Nicaragua. He has served as a consultant for most of the major multilateral agencies, including the World Bank, the Inter-American Development Bank, the Food and Agricultural Organization of the United Nations, and the International Labour Office. His publications in the areas of development economics, macroeconomic theory, and classical political economy include *The Economies of Central America* (Holmes & Meier, 1985); *The Limits to Capitalist Development: The Industrialization of Peru, 1950-1980* (Westview Press, 1985); *A Critique of Neoclassical Macroeconomics* (Macmillan, 1989); and (with Vali Jamal) *Africa Misunderstood* (Rutledge, forthcoming).

Professor Weeks obtained his Ph.D. from the University of Michigan, Ann Arbor, and has taught at universities on four continents, including the University of London, Universite Catholique de Louvain, and universities in Peru and Nigeria.